1970

THE POEMS OF ALEXANDER POPE
VOLUME XI: INDEX

The Twickenham Edition of the Poems of Alexander Pope

GENERAL EDITOR: JOHN BUTT

VOLUME I

PASTORAL POETRY and AN ESSAY ON CRITICISM.
E. Audra, formerly Professor of English, Lille University, and Aubrey Williams, Professor of English, University of Florida.

VOLUME II

THE RAPE OF THE LOCK and other poems. Geoffrey Tillotson, Professor of English, Birkbeck College, University of London.

VOLUME III i

AN ESSAY ON MAN. Maynard Mack, Sterling Professor of English and Fellow of Davenport College, Yale University.

VOLUME III ii

EPISTLES TO SEVERAL PERSONS (MORAL ESSAYS).
F. W. Bateson, Fellow of Corpus Christi College, Oxford.

VOLUME IV

IMITATIONS OF HORACE and AN EPISTLE TO DR ARBUTHNOT and THE EPILOGUE TO THE SATIRES. John Butt, late Regius Professor of Rhetoric and English Literature, University of Edinburgh.

VOLUME V

THE DUNCIAD. James Sutherland, Lord Northcliffe Professor of English, University College, University of London.

VOLUME VI

MINOR POEMS. Norman Ault and John Butt.

VOLUMES VII–X

HOMER'S ILIAD AND ODYSSEY. Editor: Maynard Mack. Associate Editors: Norman Callan, Professor of English, Queen Mary College, University of London; Robert Fagles, Associate Professor of English and Comparative Literature, Princeton University; William Frost, Professor of English, University of California, Santa Barbara; Douglas M. Knight, President, Duke University, Durham, North Carolina.

ALEXANDER POPE

VOLUME XI: INDEX

★

Edited by
MAYNARD MACK

LONDON: METHUEN & CO LTD
NEW HAVEN: YALE UNIVERSITY PRESS

First published 1969
© 1969 Methuen & Co Ltd
Printed in Great Britain by The Broadwater Press Ltd
Welwyn Garden City, Hertfordshire

SBN 416 44380 x 35

PREFACE

THESE pages contain a conflated index to the ten volumes of the Twickenham Edition of the Poems of Alexander Pope. Some of the volumes have been reset or added to since first publication, and in such cases the latest revised editions have been used.[1] For the editorial matter of the Twickenham Edition (introductions, notes, appendices, etc.), the present index records in one comprehensive alphabet whatever the individual editors included in their individual indexes, here re-verified. For the texts of Pope's poems (though not for the texts of the Homer translations in volumes VII–X), the present index affords a fresh and exhaustive listing of all proper names, including proper names in the Textual Notes. Since many proper names were omitted from the earlier individual indexes, this new index should be uniquely serviceable to readers.

The procedures followed in the index are these:

1. Titles are used for standard name entries, with cross references from family names.

2. The use of n for note (or notes) is consistent for Volumes I–VI, and for the editorial preface and Introduction to Volume VII. As stated above, the text of the Homer translation (VII–X) is not indexed, therefore n has been omitted in references to these pages, since all such references are to notes. Pope's own indexes to the characters and episodes of Homer will be found at the close of each translation.

3. Some long series of unanalysed consecutive page numbers are entered as, for example, $1n-10n$, or, in Vols. VII–X, $1-10$. This means that the entry occurs on each page, inclusively.

4. If a name appears in the Biographical Appendices contained in Volumes IV and V that reference occurs first in the entry. If a name cannot be identified in a standard reference work, or if the

1. Dates of the editions on which the index is based: Volume I (1961), Volume II (1962), Volume III i (1950), Volume III ii (1961), Volume IV (1961), Volume V (1963), Volume VI (1964), Volumes VII–X (1967).

page reference does not identify the person, he may be identified briefly in the entry.

5. All translations occur under the names of the translators.

6. "Other ref." means either other reference or other references, and does not correspond to, though it includes, the customary use of "mentioned".

Though I assume full responsibility for what is here submitted, by far the largest part of the labour (and therefore of credit for the degree of accuracy, which I believe is high) is owing to Mary Price and Annetta Bynum. Like those beautiful allegorical figures in certain Renaissance *Trionfi*, they drove the chariot which they seemed to draw. This book is dedicated to them.

M. M.

1314 Davenport College
Yale University
14 June 1968

A

Aaron, in AP poem, III.i 71

Abbey, C. J., I 301*n*, 302*n*

Abchurch Lane (London), in AP poems, VI 162, 164*n*

Abel, in AP poem, III.i 139; other ref., III.i lv

Abelard, Peter, in AP poems, II 319, 321, 322, 327, 330, 340, 345, 346; other ref., II 95*n*, 411 ff.

Abergavenny, William Nevill, 16th Baron, and his wife Catharine, IV 88–9*n*

Abscourt farm. See Aps-court

Accius, Lucius (poet, 2nd/1st c. BC), VIII 3

Acestis, in AP poem, I 436

Achaemenes, in AP poem, I 446 and *n*

Achaian, in AP poem, I 417

Achilles, in AP poems, I 459; V 127, 306

Achiz, King, in AP poem, VI 290, 293*n*

Acis, in AP poems, I 365 and *n*, 367, 370, 371, 372, 373

Acton (Middlesex), in AP poem, III.ii 25 and *n*

Adam, in AP poems, II 17, 75; IV 27; VI 186

Adams, Mr (translator of Virgil), I 67*n*

Adams, G. B., I 152*n*

Adams, J. C., III.i xxxiv *n*

Adderbury (formerly Atterbury, in Oxfordshire), VI 380–2

Addison, Joseph, Biog., IV 343; opinion of Chaucer, II 5 f., 8*n*; of the *R. of the Locke*, II 103, 121; on gardening, III.ii 141*n*; organizes benefit performance for Durfey, VI 102*n*; his "little Senate", VI 112*n*, 124*n*, 285; assists Budgell, VI 123; assists Philips, VI 139*n*; praises Philips's *Pastorals*, VI 139*n*; criticizes *E. on Criticism*, VI 144*n*; compared with Virgil, VI 204, 207*n*; connection with *Iliad* trans., VI 132*n*, 135*n*, 144*n*, 145*n*, 173, 285; VII xli–xlii; on Homer's intention, VII lxxx; other ref., I 18, 59*n*, 257*n*; II xii, xiii, 115, 140*n*, 408; V xxxix, 125*n*, 134*n*, 165*n*, 207*n*, 431, 432, 446; VI 85*n*, 140 and *n*, 141*n*, 177*n*; X 596. See also *Guardian, Spectator, Tatler*.
AP relations with, IV xxiii, 339, 343; V 26 f., 29 f., 32–3, 188*n*; VII xxvi, xxxviii, 23; X 443; AP corres., I 315*n*; in AP poems, IV 109, 213; V 110 and *n*, 114 and *n*, 301, 302; VI xv, 123, 140, 173, 202–7; as Atticus, II 240*n*; IV xxiv, 107*n*, 109–11, 212*n*, 323*n*; V 33*n*; VI 141*n*, 142–3, 144–5*n*, 205*n*, 284–5*n*

WORKS:

Account of the Greatest English Poets, I 254n, 271–2n, 294n; 424n; II 221n, 286n; *Battle of the Frogs and Mice*, II 107; *Campaign*, I 74n, 156n, 159n; II 349n; III.i 68n; X 502, 509; *Cato*, III.i 12n, 54n, 141n, 153n; IV 111n, 224n; V 185; VI 115n, 410n; VII xxv; AP Prologue, VI 96–8; epigrams on, VI 99–100, 410; *Dialogues upon Ancient Medals*, I 172n; VI 205–6n, 207n; Epilogue for Granville, *The British Enchanters*, I 68n; *Essay on the Pleasures of the Imagination*, X 605; *Essay on Virgil's Georgics*, I 32n, 135; V 106–7n; *Horace's Ode* III iii, X 510; Latin poems, II 107 and n; V 155n, 364n; *Letter from Italy*, I 149n, 154n, 194n, 320n; II 37n, 253n, 258n; III.i 79n; IV 107n; V 69n, 178–9n, 304n; *The Lover*, III.ii 72n; *The Playhouse* [?], III.i 156n; *Poem to his Majesty*, I 189n; II 182n; *Remarks on Several Parts of Italy*, I 181n, 183n, 184n, 188n, 245n, 266n, 268n; II 164n, 237n, 258n, 275n, 305n; *Rosamond*, II 121, 164n, 187n; *A Song for St Cecilia's Day*, II 259n, 279n; *To Sir Godfrey Kneller*, V 97n

Translations: Ausonius, II 254n; Claudian, II 261n; Horace, I 193n; IV 101n; Lucan, II 164n; Ovid *Metam.*, II 21n, 50n, 183n, 191n; Sappho, V 72n; Silius Italicus, I 266n; II 203n; Virgil *Georgic iv*, II 127n

Admiralty Building (Whitehall), III.ii 137n

Adonis, in AP poems, I 76, 90; III.ii 91; V 124, 305

Adrastus, in AP poems, I 424, 433, 434, 436

Adrian. See Hadrian

Adriatic, in AP poem, V 374

Adventurer, notes on *E. on Man*, III.i 59n, 96n, 139n, 165n

Aegerian, in AP poem, VI 383

Aegon, in AP poem, I 80 ff.

Aegypt. See Egypt

Aegysthus, in AP poem, IV 301

Aelianus (author of *Tactica*), VII 237

Aelianus, Claudius (author of *De nat. anim.*, 2nd/3rd c. AD), VII 34, 41, 57–8, 62–3; VIII 306; IX 134; X 97, 341

Aeneas, in AP poems, I 365; II 272; V 373

Aeolian, I 423 and n, 430; VI 45

Aeschylus, in AP poems, V 88, 185, 335; epigram, VI 300, 303n; Scholiast upon, IX 115; other ref., I 250n; II 230

WORKS:

Fragments, VII 399–400, 442, 463; VIII 545; X 101; *Persae*, IX 379; *Prometheus Bound*, VII 370; IX 202; *Seven Against Thebes*, VIII 358

Aeson, in AP poem, V 353

Aesop at the Bear Garden. See Preston

Aethiopian, in AP poems, I 395 and n; VI 117 and n

Aetna, in AP poems, I 86, 366, 371, 393 and n; III.i 139

Africk, in AP poems, II 174; IV 27

Against Chance and Fate (anon.), III.i 51n

Against the Fear of Death (anon.), II 201n

Agallias Cercyreus (commentator on Homer), VIII 350–1

Aganippe, in AP poem, VI 79
Agenor, in AP poem, I 409 and n
Agis, in AP poem, II 269 and n
Ahlers (surgeon), VI 262n
Aitken, George, VII xxxvii n
Ajax [Ajaces], in AP poems, I 282, 451, 452, 453, 454; V 81, 371
Alans, in AP poems, V 157, 324
Alaric, in AP poems, V 157, 324
Alban, in AP poem, I 380
Albion, in AP poems, I 61, 161, 179, 180, 193; V 93
Albutius, in AP poem, IV 59
Alcaeus (Greek lyric poet), in AP poems, I 394 and n; II 273
Alce [Alse 1751], in AP poem, II 70
Alciati, Andrea, I 321n
Alcibiades, I 315n
Alcides, in AP poems, I 434; II 75, 258; IV 195
Alcinous, in AP poems, I 465, 467, 468, 471; VI 103
Alcmaon, in AP poem, I 454
Alcmena, in AP poem, I 385
Alcoforado, Marianna, II 295n
Alday, John (translator), III.i li n
Aldenham, Henry Hucks Gibbs, 1st Baron, II 383, 386
Aldgate (London), in AP poem, V 314
Aldrich, Henry, V 126n
Aldus Manutius (printer), III.ii 150; VI 83, 85n
Alexander the Great, I 283n, 312n; II 236 f., 265 f.; III.i 35, 148 and n; VII 15, 59–60; X 430
Alexander the Mydian [Myndian] (writer on zoology, date uncertain), IX 425
Alexander Paphius (2nd c. AD), VII 28
Alexandrine, in AP poem, I 280

Alexis, in AP poems, I 71, 73, 75, 77, 89; VI 236
Alfred, King, in AP poems, IV 195; VI 290
Alison, in AP poem, II 69
Allatius, Leo (translator of Homer), VII xxxviii; AP debt to, VII lxxxi; De patria Homeri, VII 31, 44, 46, 54, 59; IX xiv
Allen, R. J., Clubs of Augustan London, III.ii 31n, 91n; VI 177n
Allen, Ralph, Biog., IV 344; AP corres., III.i 75n, 131n, 140n, 146n, 150n, 164n; IV xli, 64n, 97n, 169n, 282n, 304n, 308n, 346, 384; V 65n; VI 149n, 363n, 389n, 394n; in AP poem, IV 308 and n; other ref., V xxx, 251n; VII ccxxvii
Allen, Mrs Ralph, III.ii 47n
Allen, T. W. (modern editor of Homer), VII lxxv and n, lxxxi, 28–30, 34, 36, 44, 50
Allestree, Richard, Decay of Christian Piety, III.ii 101n
Almonds for Parrots (anon.), II 400
Alphaeus, in AP poems, V 140, 314
Alphëus, in AP poem, I 426
Alps, in AP poems, I 265; II 343; VI 157
Alsop, Anthony, Biog., V 427; other ref., V 361n, 364n, 365, 440
Amaranthine, in AP poems, I 94 and n; VI 33
Amasaeus, Romulus (Venetian writer, translator), IX 209
Amazon, in AP poem, II 173
Amazonia (Homeric lost work), VII 54
Amelia, Princess, Biog., IV 344; in AP poem, IV 7
Ames, Joseph (antiquary), III.ii 112n

Amhurst, Nicholas (journalist), IV xxxi

Amis, Sara Mack, VII xxiii

Ammianus Marcellinus (historian, 4th c. AD), VII 237; VIII 58, 104; IX 142

Ammon, in AP poems, III.i 35; IV 104, 320; V 380

Amory, Thomas, *Life of John Buncle*, V 115n

Amphiaraus, in AP poem, I 433

Amphion, in AP poems, I 409 and n; II 29, 259; VI 31

Amphisboena, in AP poem, VI 301

Amphisus, in AP poem, I 388

Amphitrite, in AP poem, III.ii 149

Anacharsis (hellenized Scythian sage c 600 BC), III.i 112n; X 254

Anacreon, VII 200

Anaxarchus, VII 60

Ancient v Modern controversy. See Homer scholarship

Ancus (king), VII ccxxxii n

Andover, William Howard, Viscount, VI 338n, 451

Andraemon, in AP poems, I 386, 388 and n

Andron (of Halicarnassus, genealogist), X 202

Angelo, Henry, VI 448n

Anglo-Saxon chronicler, I 132, 138, 153n

Anjou, Duke of (later Philip V of Spain), III.ii 93n

Anna Ivanovna, Czarina, III.ii 28n

Anne, Queen, in AP poems, I 181 and n; II 99, 129, 134, 169, 199, 297; III.ii 105; IV 151, 167; V 99, 297; other ref., I 39, 40, 69n, 130, 132, 134, 136, 137, 138, 140, 141, 142, 159n, 165n, 182n, 187n, 191n, 194n, 225, 299n, 324n; II 392, 399, 400; V 45; VII xxv, l, ccxvii

Annius, Biog., V 427; in AP poem, V 380; other ref., V 338n, 376n, 377 ff., 452

Annual Miscellany, VII cx

Annual Register, II 306n

Anstis, John, Biog., IV 344; in AP poems, IV 243, 326; other ref., V 416

Antimachus of Colophon (poet and scholar, 5th c. BC), VIII 202

Antiochus I (king of Syria), VII 61

Antonius, in AP poem, VI 167

Antony, in AP poem, VI 67

Aonian, in AP poems, I 112 and n, 428

Apelles (painter, 4th c. BC), in AP poem, V 325; other ref., V 158, 159; VIII 360; X 46, 600

Apian (Apion of Alexandria, compiler of Homer glossary), VII 43, 47, 66; IX 39

Apicius (supposed author of 1st/2nd c. AD cookery book), V 396n

Apollo, in AP poems, I 243 and n, 402 and n, 433, 434, 438, 443, 444, 462; IV 112; V 353; VI 25, 47, 171, 284, 360; other ref., VI 308n

Apollodorus (Athenian commentator on Homeric catalogue of ships, 2nd/1st c. BC), IX 400

Apollonius of Rhodes (2nd c. BC), *Argonautica*, VII 6; VIII 285; IX 226, 246, 329–30; X 61, 171, 414

Apollonius Glaccus (writer on internal diseases, 2nd/1st c. BC), X 222

Appius, in AP poem, I 306

Applebee's Original Weekly, III.i 73n, 131n

Applebee's Weekly Journal, V 437, 457

Aps-court [Apps-Court], in AP poem, IV 164*n*, 181 and *n*

Aquinas, Thomas, his theodicy, III.i xxxiii; *Sum. c. gent.*, 33*n*, 38*n*, 46*n*, 48*n*, 49*n*, 59*n*, 103*n*, 105*n*, 110*n*, 139*n*, 161*n*, 162*n*; *Sum. theol.*, 48*n*, 100*n*: other ref., I 289*n*; III.i xlviii; VII lxxviii

Arabia [–y, –n], in AP poems, I 397 and *n*; II 156, 279; IV 237; V 157, 324; VI 11, 22

Arachne, in AP poems, V 401

Arachnomachia (work attributed to Homer), VII 54

Aratus of Soli (editor of Homer, 4th/3rd c. BC), VII 61; VIII 225, 348–9; IX 344

Arber, Edward, I 310*n*

Arbuthnot, Anne (daughter of AP friend), III.ii xi *n*, 169

Arbuthnot, John, Biog., IV 344; AP *Ep. to*, II xii, xiii, xiv (see AP Works); intermediary in AP disputes, IV xvi, xx; dying requests to AP, IV xx–xxi, 103*n*; in AP poems, IV 98, 105; VI 129; abused, IV 121*n*, and attacked, V 91*n*, 111*n*, 138*n*; writings ascribed to, IV 127; VI 291*n*, 346*n*, 434*n*, 447*n*; conjectured authorship of two lines in AP poem, IV 127; as AP collaborator, VI 115–18*n*, 179–80*n*, 216*n*, 414*n*; member of Scriblerus Club, VI 115*n*, 116, 117, 118, 241*n*; a verse epistle to, VI 263*n*, 444–6; other ref., II xii; III.ii xxxix f., 173, 176; V xv f., 34*n*, 101*n*, 193*n*, 238*n*, 251, 343*n*, 436, 442, 448; VI 263*n*, 265*n*, 292*n*; VII xxv, xxvii

AP corres., IV 313*n*, 324*n*; V 206*n*; VI 120*n*; VII xli *n*, xxxvii *n*

WORKS:
Epitaph on Chartres, III.ii 85–7*n*; VI 346*n*; *The Quidnuncki's*, VI 439*n*; *Three Hours after Marriage* (co-author), I 307*n*; II xiii; VI 179*n*, 286*n*; *Virgilius Restauratus*, V xxv, 217*n*

Arcadia[–ns], in AP poems, I 164, 426

Arcadia's Countess, in AP poem, III.ii 48 and *n*, 49*n*

Archelaus of Priene (sculptor), VII xiii, 55

Archer, Thomas, Biog., V 427–8; other ref., IV 62*n*; V 292

Archilochus (poet, 8th?/7th? c. BC), III.i lxiv; VII 158; VIII 285

Arcturus, in AP poems, I 85, 161

Ardelia, in AP poem, VI 120, 122*n*

Arethuse, in AP poems, V 140, 314

Aretino, Pietro (poet), IV 33 and *n*

Argive[–s], in AP poems, I 423, 427, 438, 472

Argo, in AP poem, VI 31

Argos, in AP poems, I 425, 433, 434, 438, 439, 442, 443, 445

Argus, in AP poems, I 325; II 39; V 142, 192, 315, 407; VI 22, 51

Argyle, John Campbell, 2nd Duke of, Biog., IV 351–2; III.ii 174; IV xxxv, 318 and *n*; VI 119*n*, 185, 186, 188*n*, 214, 215*n*, 380, 381–2*n*, 422

Ariel, in AP poems, II 153 and *n*, 164, 166, 171, 178, 183

Ariosto, Ludovico, II 136*n*, 208*n*, 221, 252; VI 387*n*; VIII 174

Aristarchus (editor of Homer, 3rd/2nd c. BC), V 254*n*, 337*n*, 362 f., 366*n*; VII 60–2; VIII 507, 536; IX 30, 119–20, 151, 189, 269, 324, 338; X 294, 338, 345, 347, 350, 352, 357

Aristeas of Proconnesus (author of epic on the Arimaspeans), VIII 225

Aristides (sophist and orator), AP estimate of, II 269; other ref., VII 244; X 48

Aristides of Thebes (painter), VIII 360

Aristippus (5th/4th c. BC, hedonist philosopher), in AP poems, IV 280*n*, 281; other ref., III.i xxiv

Aristophanes, in AP poems, VI 27; *Acharnians*, VII 316; *Birds*, X 303; *Clouds*, X 167; *Frogs*, IX 378; X 282; other ref., VII 60

Aristophanes (editor of Homer), VIII 527; X 185, 338

Aristotle, cited by Dryden, I 250*n*, in AP poems, I 255, 270 and *n*; 271, 311; II 274; V 193, 360 and *n*; AP appeal to, II 221; image of in *Temple of Fame*, II 274; and Homeric tradition, VII lxxi; on soul of poetry, X 413; in AP MS Preface to *Iliad*, X 418, 420; in AP MS Postscript to *Odyssey*, X 452–3; other ref., I 15, 241*n*, 255 and *n*, 257*n*, 271, 311, 312*n*, 313*n*, 485–6; II 11, 109, 251, 349*n*; III.i xxxvi; V 193 and *n*, 370*n*; VII cxxviii, ccxliv, 36, 40, 60, 70, 189; IX 11, 19–20, 161, 261; X 384

WORKS:
De anima, X 173; *De coelo*, VIII 204; *De part. anim.*, III.i 43*n*; *Fragment*, IX 242; *Hist. anim.*, III.i 43*n*, 110*n*; VIII 135, 306; IX 124; X 151; *Homeric Questions*, VIII 504; *Meteorologica*, IX 210; *Nicomachean Ethics*, III.i 64*n*, 65*n*, 66*n*, 70*n*, 82*n*, 103*n*, 105*n*, 128*n*, 130*n*, 143*n*, 152*n*, 160*n*;

VIII 316; IX 310; X 367; *On Marvellous Things Heard*, IX 338–9; *Poetics*, I 26*n*, 30*n*, 210, 249*n*; II 106; V 48 and *n*; VII 5, 8–9, 30, 53, 66, 89, 126–7, 139, 288, 390, 446; VIII 2, 20, 81, 181, 342, 349, 358, 373, 462; IX 14, 24, 71, 119, 154, 260, 266, 280, 292, 298–9, 335–6, 353, 390, 427–8; X 9–10, 14, 70, 111, 187, 205, 215, 217–18, 233, 270–1, 317, 330, 355, 378, 395–6, 480; *Politics*, III.i 114*n*, 116*n*, 123*n*; VII 102, 139; *Problemata*, IX 210; *Rhetoric*, III.i 99*n*; IV 340; IX 46; X 214, 306; *Topics*, VII 77

Arius, in AP poem, II 76

Army, standing, maintenance of, IV 11*n*, 67

Arnall, William, Biog., IV 345; V 428; attacks AP and his friends, V 211 f., 312*n*; in AP poems, IV 102, 320; V 138, 148, 312; other ref., V 134*n*

Arnobius (Christian propagandist, 4th c. AD), VII lxxxi, 64

Arnold, Matthew, on Homer trans., VII l; *On Translating Homer*, VII lxiii and *n*; on AP trans., VII xciv, xcv, xcvi, ciii; other ref., III.i lxvii

Arria, in AP poem, II 47

Arrian (Flavius Arrianus, historian, 2nd c. AD), X 39, 242, 303

Art of Dress, II 177*n*, 183*n*, 190*n*, 197*n*

Artemon of Miletus (author of book on dreams), VIII 282–3

Arthur, King, in AP poems, V 144 and *n*, 316; VI 290; other ref., I 135

Artimesia, in AP poem, VI 48

Arundel, Richard (original of AP Paridel (?)), V 376*n*, 398*n*

Arundel, Thomas Howard, 2nd Earl of, IX xiii; Arundelian Marble, VII 42

Ascapart, in AP poem, IV 49 and *n*

Ascham, Roger, I 274*n*

Asclepiades (physician), VIII 70

Ashley, Maurice Percy, *Finan. and Commerc. Policy under Cromwell*, IV 64*n*

Ashurst, Dr (poet), in AP poem, VI 173

Asia[–n], in AP poems, II 174; IV 111, 229

Assyrian, in AP poems, II 18, 260

Aston, Lady Catherine, II 353*n*

Astraea, in AP poem, IV 219

Astrophil (sig. in *Gent. Mag.*), II 4

Asturian, in AP poem, III.ii 104

Atalantis, in AP poems, II 131, 181

Athenaeus of Naucratis (author of a symposium), III.ii 35*n*; VII 361; IX 39, 119–20, 124, 129, 205, 244, 266, 300, 308, 425; X 85, 101, 218, 222, 248, 266, 361

Athenian, in AP poems, I 270; VI 378, 379

Athenian Oracle, II 147*n*, 201*n*, 253*n*, 320*n*, 323*n*, 379

Athens, in AP poems, I 311; II 296; IV 197, 225; VI 151, 152

Atkins, J. W. H., I 210*n*, 313*n*

Atkyns, Sir Robert (historian), III.ii 172*n*

Atlantic, in AP poem, VI 151

Atlas, in AP poems, I 415; II 256; VI 268

Atossa, in AP poems, III.ii xi f., 59 ff., 159 ff.; VI 402–3, 404*n*; VII ccxlviii

Atreus, in AP poem, I 429 and *n*

Attalus (unidentified ancient commentator), X 222

Atterbury, Francis, Bishop of Rochester, Biog., IV 345; AP corres., I 8*n*, 10*n*, 205, 302*n*; II 170*n*, 240; III.i 88*n*, 135*n*, 141*n*, 161*n*; III.ii xx *n*, 38*n*; IV 64*n*; VI 345*n*; VII xliii and *n*; AP *Epitaph for*, III.ii 38*n*; VI 343–5; AP witness at trial of, VII xxvi; other ref., I 8*n*, 278–9*n*; II xiii; III.ii 97*n*; IV xxix, 105 and *n*, 121*n*, 122*n*, 317, 323*n*, 346; V 13*n*, 125–6*n*, 134*n*, 145*n*, 168*n*, 281*n*, 313*n*, 342*n*, 361*n*, 367 and *n*, 429, 439, 445; VI 20*n*, 68*n*, 200*n*, 294, 295*n*, 456; VII xliv

Attic, in AP poems, IV 317; V 365

Atticus. See Addison

Atticus, Titus Pomponius, in AP poems, I 172, 172–3*n*; other ref., I 141

Attila (king of the Huns), in AP poems, V 157, 324

Attys, in AP poem, V 378

Aubin, R. A., *Grottoes, Geology, and the Gothic Revival*, II 307*n*

Auden, W. H., II 118*n*; VII ccxiv *n*

Auditor, III.i 37*n*

Audra, Emile, II 105*n*, 243, 295*n*, 297*n*, 302*n*, 308*n*; III.i xvi *n*, xviii *n*, xix *n*, xx *n*, xxii *n*; III.ii 16*n*, 20*n*, 27*n*, 35*n*, 106*n*; IV 165*n*, 278*n*; V 18*n*; with Aubrey Williams, ed. TE Vol. 1: X 495, 501, 503–4, 510

Auerbach, Erich, VII lvi and *n*, ccv and *n*, ccviii *n*

Augusta, in AP poems, I 182 and *n*, 187

Augustine. See St Augustine

Augustus (Roman emperor), in AP

poems, II 273 and *n*; IV 299; V
186, 320, 335; other ref., I 132,
136, 137, 138, 142, 143
Augustus II, King of Poland, III.ii
103*n*
Ault, Norman, on pronunciation,
III.ii 56*n*; his *New Light on Pope*,
I 63*n*, 128*n*, 150*n*, 165*n*, 292*n*,
336*n*; II 37*n*; III.ii 49*n*, 63*n*, 174;
IV 343, 348; VI v, 72*n*, 92*n*, 115*n*,
144*n*, 158*n*, 165*n*, 198*n*, 201*n*,
205*n*, 209*n*, 223*n*, 231*n*, 247*n*,
255*n*, 258*n*, 267*n*, 291*n*, 342*n*,
345*n*, 347*n*, 349*n*, 360*n*, 370*n*,
377*n*, 401*n*, 409*n*, 415*n*, 438*n*,
457*n*, 458*n*; VII xxxviii *n*, xlii n;
(ed.) *Poems on Several Occasions*,
III.ii 68*n*; his *Pope's Own Miscellany*, I 8*n*, 162*n*, 397*n*, 400*n*, 402*n*;
VI v, 8*n*, 13*n*, 68*n*, 109*n*, 281*n*,
416*n*, 417*n*, 418*n*, 419*n*, 420*n*,
435*n*; *Pope's Prose*, I 13*n*, 14*n*, 38*n*,
242*n*, 243*n*, 484*n*; II 102*n*; IV
xv n, 121*n*, 348, 351, 356; V cited
passim; VII xxvi; other ref., I
xiii; IV xlii *n*, 35*n*, 105*n*, 157*n*;
V 12*n*, 33*n*, 79*n*, 81*n*, 82*n*, 170*n*,
350*n*, 441; X 495, 501–3, 506,
510
Aulus   Gellius   (translator   of

Homer), VII xxxviii, cvi, 44;
AP use of, VII xl, and debt to,
VII lxxxi; his *Attic Nights*, I 296*n*;
V 365*n*; VII 77, 244; VIII 40,
316; IX 211, 303, 315; X 222
Aurangzeb (Mogul emperor), I
186*n*
Aurelius Antoninus, Marcus, in AP
poem, II 268 and *n*; other ref.,
III.i xxviii, 22*n*, 45*n*, 148, 149*n*,
153*n*; VIII 579
Aurelius, Victor (author of *De
viris illust.*), VIII 427
Aurora, in AP poems, I 62, 398
and *n*
Ausonius, Decimus Magnus (poet),
in AP poem, II 273 and *n*; other
ref., I 132, 163*n*, 169*n*, 183*n*,
185*n*; II 332*n*; VII 205–6
Austen, Jane, II 310
Auster, in AP poems, I 430 and *n*;
IV 139; VI 79
Automedon, in AP poem, I 460
Avidien, in AP poems, IV 57–9, 57*n*
Avon (river) in AP poem, IV 205
Ayre, William (poet and bio-
grapher of AP), III.i xxi; III.ii
46*n*, 67*n*; V 79*n*, 93*n*, 101*n*, 149*n*,
166*n*, 174*n*, 456; VI 179*n*, 448*n*
Ayres, Philip (translator), II 378

B

Baal, in AP poem, V 350
Babb, James T., III.i vi; VII xxiii
Babb, Laurence, II 184*n*, 187*n*, 188*n*, 189*n*
Babel, in AP poem, IV 33
Baber, J., V 93*n*
Babo, in AP poem, III.ii 138, 139*n*, 182
Babylon, in AP poem, II 257
Bacchus, in AP poems, I 394 and *n*, 427 and *n*, 429; II 30; VI 289
Baccylides (poet), VIII 285
Bacon, Francis, AP opinion of, II 251; his conception of ruling passions, III.i xxxvi, 153*n*, 154 and *n*; accessibility of works to AP, IV 176–7*n*; in AP poems, IV 69, 177; V 175, 176, 331; VI 204; other ref., IV 68–9*n*
WORKS:
Adv. of Learning, II 221, 234*n*, 236, 268–9*n*; III.i 64*n*, 71*n*, 117*n*, 130*n*, 157*n*, 158*n*, 160*n*; IV 110*n*; VII 209; *Apophthegms*, III.i 145*n*; *De augm.*, III.i 26*n*, 110*n*; *De sap. vet.*, III.i 123*n*; *Nat. Hist.*, III.i 72*n*; *Nov. org.*, III.i 110*n*, 115*n*; *Of Atheism*, I 264–5*n*; *Of Beauty*, I 211, 255*n*; *Of Death*, III.i 86*n*; III.ii 34*n*; *Of Empire*, III.i 121*n*; *Of Goodness and Goodness of Nature*, III.i 158*n*; *Of Seditions and Troubles*, III.ii 111*n*; *Of Studies*, III.i 64*n*; *Of Truth*, III.i 89*n*; *Wisdom of the Antients*, II 251

Bacon, Sir Nicholas, IV 68–9*n*
Bacon, Roger, in AP poems, V 158, 325
Bæotia, in AP poem, V 62. See also Bœotia
Bailey, Nathan, his dictionary, III.i 37*n*, 64*n*, 68*n*, 72*n*, 102*n*
Bainbrigg, Charles, II 333*n*
Baker, C. H. Collins, *Life of Chandos*, III. ii 23*n*, 147*n*
Baker, H. K., III.i 154*n*
Baker, Henry, Biog., V 428; other ref., III.i 39*n*; V 172
Baker, Sir James (journalist), V 102*n*, 136*n*, 460; VI 135, 136*n*, 191*n*
Baker, Thomas (dramatist), in AP poem (?), VI 40 and *n*
Balaam, in AP poems, III.ii xxi, 121 and *n*; 122, 123, 124, 125; IV 9; AP portrait of, VII ccxlviii
"Balance of Things", III.ii xxi, xxiii f., xxvi, 106 f., 153*n*
Balbus, in AP poem, IV 115 and *n*
Balderston, Katherine C., VI 150*n*
Balguy, John (divine), III.i 132*n*, 136*n*, 137*n*, 141*n*
Bamford (playing-card maker), II 391 f.
Bancks, John (poet), VI 393*n*
Banier, Abbé Antoine, V 272–3*n*

Banks, John (dramatist), V 92, 93*n*,
280, 280–1*n*
Banks, Joseph, II 416
Banks, T. H., I 173*n*; X 541
Bansted-down (Surrey), in AP
poem, IV 67
Barbarus, Hermolaus (author of
Allégories d'Homère), IX 209
Barber, John, Biog., V 428; in AP
poem, VI 395, 396*n*; other ref.,
IV 213*n*, 319*n*; V 118*n*, 238, 354*n*
Barber, Mary (poet), IV 97*n*
Barca, in *Dunciad*, V 68 and *n*, 275
Barfield, Owen, III.i 62*n*
Barker, R. H., *Mr. Cibber of Drury
Lane*, V 185*n*, 279*n*, 335*n*, 433 f.
Barnard, John, VII xv *n*; X 575
Barnard, Sir John, Biog., IV 345;
in AP poems, IV 285 and *n*, 318
and *n*; other ref., IV xxxi, xxxv,
367; V 373*n*
Barnard, Lady Mary. See Fitz-
williams
Barnard, Christopher Vane, 10th
Baron, VIII xiii
Barnes, Joshua, AP debt to, VII xl,
lxxxi, cvi–cvii; modern recog-
nition of his view of Homer, VII
lxxv and *n*; his *Iliad*, VII lxxx
and *n*; his Latin gloss, VII xciv
and *n*, xcv; trans. and ed. of
Homer, V 399*n*; VII xxxviii,
lxxii and *n*, lxxvii and *n*, 313, 427;
VIII 2, 16, 22, 132, 144, 194,
240, 381, 530, 536; IX 141, 204;
in AP MS Preface, X 441
"Barnivelt, Esdras" (pseud.), in
AP poems, VI 132*n*, 133–6
Baron, The. See Petre, Lord
Robert
Baron, Robert (poet), III.i 160*n*
Barrow, Isaac (divine), III.i 39*n*,
40*n*; in AP poem, V 367

Bartlett, Phyllis, VII ccxix *n*
Basnage de Beauval, Jacques, II
157*n*; X 317
Basto, in AP poem, II 172
Bateman, Sir William, III.ii 37*n*
Bateson, F. W., III.i 165*n*; VI 287*n*
Bath (Somersetshire), in AP poem,
V 327 and *n*
Bath, Earl of. See Pulteney
Bath, The Marquess of, IV 148
Bathsheba, VI 375*n*
Bathurst, Allen, Earl, Biog., III.ii
83*n*; IV 345; on Warburton text,
III.ii 79; on AP intemperance,
IV 65*n*; connection with publi-
cation of Dunciad, V xxviii, 31,
461, 463; AP bequest to, VI
213*n*; other ref., III.ii x *n*, xlii,
173; IV xx, 10*n*, 121*n*, 248*n*,
321*n*, 370; V xxii *n*; VII ccxxii,
ccxxviii; AP corres., III.i 14*n*,
58*n*; III.ii 60*n*; IV 182–3*n*; VI
195–6*n*, 454*n*; in AP poems, *Ep.
to*, III.ii 83–125; others, III.ii
154; IV 87–9, 183, 333 and *n*;
VI 195–6, 368
Bathurst, Benjamin (son of
above), III.ii 181*n*
Bathurst, Ralph, I 185*n*
Batrachomyomachia, V 109*n*, 339*n*;
VII lxxxii, 47, 52, 55
Battaille, M.-L., VIII xii
Bavius (poetaster, 1st c. BC), in AP
poems, IV 102 and *n*, 114; V 151,
154, 186, 321 f.; VI 16
Baxter, Richard (divine), III.i
110*n*
Bayle, Pierre (philosopher, author
of *Dictionnaire historique et critique*),
III.i 23*n*, 84*n*, 85*n*, 141*n*; V 157*n*,
158*n*, 378*n*; VI 122*n*; VII 461;
IX, xiv; X 310, 317–18
Bayonne hams, in AP poem, V 397

Beach, J. W., III.i 93n, 103n

Beales, H. L., III.ii 156n

Beardsley, Aubrey, II 118n

Beattie, James, II 107; X 506

Beattie, L. M., *John Arbuthnot*, III.ii 87n; IV 37n; X xxv

Beauclerc, Lord Sidney (collector), III.ii 134n; IV 288n

Beaufort, L. de, III.i 17n, 103n

Beaumont, Francis, III.i 94n; IV 200n, 201; and Fletcher, II 32n, 188n

Beaumont, Sir John (poet), I 193n; III.i 129n

Becan, Jean. See Goropius

Beccaficos, in AP poem, IV 56n, 57

Beckingham, John, II 415

Bedford, John Russell, 4th Duke of, V 402n

Bedford, Wriothesley Russell, 2nd Duke of, in AP poems, III.ii 91n; IV 141 and n

Bedford Head, Covent Garden (London), in AP poems, IV 57 and n, 87

Bedingfield, E., II 87n, 96 ff., 373

Bedlam, in AP poems, IV 96, 107, 231; V 150, 320; VI 142, 277, 283

Behn, Aphra, translator of Ovid, I 340, 393n, 399n; II 293n, 296, 307, 328n; of Tallemant's *Voyage to the Isle of Love*, II 216n, 276n, 347–8n; of Fontenelle, II 209n; in AP poem, IV 219 and n; other ref., IV xvii; X 512

Bekker, B., II 157n

Belerium, in AP poem, I 179 and n

Belgian, in AP poem, I 300

Belinda, source of name, II 143n; in AP poems, II 125, 127, 130, 134, 135, 137, 139, 144, 147, 154, 162, 171, 173, 178, 183, 190, 191,

199, 201, 206, 207, 212; VI 107, 158. See Fermor, Arabella

Belisarius, in AP poem, VI 355

Beljame, Alexandre, I 307n

Bellarmine, Roberto (Jesuit theologian), III.i 48n, 59n, 123n, 144n

Bellenden, Margaret and Mary, in AP poems, VI 180, 184n, 185, 186, 187n

Bellers, Fettiplace, V 101n

Bellucci, Antonio, III.ii 151n

Bembo, Pietro, I 319n

Benedict XIII, Pope, III.ii 28n

Bénézit, E., VII xiii

Benham, W. G., II 391 f.

Beni, Paolo, IX 36

Benlowes, Edward (poet), in AP poems, V 99n, 321 and n

Bennet, William, Bishop of Cloyne, III.ii 104n, 116n

Benson, Martin, Bishop of Gloucester, Biog., IV 345–6; in AP poem, IV 316; other ref., IV 382

Benson, William, Biog., V 428–9; in AP poems, V 188, 336, 352; VI 395, 396–7n

Bentham, Jeremy, VII ccxxviii

Bentinck, Willem. See Portland

Bentivoglio, Guido, Cardinal, *Letters of Wit*, II 169n, 194n, 400

Bentley, Richard, Biog., IV 346; V 429; in AP poems, IV 29 and n, 108 and n, 203 and n; V 59n, 175n, 238n, 254n, 267n, 268n, 275n, 305–6n, 340n, 356n, 361n, 362 ff., 363n, 372n, 395n; VI 283, 286n, 328, 332–3n; notes attributed to him, IV 74n, 77n, 78n, 80n, 82n, 86n, 88n; V *passim*; ed. of Horace, IV xliii, 72; ed. of Terence, IV 77n; V 306n; his emendations parodied, V 217 ff.; on AP Homer, VII xlii and n,

B

lxxvi–lxxvii, cxciii; his Homer
scholarship, VII lxxiii *n*, lxxvi,
lxxxi; other ref., I 251*n*; III.i
38*n*; IV 372; V xl, xlii, 427, 432,
440, 446–7, 457, 458; VI 255*n*;
VII xxii, lxxviii
Bentley, Thomas, Biog., V 429; in
AP poems, V 124*n*, 305–6 and *n*;
IV 121–2*n*, 346; other ref., VII
xlii *n*
Beowulf, VII lxxvi
Berecynthia, in *Dunciad*, V 160,
326; in minor poem, VI 368
Berenice, in AP poem, II 137, 210
Bereshi[t], Rabbi, II 157*n*
Berglerus, Stephanus, AP copy of
his Homer, VII lxxvii *n*; in AP
MS Preface, X 441
Berington, Joseph, II 297*n* f.
Berkeley, George, Bishop of Cloyne,
Biog., IV 346; his *Alciphron*,
III.ii 23*n*; V 387*n*, 390*n*; in AP
poem, IV 317; comment on AP
Homer, VII cvii; other ref.,
III.i xxiii, 104*n*; IV 352
Berkeley, George (politician), VI
28*n*, 392*n*
Berkeley, James, 3rd Earl of, V
392*n*
Berkeley, Louisa (Lennox), Lady,
VI 158*n*
Berkeley, William, 4th Baron B. of
Stratton, II 93*n*
Berks[hire], in AP poem, IV 243
Bernini, G. L., in AP poem, IV
226*n*, 227; other ref., VII cciv;
IX xiii
Bernouilli, Jean (natural philo-
sopher), III.i 56*n*
Bertie, James, M.P., III.ii 25*n*
Bertrand's toy shop, in AP poem,
VI 378, 379*n*
Bess. See Elizabeth

Bestia, in AP poems, IV 126, 285
Bethel, Hugh, Biog., IV 346–7; AP
corres., III.i 140*n*, 158*n*, 159*n*;
III.ii 59*n*, 97*n*; IV xix, 54*n*, 67*n*,
391; V 322*n*, 360*n*, 361*n*; VII
ccxxvii and *n*, ccxxix; in AP
poems, III.i 140; IV 55, 65; V
128, 131*n*, 232, 233*n*, 321, 322*n*;
other ref., III.i lv; V 34
Bettenham, James (printer), V
xviii ff., 463; X 589
Betterton, Thomas, Biog., IV 347;
in AP poem, IV 205; other ref.,
II 6, 7
Betty, in *R. of the Lock*, II 158 and *n*;
in *Ep. to Cobham*, III.ii 36 and *n*
Bevan, Ernest, III.i 119*n*
Bevismount (Hants, seat of Lord
Peterborough), III.ii 140*n*
Bible, King James Version, I 102,
112*n*, 113, 114*n*, 115*n*, 117*n*,
118*n*, 119*n*, 120*n*, 121*n*, 122*n*;
Rheims-Douai Version, I 102,
112*n*, 113*n*, 114*n*, 115*n*, 116*n*,
117*n*, 118*n*, 119*n*, 120*n*, 121*n*,
122*n*, 155*n*, 174*n*; in AP poems,
II 74, 156, 401; V 107, 284, 299;
other ref., I 101–3, 132; VII
ccxxix
New Testament: allusions to, VII
ccxxvii; Sermon on the Mount,
X 581
Acts, VIII 302; IX 458–9;
I Cor., III.i lxviii, 25*n*, 46*n*, 47*n*,
54*n*, 123*n*, 125*n*, 157*n*, 159*n*,
161*n*; IV 281*n*; VI 95*n*; 2 Cor.,
II 256*n*; Hebrews, III.i 26*n*, 47*n*,
125*n*; X 267; James, III.i 87*n*,
125*n*; John, I 118*n*; III.i 28*n*,
125*n*; IV 104*n*; VIII 205; Luke,
V 287*n*; VIII 382; X 225;
Matthew, I 286*n*; II 148*n*, 160*n*;
III.i xxiv, lxviii, 24*n*, 28*n*, 50*n*,

68n, 87n, 95n, 161n, 163n; VIII 209, 564; X 198; 1 Peter, III.i 25n; Philippians, IV 281n; Revelation, VII 175; Romans, III.i 18n, 26n, 59n, 90n; 1 Timothy, III.i 66n, 96n; Titus, X 55

Old Testament: allusions to, III.ii 107n, 177n; V 465n; AP relates Homer to, VII 18, 175; referred to in Essay on Battles, VII 254, 257; language of, IX 23; Abraham mentioned, IX 63; in AP MS Preface, X 419, 436; in AP Postscript, X 455; *Odyssey* parallels to, X 508 ff.; other ref., I 143; VII ccxxvii

Chronicles, VII 127, 201; VIII 75; X 41; Daniel, II 165n, 380n; VII 399–400; Deuteronomy, III.i 96n; VII 407; VIII 418, 465; IX 112, 183, 315; Ecclesiastes, III.i 61n, 137n, 139n; VII lix; VIII 573; IX 264; X 234; Ecclesiasticus, VII 335; VIII 444; IX 264; Esther, II 18n; X 207; Exodus, II 260n; III.i lxviii, 71n, 139n; IV 104n; V 466n; VII 258, 260, 265; VIII 109, 334, 421; IX 32, 206; X 113, 184; Ezekiel, VIII 342, 495–6; X 198, 308, 366; Genesis, I 155n, 293n; II 17n, 18n, 157n, 172n; III.i lxiv, 51n, 79n, 95n, 109n, 116n; III.ii 107n; VII 235, 274, 323, 336, 351, 407, 442; VIII 36, 266, 478, 492; IX 108, 206, 214; X 74, 86, 131, 166, 211, 251, 318, 510; Hosea, III.i 51n; VIII 456; Isaiah, I 101–5, 111, 112 and n, 113n, 114n, 115n, 116n, 117n, 118n, 119n, 120n, 121n, 138, 142 ff., 156n, 188n, 190n, 191n, 192n; II 330n; III.i lxviii, 25n, 32n,

56n; IV 305n; VII 435; VIII 50, 94, 169, 175, 376, 456; X 92, 236, 308, 511; Jeremiah, III.i 102n; VIII 142, 175, 483; Job, II 65, 399; III.i lxviii, lxx, 17n, 30n, 35n, 46n, 53n, 56n, 59n, 95n; VII 399; VIII 463, 483; X 236, 310, 314; Jonah, VIII 209; Joshua, VII 355; VIII 129; X 198; Judges, VII 267, 342, 402; VIII 14; IX 205; X 113, 207, 312; Judith, II 18n; 1 Kings, III.i 68n; VII 91; 2 Kings, VII 402; VIII 40; X 320, 323; Lamentations, VIII 175, 447; Maccabees, VIII 372; X 207; Micah, III.ii 177n; Numbers, VII 175, 274, 342; X 83; Pentateuch, VIII 379–80; IX 32, 310; Proverbs, III.i 87n; III.ii 107n; VII 399; VIII 564; IX 222, 285, 432; X 510; Psalms, I 120n, 174n, 253n, 291n; III.i xxxix, lx, lxviii, 18n, 27n, 28n, 35n, 36n, 68n, 87n, 95n, 97n, 109n, 135n; IV 214n, 215; V 160n; VII 245, 260, 293, 309, 337, 401; VIII 50, 81, 106, 169, 326, 456, 564; IX 219; X 235, 509, 511; 1 Samuel, II 18n, 164n; V 363n; VII 91, 326, 334, 367, 384, 401, 442; VIII 9, 17, 22, 476; IX 27, 264, 378–9; X 211, 239, 285; 2 Samuel, VII 386, 462; VIII 139, 489; X 233, 502; Solomon, IX 247; Song of Solomon, I 116n; Wisdom of Solomon, III.i 49n; Tobit, VIII 555

Bibliothèque de l'Arsenal, discovery of AP *Iliad* proofs in, VII xxxvii n

Bickham, George, I 177n, 178n; III.ii 143n

Bicknell, Mrs M. (actress), in AP poems, VI 129, 132n

Biddel, in AP poem, VI 276

Bidez, J., III.i 139n

Bill, C., II 402

Billingsgate (London), in AP poem, V 292, 342; VI 44

Billy, in AP poem, II 65. See also Yonge, Sir William

Binfield (Berks.), in AP poem, VI 26; other ref., VI 130n; VII xxv, xxvi, lx

Biographia Britannica, V 144n

Bion (poet, fl. *c* 100 BC), I 20, 47, 90n, 91n; V 229

Birch, Thomas (antiquary), VI 224–5n, 374n

Blackburne, Lancelot, Archbishop of York, Biog., IV 347; in AP poems, IV 78n, 79, 335 and n; other ref., III.ii 34n

Black Joke (musical air), in AP poem, IV 220–1n, 221

Blacklock, Thomas, II 358

Blackmore, Sir Richard, Biog., IV 347–8; V 429; quarrel with wits, including AP, I 225, 291 and n; IV 348; V 16n; VI 175n; in AP poems other than *Dunciad*, I 291; IV 6n, 7, 173, 227 and n, 279 and n; on melancholy, II 188n, 189n; his poetry, I 267n, 295n, 309n; II 156n, 163n, 169n; III.i 102n, 110n, 111n, 142n, 150n; V xvi, xxxviii n, xxxix, xlv, 53, 144n, 146n; knighted, IV 227 and n; in *E. on Criticism*, I 291 and n; V 12n, 447; in *Dunciad*, V 71n, 72, 129, 131–2n, 134n, 137, 142, 206n, 210, 239n, 276 and n, 308, 310 and n, 315, 340n; in *Verses*, VI 290–3

Blackwell, Alexander (gardener), III.ii 148n

Blackwell, Thomas, VII lxxiv

Bladen, Col. Martin, in AP poems, V 91n, 397; other ref., V 473

Bladen, Thomas, Biog., V 430; in AP poem, V 397 and n; other ref., V 473

Blaeu, Willem Janszoon (printer), in AP poem, VI 82, 84n

Blair, Hugh, VII ccxxii

Blake, William, II viii

Blakeney, E. H., V 255n, 395n

Blanchard, Rae, II 243n; VI 102n; VII 23

Blanchet, L., III.i 158n

Bland, Desmond, VI xix

Bland, Henry, Biog., IV 348; V 430; in AP poems, IV 304, 303–4n; V 287, 311n, 315n

Blenheim Palace (Oxon.), III.ii 19n, 148n, 151n, 170, 187

Blois (French town), in AP poem, IV 164n, 165

Blome, Richard (publisher), in AP poem, V 78, 79n, 80n

Blomfield, J. C., II 371 f.

Blomfield, Sir Reginald, *Renaissance Architecture in England*, III.ii 138n; *Formal Garden in England*, III.ii 141n, 145n

Bloom, Lillian D., IV xliii n

Bloomsbury Square (London), in AP poem, IV 171

Blount, Charles, Biog., IV 348; in AP poem, IV 307 and n; other ref., III.i 117n; V 92n

Blount, Edward, AP corres., III.i 125n, 135n; III.ii 172n; IV 126n; VI 193n, 248n; VII xli n, ccxxvi n

Blount, Martha (called Patty), Biog., III.ii 46–7n; AP corres., I 100; II 88n, 94, 100, 311, 366n; III.i 21n, 50n, 51n, 95n, 156n, 163n; III.ii 63n, 71n, 72n, 74n,

148n; IV 153, 352; VI 126n, 132n, 194n, 198n, 231n, 381n, 411n; VII xxxvii n; connection with *Eloisa to Abelard*, II 311-13, 325n; AP poems to, VI 232-3 and n, 65n, 126n, 231, 244-7, 308n; in other AP poems, III.ii 46-74; VI 158; her copy of *The Temple of Fame*, VI 128n; other ref., II xii; III.ii xiii n, 72n, 73n, 131n; IV 153n, 344, 347; V 13n, 119n; VI 230n, 317n; VI xviii, 127n

Blount, Teresa, AP corres., II 94; VI 194n, 201n, 411n; AP poems to, VI 65n, 126n, 189-92, 232-3; in other AP poem, VI 158; her character, VI 190-1n; other ref., III.ii 47n, 71n, 230n

Blount, Thomas, *Glossographia*, III.i 12n

Blount, Sir Thomas Pope, *De Re Poetica*, II 3

Blount, Walter, of Mapledurham, V 321n

Bluhm, Heinz, III.i xxvii n

Blunt, Sir John, Biog., IV 348; in AP poems, III.ii 99, 104 and n; IV 298; other ref., III.ii 85n

Boas, George, III.i 100n, 108n

Boccaccio, Giovanni, I 309n; II 220, 251

Bochart, Samuel (geographer), VIII 410; IX 44, 143, 155, 190, 309, 337, 340, 345, 429, 434; X 60, 91-2, 255, 341

Bodenham, J., III.i 88n

Bodin, Jean, II 233

Bodleian Library, VII xxii; VIII xii

Bœotia[-n], in AP poems, I 420; V 154, 271, 322; VI 307. See also Bæotia

Boethius, III.i 50n, 92n, 135n

Bohea, in AP poems, II 134, 197; VI 125

Boiardo, Matteo Maria, II 221

Boiastuau, Pierre (moralist), III.i li

Boileau-Despréaux, Nicolas, Biog., IV 348-9; AP use of, I 279n; VII xxxix, xl; in AP poems, I 323 and n; IV 15, 227, 326; VI 37, 450; Cleland on, V 17; his defence of Homer, VII lxxii; his trans. of Longinus and his commentary, VII 15, 160, 244-5, 356; VIII 64, 285, 316-17, 437; IX 113, 228, 280, 334, 457-8; X 32-3, 90, 233-4; in AP MS Preface, X 419, 429; other ref., I xvi, 253n, 285n; IV xxviii, 226n, 519n; V xxxviii, 9, 20, 114n

WORKS:

Art poétique, I 210-11, 244n, 252n, 255n, 256-7n, 267n, 268n, 281n, 310n, 311n, 320n, 323n, 326n; II 36n, 272n; III.i 165n; IV 12n, 96n, 97n, 99n; *Discours*, II 272n; IV 325n, 326n; *Epîtres*, I 290n; III.i 53n, 56n, 129n, 142n; III.ii 25n; IV 105n, 115n, 123n, 179n, 278n; V 377n; VI 388 and n; *Le Lutrin*, II 93 f., 107-12, 115 ff., 145n, 146n, 147n, 170n, 174n, 183n, 189n, 191n, 192n, 199n, 203n, 378, 394 f.; V 96n, 121n, 198, 292n, 450; VI 37-8 and n; VIII 174; X 387; Preface to *Œuvres Diverses*, I 273n, 316n; *Sat.*, III.i 31n, 100n, 101n, 104n 110n, 114n, 146n, 147n, 148n; IV 104n, 230n, 297n, 327n; V 188n, 289n; trans. of Longinus, I 247n, 248n, 255n, 316n; VI 95n

Boivin de Villeneuve, Jean (author of *Apologie d'Homère*), VII xl,

360; VIII xii–xiii, 105, 358, 362, 379, 395; IX 169, 334

Bolgolam, in AP poem, VI 278

Bolingbroke, Henry St John, 1st Viscount, Biog., IV 383; AP bequest to, I 318n; presence a stimulus to AP work, III.i xlvii; IV xiii; at Dawley Farm, II xiv; III.ii 187n; IV 181n, 390–1; VI 452–5; returns from exile, III.i xii; VII xxvii; and visits AP, VII xxviii
Connections with AP *E. on Man*, III.i: his letters to Swift describing, xii ff.; authorship attributed to, xv; criticism of AP for addressing *Essay* to him, xvii n; his deism, xxiv; *Essay* not sufficiently heterodox to suit him, xxv; influence on, xxvi, xxvii, xxix ff.; his surviving works written later than, xxix, 169; differences between his thought and that of *Essay*, xxx f., lxviii; *Essay* had deeper roots than his suggestion, lxiii, lxxii; other connections, III.ii x, xiv n, xxi
Suppresses *Ep. to Several Persons*, III.ii xi f., 166 f.; AP prints his *Idea of a Patriot King*, III.ii xiii; opinions, III.ii xxvii n, 27n, 33n, 46n, 120n, 145n; publishes AP character of Atossa, III.ii 168; as political figure, III.ii xlii, 105n; IV xxxi–xxxiii, 380; V 13n, 19n, 306n, 312n, 342n, 352n, 359n, 430, 439, 445, 459; as addressee of AP Horatian epistles, IV xxxviii, 268n, 279; influence on *Dunciad* passage, V 385n–389n; shares in "Cheddar" letter to Swift, VI 254–5n; writings ascribed to, VI 412n; as

Odysseus figure, VII ccxxxiv; acknowledgement in AP Preface, VII 24
AP corres., III.ii xiv, xxvii n; IV 115n; VI 308n, 384n
In AP poems, III.i (pseud. "Laelius"), 11 and n, 129; IV 17, 81 and n, 105, 255, 279, 292n, 293 and n, 320–1 and n; VI 307, 309n, 333, 334n, 383, 452–5; VII ccxxxi
Other ref., I 245n, 315n; III.i v, xxvi, 38n, 76n, 86n; III.ii 173; IV 281n; V xxv, xxxi n, 34, 114n, 193n, 447; VI 459n

Bolingbroke, Marie Claire, Viscountess, in AP poem, VI 307, 308n, 309n; other ref., III.ii 35n

Bolton, Charles Paulet, 3rd Duke of, V 126n, 127n, 190n, 371n, 432, 458, 467

Bond, Denis, Biog., IV 349; in AP poems, III.ii 98; IV 9, 307

Bond, D. F., III.i 59n

Bond, R. P., I 191n; II 105n, 106n, 293n

Bond, William, Biog., V 430; attacks AP, V 41n, 110n, 430; in AP poems, V 111, 164, 301; other ref., V xx n, 433

Bonducci, A. (translator), II 105n

Bonnard, G. A. (scholar), III.i xx n, xxi n

Bonutius, Juda (printer), VII 44

Book of Common Prayer, III.i xliv

Boötes, in AP poem, I 432

Booth, Barton, Biog., IV 349; in AP poems, IV 205 and n, 222n, 223; V 179 and n, 333 and n

Boreas, in AP poems, I 95, 421; IV 139; VI 79, 231, 289

Borellus (Giovanni Alfonso Borelli), *De motu anim.*, VIII 133

Borgia (family name), in *E. on Man*, III.i xxxiii, xxxvii, lxi, 35

Borgman, Albert Stephens, *Life of Mountford*, IV 376n; *Thomas Shadwell*, V 141n, 454

Bossu. See Le Bossu

Bossuet, Jacques Benigne (preacher), III.i 97n; V 344n

Boswell, James, *Life of Johnson*, III.i 26n; IV 69n; V 116n, 436n, 450; VII lxxxviii n

Bottkol, J. M. J., VII cxiii n

Bouhours, Dominique (critic), I 210, 247n, 248n, 267n; V 347n; VII lxxiii

Boulter, Edmund (John Hopkins's executor), III.ii 116n

Boulter, Hugh, Bishop of Armagh, IV 102n

Bounce, in AP poems, VI 366, 367, 368, 369, 370; VI 405

Bourbon, in AP poem, V 373

Bourbon, Charles, Duke of, I 322n

Bowles, William (translator), I 83n

Bowles, William Lisle (editor of Pope), I viii, 73n, 79n, 112n, 149n, 176n, 183n, 184n, 188n, 297n, 308n, 418n; III.i 17n, 68n, 94n, 119n; IV ix, xxiv, 210n, 332n, 335n, 337n; V 126n, 174n, 388n, 404n; VI 138n, 212n, 332n, 413n, 419n

Bowra, Sir Maurice, VII clxxiv–clxxvi and n, clxxxv, cciv n

Bowyer, William, AP corres., III.ii x; connection with early printings of *Iliad*, X 587–9, 591–2, 606; other ref. to him as AP printer, I viii, 60n, 389n; II x; III.ii x, xii, xv n; IV ix; V 296n, 353n

Boyer, Abel, Biog., V 430; *Letters of Wit*, I 80n, 81n; *Achilles*, I 306n;

Political State, IV 89n, 240n, 356; V 146–7n; in AP poems, V 146, 317; VI 123, 124n; other ref., III.i 111n

Boyle family, genealogical table, IV 350. For individuals, except next entry, see Orrery

Boyle, Charles (later 4th Earl of Orrery), VII lxxviii

Boyle, Richard, Earl of Burlington. See Burlington

Boyle, Robert, in AP poem, VI 48, 51n; *Works*, III.i 19n, 20n, 22n, 39n, 41n, 111n; other ref., III.i 56n, 104n

Boyle Lecture Sermons (BLS), III.i 38n, 39n, 95n, 98n, 101n

Boynton, Henry W., I viii

Boys, R. C., I 225n

Brachmans, in AP poem, II 260 and n

Bradley, Richard (natural philosopher), III.i 32n, 42n

Brady, Nicholas (poet), in AP poem, VI 173, 176n; other ref., I 253n

Bra[h]mins, in AP poem, III.ii 109

Bramante, Donato d'Agnolo, I 319n

Brampton Bryon (Herefordshire), VI 241n, 242n

Bramston, James, *Art of Politics*, IV 43n; V 294n, 444; *Man of Taste*, IV 60n, 143n; V 398n; in AP poems, V 174–5n; other ref., V xlv n

Brandon, Samuel, II 294

Brasil, in AP poem, VI 25, 26

Brathwait, Richard, II 7

Brébeuf, Georges de (poet), VI 418

Bredvold, Louis I., I 220n, 221n; II 267n; VII ccxix n

Brerewood, Edward, VII 324

Brett, Col. Henry, V 282*n*

Brett, R. L., I 252*n*

Breval, John Durant, Biog., V 430–
1; in AP poems, V xx *n*, 111 and
n, 128 and *n*, 301 and *n*, 307 and
n, 372*n*, 375*n*; *The Confederates*, V
91*n*, 110–11*n*, 208, 210; other
ref., III.ii 178; IV 243*n*

Briareus, in AP poems, V 348; VI
22

Brice's Weekly Journal, V 116*n*, 153*n*

Bridewell (prison), in AP poems, V
132, 308

Bridges, Mr (author of *On Divine
Wisdom and Providence*), III.i xvii
n, xxi *n*

Bridges, Brook (nephew of Ralph
Bridges), I 355

Bridges, Ralph, corres. with Sir
William Trumbull, I 41*n*, 126,
127, 201, 202, 348, 355; VII
xxxv and *n*; comment on AP
Episode of Sarpedon, I 354–6, 358;
AP corres., I 353; VII lxxxv,
lxxxviii, ccxxii and *n*

Bridgewater, Elizabeth Egerton,
Countess of, in AP poem, VI 157,
158, 159–60*n*

Bridgman, Charles (gardener), in
AP poem, III.ii 141*n*, 143*n*, 144,
149*n*

*Brief Journal of what passed in the
City of Marseilles While it was
Afflicted with the Plague, In the Year
1720*, III.i 138*n*

Brillante, in AP poem, II 166

Bristol, Elizabeth Hervey, Countess of, III.i 58*n*

Bristol, John Hervey, 1st Earl of,
III.ii 91*n*

Britain, in AP poems, I 179, 189; II
129, 169; III.ii 21, 26, 29, 104,
105, 110, 111, 124, 156; IV 126,
207, 209, 217, 332, 334, 335, 336,
337; V 82, 159, 325; VI 64, 151,
204, 280, 310, 311, 404

Britannia, in AP poems, I 159 and
n, 161; V 175, 269, 330, 407; VI
120

Britannia Illustrata, III.ii 172*n*

British, in AP poems, I 169, 186,
189; II 129, 131, 165, 170, 181;
III.ii 89; VI 86, 96, 97, 229, 270,
311, 383

British Apollo, III.i 70*n*

British Journal, V xxxix, 134*n*, 165*n*,
209, 211*n*, 235*n*, 428, 441; VI
247*n*, 447*n*

British Museum, Egerton MS
(1950), III.i 124*n*, 170; other
ref., VII xiii, xiv, xxii, xlvi; VIII
xiii; IX xiii

Briton[s], in AP poems, I 323; IV
197, 221, 327; VI 97, 232, 281,
320, 355, 356, 400

Broadus, E. K., *The Laureateship*, IV
7*n*, 226*n*

Brobdingnag, in AP poems, III.ii
147; VI 271, 272, 279, 280

Brocas, "Beau" (poet), in AP
poems, VI 24, 25, 28*n*, 131*n*

Brome, Richard (Caroline dramatist), in AP poem, V 280, 281*n*;
other ref., III.ii 56*n*

Brompton Park (London), in AP
poem, VI 222

Brooke, Fulke Greville, Lord, III.i
31*n*, 61*n*, 73*n*, 112*n*, 116*n*, 117*n*,
118*n*, 120*n*, 121*n*, 122*n*, 125*n*

Brooke, Henry (poet), II 4

Brooke, W. T., his copy of "death-
bed" edition, III.ii xiv *n*

Brooks (name of London brothel),
in AP poem, VI 232, 233*n*

Brooks, Cleanth, I xiii, 215*n*

Brooks, Roberta, VII xxiii

Broome, William, Biog., V 431; his poetry, II 319n; V 113n; VI 437n; his *Habbakuk*, X 504; portrait illus., X xii; quoted on AP, V 37; VI 448n; AP corres., III.i 34n, 160n; V 31n, 191n; VI 213n, 319n, 329n; VII xli n, lxxxiv n, cvi and n, cxcvii n, ccxxi and n; in AP poems, II 144; V 191, 280, 339n; other ref., IX 279, 348, 361, 373; X 119, 205, 266, 286
Homer translation: as translator of Dacier *Iliad*, VII xiii, xvii–xviii n, xl n; VIII xii, 104; X 500, 503 (see Ozell for Ozell–Broome–Oldisworth trans.); as AP collaborator in *Odyssey* trans., I 350; III.i 32n; III.ii xvi n; V 32n, 191n, 236; VII xviii, xliii, xliv–xlvi, l, lxiii, cxxii–cxxiii, cxxvii, clvi, cxciii and n, cxciv, cxcv, cxcvi and n, cci–ccii, ccviii, ccix, ccx, ccxv n, ccxlii, ccxliii; IX xii; assists AP in work for *Iliad* trans., VII xxxix; tribute to AP, VII lxiii; his trans. of *Odyssey*, VII lxviii and n, cxii, cxxiii; X 506, 507, 509, 510–12, 599, 602–3; on AP and Eustathius, VII lxxxiv and n; his own trans. of *Iliad*, VII cxii n; X 585–6; AP debt to, VII cvi; acknowledgement in AP end note, VIII 578

Brossette, Claude, I xvi f.

Brower, Reuben, V 460, 470, 472; VII li n, lviii and n, cxciv n, ccii n, ccxxvii and n, ccxxix and n

Brown (printer, probably Jonas Browne), Biog., V 431; in *Dunciad*, V 152 and n, 321 and n, 447

Brown, Father (chaplain to John Caryll), VI 78n

Brown, John (author of *Estimate*), III.ii xix n

Brown, Lancelot ("Capability"), II 225; III.ii 143n; IV 225n

Brown, Tom (satirist), II 153n; IV 370; V 151n, 452, 454

Browne, Anthony, of Abscourt (possible addressee of *Imit. Hor., Ep. II.ii*), IV 164n, 181n

Browne, Daniel, Biog., V 431

Browne, Sir George, Biog., II 376 f.; as "Sir Plume", in AP poems, II ix, 81n, 87 ff., 93, 108, 133, 194, 206

Browne, Isaac Hawkins (poet), V 263n; VI 279n

Browne, Sir Thomas, *Pseud. Epidem.*, III.i 122n; *Rel. Med.*, III.i 15n, 25n, 36n, 50n, 61n, 95n, 101n, 112n; IV 120n; *Vulgar Errors*, II 341n

Browne, William (of Tavistock), II 294

Browning, Robert, II 301n

Brudenal, Frances (Granville's "Myra"), I 176n

Brunswick (Germany), in AP poems, IV 7, 279

Brussels, in AP poem, III.ii 36

Brutus, in AP poems, II 270; III.ii 120; VI 152, 153

Bruyère. See La Bruyère

Bryce, J. C., IV 120n; VI xix

Brydges, James, Duke of Chandos. See Chandos

Bubb, George. See Dodington

Bubo, in AP poems, III.ii 138, 182. For other ref. see Dodington

Buchanan, George (poet), II 160n; III.i 11n, 96n

Buckenburg. See Bucquenbourg

Buck, Lady, IV 89, 366

Buckingham and Normanby, Edmund Sheffield, 2nd Duke of, AP *Epitaph on*, VI 362-3 and *n*; other ref., VI 155*n*

Buckingham and Normanby, John Sheffield, 1st Duke of, and 3rd Earl of Mulgrave, Biog., IV 385; *Essay upon Poetry*, I 208, 239*n*, 247*n*, 262*n*, 268*n*, 274*n*, 292*n*, 297*n*, 308*n*, 316*n*, 323-4*n*; II 204*n*; III.i 151*n*, 152*n*; V 27*n*; AP edition of his *Works*, II xiii, 217*n*; III.ii 59*n*, 89*n*; V 168*n*; VI 154-5*n*; VII xxvi, xlii, xliv; his *Brutus*, and AP choruses, III.i 12*n*, 86*n*; IV 62*n*; VI 151-4, 155*n*; other works, III.i 122*n*, 132*n*, 152*n*; III.ii 56*n*, 89*n*; IV 66*n*; V 187*n*, 276*n*; procures Dryden a tomb in Westminster Abbey, VI 209*n*, 237, 238*n*; in AP poems, IV 105; VI 188 and *n*; acknowledgement in AP Preface, VII 24; other ref., I 38, 298*n*, 339, 356; II 216*n*, 257*n*; III.ii 60*n*, 62*n*; V xxxix, 35*n*, 104*n*, 113*n*, 114*n*, 430, 440, 444, 455 f.; VI 362*n*; VII cxliii

Buckingham and Normanby, Katharine (Darnley) Sheffield, Duchess of, as Atossa, III.ii 59*n* ff., 74*n*, 160 ff.; AP corres., III.ii 60*n*; other ref., IV 289*n*, 319*n*; V 153*n*; VI 155*n*, 362 and *n*

Buckingham, George Villiers, 2nd Duke of, his *Rehearsal* in AP poems, V 277 and *n*; VI 25-6, 28-9*n*; other ref., I 291*n*, 298*n*, 300*n*; III.ii 60*n*, 118; IV 69 and *n*; VII ccxlviii

Buckingham House (London), III.ii 170; VI 155*n*

Bucquenbourg, Sophie C. De Lippe, Countess of, in AP poem, VI 181, 184*n*, 465*n*

Budgell, Eustace, Biog., IV 351; V 431-2; his writings and speeches, IV 6-7*n*; V 144*n*, 428, 458; forged Tindall's will, IV 124-5*n*; his *Bee* cited, V 43*n*, 430, 441, 449, 451; identified as Umbra, VI 141*n*; in AP poems, IV 7, 15, 29, 80-1 and *n*, 124 and *n*; V 144 and *n*, 316, 416; VI 112-13 and *n*, 123, 124*n*, 172 and *n*

Buffon, Georges Louis Leclerc, comte de, III.i 42*n*

Bufo, in AP poems, 112-44; other ref., IV xxiv

Bug. See Kent, Henry de Grey, 1st Duke of

Bull, in AP poem, VI 259

Bulstrode, William, III.i 99*n*

Bunbury, Sir C., V 351*n*

Bundy, M. W., III.i 72*n*

Buononcini, G. B. (musician), III.ii 56*n*; VI 155*n*, 447*n*

Buononcini, M. A. (musician), II 205*n*

Burckhardt, J. C. (historian), II 216*n*

Burgersdyck, Francis (logician), in AP poem, V 361, 362*n*

Burke, Edmund, IV 368

Burke, H. F., II 82*n*

Burleigh, R. (publisher), V 208*n*

Burleigh, Mrs R. (bookseller), VI 183*n*, 187*n*

Burlington, Dorothy (Savile) Boyle, Countess of, in AP poems, VI 336-8, 390; her drawing, VI 384*n*, 393*n*; other ref., III.ii xxx

Burlington, Richard Boyle, 3rd Earl of, Biog., III.ii 134*n*; as architect, III.ii 156*n*; V 189*n*;

Palladian interests, III.ii xxv f., 128*n*, 139*n*, 155, 156*n*, 177*n*; connection with *Dunciad*, V xxviii, 33, 116*n*, 336, 461, 463; as AP friend, V 441–2; VI 305*n*; his house at Chiswick, VI 216*n*, 341*n*, 368, 434*n*; AP *Ep. to*, III.ii xxv–xxvi, 127–56; VI 334, 338*n*; in other AP poems, V 189, 336; VI 130, 132*n*, 355, 368; AP corres., III.ii xxv–xxvi, xxvii, xxx, 131*n*; VI 175*n*, 337*n*; other ref., II xiii; V 376*n*, 377*n*, 452, 453; VI 395*n*; VII xxvi

Burmann, Peter, Biog., V 432; in AP poem, V 366; *Anthologia Vet. Latin. Epigr.*, VI 249*n*

Burnet, Gilbert, Bishop of Salisbury, I 301*n*, 302*n*; III.i 146*n*; III.ii 26*n*, 92*n*; IV 30*n*, 31, 106*n*, 285*n*, 350; V 34*n*, 168*n*, 344*n*, 386*n*, 432; VI 234*n*

Burnet, Thomas, Biog., IV 351; V 432; relations with AP, III.i xvii *n*; V 16*n*, 18*n*, 168*n* f., 207, 212*n*, 401*n*; VI 132*n*, 135*n*, 145*n*; *Letters to Duckett*, IV 111*n*; VI 100*n*, 423; VII lxxxvii *n*; in AP poems, IV 106 and *n*; V 168, 329; VI 173, 301, 304*n*; other ref., IV 343; V 170*n*, 235*n*

Burnet, Thomas, *Sacred Theory of the Earth*, III.i 34*n*

Burney, Dr Charles, *General History of Music*, II 205*n*; V 128*n*, 347*n*, 435

Burton, Hezekiah (divine), III.i 31*n*, 61*n*, 63*n*, 64*n*, 79*n*, 94*n*, 106*n*, 118*n*, 126*n*, 134*n*, 137*n*, 157*n*, 159*n*, 160*n*, 161*n*, 162*n*, 164*n*

Burton, Robert, II 155*n*, 185*n*, 186*n*, 187*n*, 380, 381; III.i 68*n*, 70*n*, 72*n*, 125*n*; V 470

Burtt, E. A., III.i lxv *n*, 93*n*

Bury, J. B., II 233*n*, 270*n*

Busby, Richard (headmaster of Westminster School), V 355 ff., 355*n*, 357*n*

Bush, Douglas, III.i xlviii *n*, lxxii; VII cxliv

Bussy, Roger de Rabutin, comte de, II 297

Butler, C., *Reminiscences*, IV 238*n*

Butler, H. E. (translator), I 213*n*

Butler, Joseph (bishop), III.i 78*n*, 106*n*, 126*n*

Butler, Samuel, *Hudibras*, II 106, 110, 112*n*, 160*n*, 171*n*, 177*n*, 191*n*, 201*n*, 210*n*, 228, 294, 325*n*, 341*n*, 394, 395; III.i 64*n*; III.ii 47*n*; IV 219*n*; V 159*n*, 286*n*, 348*n*, 407*n*; *Thoughts*, IV 323*n*; in AP poem, VI 59; other ref., I 298*n*, 318*n*; V 354*n*, 428; VI 396*n*; VII cxxiv, clxxxv

Butt, John, I vii, ix, xiii, 17*n*; III.i vii, xvi *n*; III.ii xxx, 175 ff.; V 18*n*, 222*n*, 346*n*; VII xxiv; X 495

Butter, Nathaniel (Eliz. publisher), X 474

Button, Daniel (coffee-house manager), in AP poems, VI 135 and *n*, 140, 141*n*, 162; the Coffee House, VII xxxviii

Bykowski, Ignacy (translator), II 105*n*

Byron, George Gordon Noel, 6th Baron, II 301; VII cxxiv

C

Cadmus (founder of Thebes), in AP poems, I 409 and *n*, 410, 420, 423, 443

Cadmus of Miletus (historian, 6th c. BC), VII 77

Cadogan, Charles, 2nd Baron Cadogan of Oakley, III.ii 139*n*, 182*n*

Cadogan, William, 1st Earl Cadogan, 1st Baron Cadogan of Oakley, III.ii 97*n*, 187*n*

Caelius Aurelianus (physician, 4th/5th c. AD), VIII 70

Caesar [Domitian], in AP poems, I 410 and *n*, 411 and *n*

Caesar, Julius, in AP poems, II 266, 326; III.ii 56; IV 7, 159; V 289, 378; VI 66, 96, 97; other ref., I 81*n*, 138; II 116, 264*n*, 265*n*; III.i lv, 35, 141*n*, 142, 149*n*, 150 and *n*, 152; III.ii 21, 33

Cain, III.i lv, 139

Caius, in AP poem, VI 26, 87

Caley, "Mr." (poet), VI 421*n*

Calista, in AP poem, III.ii 52 and *n*

Callan, Norman, V 470; VII xv, xxxvii *n*, lxxxiv *n*

Callimachus (poet, 3rd c. BC), I 114*n*, 118*n*; II 210*n*, 398; IX 218, 226, 340, 371; X 56, 194

Callista, VI 224

Callisthenes (historian, 4th c. BC), VII 60

Calvin, John, in AP poem, III.i 141 and *n*

Calydon[-ian], I 434, 443

Calypso, in AP poem, III.ii 53 and *n*

Cam, in AP poems, I 74; V 360, 399

Cambridge, Richard Owen (poet), III.ii 63*n*

Cambridge University, in AP poems, V 143, 360, 339; other ref., V 472

Camden, William, *Britannia*, I 132, 138, 152*n*, 155*n*, 157*n*, 177*n*, 184*n*; II 264

Cameron, J. M., I 222*n*

Camilla, in AP poem, I 282, 283*n*

Camoëns, Luis de, V 205, 340*n*; VII clxxxiii

Campbell, Archibald (moralist), III.i 105*n*

Campbell, John, 1st Baron, *Lives of Lord Chief Justices*, IV 238*n*, 374

Campbell, Kathleen, III.ii 161

Campbell, Thomas, II 225

Campden House (London), in AP poem, VI 222, 224*n*

Cancer, in AP poems, I 163 and *n*, 164*n*; II 34

Cannons House (Middlesex, Chandos's mansion), in AP poems, IV 117; VI 339 and *n*; other ref., III.ii xxvi, xxx, 147*n*,

148*n*, 149*n*, 150*n*, 151*n*, 152*n*, 154*n*, 185

Cantharides, in AP poem, II 32 and *n*

Capaneus, in AP poem, I 412*n* and 413

Caracci, Annibale, VI 157, 159*n*; the Caracci, VII lvii

Carew, Thomas, II 264*n*; IV 204*n*, 205; V 66*n*

Carey, Henry (poet), V 399*n*

Carey, Walter, as Umbra (?), III.ii 24*n*; VI 141*n*; in AP poems, VI 112 and *n*, 123, 124*n*, 172

Carleton, Henry Boyle, 1st Baron, Biog., IV 349–50; in AP poem, IV 317 and *n*

Carlisle Papers, IV xxxv *n*

Carlos, Don (later Charles III, King of Spain), III.ii 93*n*

Carlyle, A., *Autobiography*, III.ii 87*n*; IV 77*n*, 353, 368

Carmel, in AP poem, I 115 and *n*

Carnarvon. See Chandos

Caroline (queen of George II), Biog., IV 352; political influence, IV xxxi, xxxvii, 300*n*; V 341*n*; death, IV xxxiv, 303*n*, 304 and *n*; VI 390, 392–3*n*; in AP poems, III.ii 24*n*, 40, 42, 43, 64–5, 65*n*, 93–4*n*; IV 7, 33, 36*n*, 37, 101 and *n*, 118–19*n*, 304 and *n*; V xxxi, 184*n*, 285*n*, 350*n*, 371, 381*n*, 382 and *n*, 392*n*; other ref., IV 224–5*n*, 381; V 189*n*, 377*n*, 387*n*, 413*n*, 438, 440; VI 184*n*, 331*n*, 342*n*, 394

Carruthers, Robert (editor of AP), I viii, 254*n*; III.i 96*n*, 153*n*; III.ii 7 f., 25*n*, 38*n*, 121*n*; IV ix, 229*n*, 333*n*, 335*n*; V 392*n*; VI 78*n*, 127*n*, 329*n*, 332*n*, 340*n*, 354*n*, 376*n*, 380*n*, 451*n*; VII xlii *n*

Carter, Charles (cook), IV 8*n*

Carter, Elizabeth (translator), III.i xxi *n*

Carter, S., II 288*n*

Carteret, The Hon. Bridget, VI 342, 343*n*

Carteret, John (later Earl Granville), Biog., IV 352; AP corres., IV 16*n*; in AP poem, IV 332 and *n*, 333 and *n*; other ref., III.ii x; IV xxxi–xxxiv, 299*n*

Carthusian, in AP poem, IV 142, 143

Cary, Lucius. See Falkland

Caryll, Edward, II 81*n*

Caryll, John, Biog., II 375; in AP poems, II 3, 127, 144 and *n*; suggests *R. of the Locke*, II 81 ff., 93, 115; AP sends *Rondeau* to, VI 61*n*; AP corres., I 99, 100, 128, 129, 188*n*, 189*n*, 198, 203*n*, 204, 205*n*, 206, 285*n*, 286*n*, 299*n*, 317*n*, 318*n*, 325*n*; II 144*n*, 355*n*; III.i xv, xxv, 22*n*, 34*n*, 47*n*, 50*n*, 53*n*, 117*n*, 118*n*, 119*n*, 125*n*, 162*n*; III.ii xxxv f., xl *n*, xlv, xlvi, 15*n*, 18*n*, 32*n*, 46*n*, 58*n*, 62*n*, 74*n*, 90*n*, 104*n*, 131*n*; IV xiii, xiv, xxii, xxiv, xxv, 10*n*, 106*n*, 107*n*, 118*n*, 356, 388, 389; V 70*n*, 84*n*, 155*n*, 157*n*, 172*n*; VI 78*n*, 82*n*, 91*n*, 92*n*, 97*n*, 98*n*, 105*n*, 106*n*, 108*n*, 121*n*, 169*n*, 200*n*, 230*n*, 231*n*, 237*n*, 256*n*, 267*n*, 332*n*, 344*n*, 410*n*, 415*n*, 446*n*; VII xxxvii *n*, xxxviii *n*, xxxix, xli *n*, xliii *n*, ccxx *n*; other ref., I 342, 371; II xii, 353; VI 35*n*, 78*n*, 81*n*, 323*n*

Caryll, John, titular 1st Baron (uncle of above), I 75*n*, 84*n*, 99*n*; II 83 f., 375; III.i 56*n*; VI 81*n*

Caryll, John, Jr., AP corres., VII ccxxiii *n*

Caryll, John (grandfather of AP friend), II 371

Caryll, Richard, II 375

Caryll family, II 81 f., 93n, 371

Casaubon, Isaac, *Commentary on Athenaeus*, IX 120; X 361; *Commentary on Strabo*, X 126–7, 202, 338; other ref., X 367

Case, Arthur E., II 210n; IV xxiii, 107n, 343n; VI 416n, 417n, 419n, 420n; VII cix n, cx, cxi, cxliii n

Cassini, Giovanni (natural philosopher), III.i 56n

Cassius, in AP poem, VI 153

Castalia[-n], in AP poems, I 438, 444; IV 112; V 162, 321

Castiglione, Baldassare, AP trans. of, I 319n; VI 66, 68n; *Courtier*, III.i 58n

Castlemaine. See Cleveland

Castlemaine, Richard Child, 1st Earl Tylney of, III.ii 145n

Castleton, Nathaniel (author), VI 133 and n

Cat, Christopher (pastry cook), VI 177n

Catherine I, Czarina, III.ii 21n

Catholic Primer. See *The Primer*

Catholics, taxation of, VII xliii

Catiline, in AP poems, III.i 35, 79; III.ii 33; other ref., III.i xxxiii, xxxvii, lxi, lxii

Catius, in AP poem, III.ii 25

Cato The Censor, in AP poems, III.ii 93; VI 27; other ref., III.i 88n, 129n, 152n, 163n; IX 371; X 48

Cato Uticensis, in AP poems, II 269; IV 111, 224n, 225, 320 and n; V 185 and n, 335; VI 96 f., 99, 114 and 115n, 143, 285; other ref., I 172n; III.i 141n

Cato, Dionysius, II 18n

Catullus, Caius Valerius, I 185n; II 182n, 198n, 210n, 398; V 381n; VI 417; X 103, 162, 253

Cave, Edward (publisher), III.i xxi n

Cavendish. See Devonshire

Caversham House (Oxon.), III.ii 139n, 183n

Cawthorn, James, II 415

Caxton, William, his *Virgil*, V xxiv n, 79, 79–80n, 82n, 83n, 213–16, 281

Cebes of Thebes, V 356n, 465

Cecil, Mrs Evelyn, *History of Gardening*, III.ii 141n

Cecilia, St, in AP poems, III.ii 49; V 65; VI 34

Cecrops, in AP poems, V 378 and n; VI 204, 207n

Cédoz, Abbé F.-M.-Th., II 372n, 373n

Cedrenus, Georgius (author of *Historiarum Compendium*), IX 309

Celebrated Beauties, II 374

Celia, in AP poems, IV 153; VI 12, 99

Celsus, Aulus Cornelius (author of encyclopedia), IV 6n, 7; VII 78, 284; VIII 62

Centaur, in AP poem, I 380 and n

Centlivre, Susanna, Biog., V 432–3; other ref., IV xvii; V xlvi, 99n, 125n, 146 and n, 162, 207, 317, 447, 452

Cephalus, in AP poem, I 398 and n

Cercidas of Megalopolis (Cynic philosopher and poet), VII 173

Cercopes (work attributed to Homer), VII 53

Ceres, in AP poems, I 67, 77, 152; III.ii 154; VI 289

Certain Epigrams, V 138n

Certon, Solomon (French trans-

lator of Homer), in AP MS Preface, X 441

Cervantes, Miguel de, I 270n, 484; II 106, 233n; III.ii 153n; V 62, 261n, 270; VI 307; VIII 70, 283; X 388, 604

Chadwick, H. M., VII lxxv n

Chaerilus, in AP poem, VI 16

Chalcis, in AP poem, V 378 and n

Chaldeans, in AP poem, II 260 and n

Chalmers, G. K., III.i 40n

Chamberlen, Hugh (physician), III.ii 61n; VI 255n

Chambers, Ephraim, Cyclopaedia, III.i 16n, 41n, 56n, 72n, 74n, 76n, 104n

Chambers, E. K., William Shakespeare, V 267n

Champion, V xxxv n, 285n, 360n, 398n, 452

Chancellor, E. B., Lives of the Rakes, III.ii 87n

Chanc'ry, in AP poems, IV 69, 291

Chanc'ry-lane, in AP poems, V 130, 308

Chandos, James Brydges, 1st Duke of (Earl of Carnarvon), Biog., III.ii 23n; IV 351; not Timon, III.ii xxvi ff., xliii, 147n, 170 ff.; IV xiii, 8n, 358; VI 339n; AP compliments, III.ii xxxii f.; in AP poem, III.ii 23; AP corres., III.ii xxviii f., xxix n; acknowledgement in AP Preface, VII 24; other ref., III.ii 112n; IV 123n, 332n; V 441; VI 432–3n

Chapelain, Jean, I 210

Chapman, George, AP annotated copy, VII xiii; X 474–91; his trans. of Iliad, VII xxxix, lxxi n, cxxxix n, clxxxv; X 575, 576–7, 578–81, 584; AP debt to, VII xl,

lxxxv, cxii, cxiii–cxiv and n, cxv–cxvi, cxxxvi, clii, clvi, clix; X 494–500, 506–8; text selection Iliad, X 512–14

Traditions followed in trans., VII lii, lxxi; comparative study of a trans. passage, VII xciv and n, xcv, xcviii n, cxv, cxlviii, clxi, clxii; trans. compared to AP, VII civ, to Ogilby, cxix, cxx, to Hobbes, cxxi, cxxii

Facts about his Homer, VII cix, cxi; characteristics of trans., VII cxv–cxviii

Odyssey trans., VII cxi, ccvi n; compared to AP, ccxviii–ccxix and n, ccxx and n

Other ref. to his Homer, I 353, 356–7, 460n, 465n, 466n, 468n, 473n; IV 185n; VII l and n, lxxxiv, lxxxviii n, xc, cviii n, cxxvii, cxxix, cxxxiii n, cxlvii, cxlix and n, cl n, clvi n, clxxxviii, cxciii, 21–2, 85, 117, 124, 133, 166, 206, 306, 338; VIII 140–1, 187, 199–200, 243; IX 437; X 180, 440, 441

Bussy d'Ambois, VII 21; other ref. to poetic works, II 310; III.i 79–80n; V 340n

Chapman, Samuel, Biog., V 433; other ref., V 121n, 431

Chapple, A. J. V., I xii

Characters of the Times, V xlviii n, 24n, 91n, 131n, 149n, 166n, 169n, 208, 429, 439, 455; VI 140n

Charing-Cross, in AP poems, IV 49, 256n; 257

Charitable Corporation for Relief of Industrious Poor, III.ii xxxiv, 98n; IV 36n, 288n, 298n, 349

Charke, Charlotte (Cibber), IV 339; V 287n

Charlemagne, in AP poem, III.ii 56

Charles (generic use), in AP poem, III.ii 56, 57*n*

Charles I, in AP poems, I 180 and *n*; IV 203, 226*n*, 227; VI 110, 328; other ref., I 142, 159*n*, 177*n*, 180 and *n*, 303*n*

Charles II, in AP poems, IV 15 and *n*, 83, 203, 207 and *n*, 213; other ref., I 40, 69*n*, 177*n*, 178*n*, 180*n*, 276*n*, 297*n*, 298*n*, 299*n*, 307*n*, 324*n*; II 396, 399; VII ccxviii

Charles V, Emperor, in AP poem, III.ii 19 and *n*; other ref., I 322*n*

Charles X of Sweden, I 246*n*

Charles XII of Sweden, I 186*n*, 246*n*; III.i 148 and *n*

Charles the Hardy, X 430

Charleton, Walter (physician), III.i 43*n*, 65*n*, 69*n*, 72*n*, 78*n*, 101*n*, 104*n*, 131*n*, 151*n*, 160*n*

"Charming", use of in AP poem, III.ii 53, 58

Charon, in AP poem, V 321

Charron, Pierre, III.i l, lii, 54*n*, 72*n*, 96*n*, 100*n*, 146*n*, 162*n*; III.ii 27

Chartres (or Charteris), Francis, Biog., IV 353; Arbuthnot's epitaph, III.ii 86*n*; VI 346*n*; in AP poems, III.i 140 and *n*; III.ii 54*n*, 55 and *n*, 85 and *n*, 87*n*, 95; IV 5, 13, 135, 245, 324; VI 287, 297, 298*n*; other ref., III.i lv; V xxvi, 148*n*

Chartreux, in AP poem, III.ii 109

Charybdis, in AP poem, I 365

Chateaubriand, François-René de, II 302

Chatham. See Pitt

Chaucer, Geoffrey, texts of, II 3, 4*n*, 9, 12, 325*n*; AP opinion of, II 7, 251; AP use of in *Eloisa to Abelard*, II 325-6 and *n*; in AP poems, I 293 and *n*, 294*n*, 484; II 13, 55; IV 196*n*, 197; other ref., I 309*n*; II 161*n*, 171*n*, 330*n*; III.i 92*n*, 164*n*; VII cxxv, cxxxi, cli and *n*; VIII 494

Chauncy, Charles (owner of AP MSS), III.ii xxxvi, 41*n*

Chavanne, J., II 411

Chavasse, Rev. S. E. II 373*n*

Cheapside (London), VI 317*n*

Cheek, Mr, in AP poem, VI 40

Cheek, T., I 306*n*

Cheops, King of Egypt, in AP poem, V 379

Cheron, Louis, II 244

Cheselden, William, Biog., IV 353; other ref., III.i 38*n*, 39*n*, 42*n*; III.ii 47*n*; IV 283

Chesterfield, Philip Dormer Stanhope, 4th Earl of, Biog., IV 387; *Letters*, III.ii 48*n*, 56*n*; IV xxxii, xxxiii, 356, 370; in opposition to Walpole, IV xxxii, xxxiv, xxxv, 313*n*; in AP poems, IV 317, 333; V 345; VI 442; other ref., III.i xxiv *n*; III.ii x *n*, 134*n*; IV 9*n*, 378; VI 374*n*

Chetwood, Knightly, Dean of Gloucester, Preface to Dryden trans. Virgil's *Pastorals*, I 16-17, 19, 24*n*, 25*n*, 26*n*, 27*n*, 28*n*, 30*n*, 49 and *n*, 69*n*, 259*n*; *To the Earl of Roscommon*, I 180*n*, 311*n*, 312*n*, 316*n*; trans. from *Iliad*, VII cx, cxv, cxxxvi and *n*, cxxxvii, cxlii–cxliii and *n*; AP use of trans., X 495, 497; text selection *Iliad*, X 550-3; other ref., III.ii 152*n*; X 188

Chetwood, William Rufus, Biog., V 433; in AP poem, V 124;

other ref., IV 205*n*; V 121 f., 121*n*

Cheyne, George (physician), III.i 38*n*, 72*n*

Child, Sir Francis, Biog., IV 354; III.ii 25*n*; in AP poem, IV 273

Child, Francis James, X 502

Child, Richard. See Castlemaine

China, in AP poems, II 130, 176

China-Jordan, in AP poem, V 120, 303

Chiswick, AP family at, VII xxvi; AP leaves, VI 213*n*

Chiswick House (Surrey), III.ii 180

Chloë, in AP poems, II 135, 206; IV 151, 238*n*, 239

Choroebus [Choraebus 1712–17], in AP poem, I 440

Christ Church College (Oxford), V 361

Christianity, III.i: *E. on Man* accepted as Christian, xvi–xviii; said to be Christian in intent, xvii *n*, xxii *n*; personal religion of AP, xxiii–xxv; his address to the Saviour, xxiii; his inscription on MS of *Essay*, xxiv; probable intent in *Essay*, xxv–xxvi; traditional Christian theodicy in *Essay*, xxxii–xxxv, xliv; fusion of theodicy and ethics, xlvi; redemption, li; St Paul's parable of unity in Christ, lvi; Roman Catholicism and *Essay*, lxxiv–lxxv

VII: Virgil and Homer's connection with tradition of, lxxii, 63; Dacier's Christianization of Homer and AP disagreement, lxxix and *n*; theological parallels between Milton and AP Homer, cxxxiii; the 18th c. tradition extended by non-Christian in-

sights, clxxxiv; AP does not "Christianize" Homer, clxxxviii Other ref., III.i 28

Christis Kirk of the Green, IV 197 and *n*

Chrysander, F., *Works of Handel*, VI 433*n*, 434*n*, 435*n*

Chrysippus, in AP poem, II 74; other ref., VII li, lxxviii

Chrysostom, in AP poem, VI 110

Chubb, Thomas (divine), III.i 119*n*, 154*n*

Chudleigh, Mary, Lady, II 379; III.i 16*n*, 31*n*, 49*n*, 59*n*, 78*n*, 81*n*, 83*n*, 86*n*, 119*n*, 123*n*, 124*n*, 143*n*, 158*n*, 160*n*

Churchill. See Marlborough

Churchill, Sir Winston, III.ii 26*n*; IV 74–5*n*; VII clxxxi

Chute, Francis (poet), V 111*n*

Cibber, Caius Gabriel (sculptor), IV 207*n*; V 263*n*, 271 and *n*

Cibber, Colley, Biog., IV 354; V 433–4; as actor, IV 100, 222*n*, 223, 279; on Addison (Atticus), IV 212*n*; in *Dunciad B*, II xv; V *passim*, 415 ff., 433 f., 456; displaces Theobald, VII xxviii; as King of the Dunces, V xxxii f., xxxv f., 248, 276*n*; in *Dunciad*, V 91 and *n*, 161, 179 and *n*, 184, 187 and *n*, 271, 286, 290, 291, 293, 294, 296, 326, 333, 334, 375, 394; AP epigrams on, VI 302, 305*n*, 327, 330–1*n*, 360–1 and *n*, 397–8, 402, 451*n*; in other AP poems, IV 7 and *n*, 102, 123, 175, 201, 221, 223, 279, 306 and *n*; other ref., III.ii 91*n*, 112*n*, 178*n*, 184*n*; IV 215*n*; V ix, 99*n*, 185*n*, 203*n*; VI 299*n*

WORKS:

Another Occasional Letter, V xxxiii

C

n, 434; *Apology*, I 200; IV 226*n*;
V xxxv, *179n*, 257 ff., 434, and
Dunciad B passim; *Caesar in Egypt*,
V 288*n*, 289, 416, 474; *Careless
Husband*, IV 202*n*, 203; V 283*n*,
302*n*; *Letter to Mr P*, IV 202*n*; V
xxxiii, xliii *n*, 42*n*, 46*n*, 52*n*, 203*n*,
212, 251, 258 ff., and *Dunciad B
passim*; VI 299*n*; *Love's Last Shift*,
V 282*n*; *Non-Juror*, V 279*n*, 289;
Ode for His Majesty's Birthday, VII
ccxl and *n*; *Ode for the New Year*
(ascribed to), VI 458*n*; *Papal
Tyranny*, V 278*n*, 288*n*, 289;
Second Letter to Mr P, V xxxiv,
296*n*; *Tryal of Colley Cibber,
Comedian*, V xxxv; other plays, V
279*n*, 281*n*, 288–9*n*, 334–5*n*
Cibber, Susanna Maria, V 326*n*
Cibber, Theophilus, Biog., IV 354;
V 434; *Lives of the Poets*, V 455 f.;
other ref., IV 306, 349; V 161,
269*n*, 287*n*, 326
Cicero, Marcus Tullius (Tully), in
AP poems, II 274 and *n*; III.i
150; III.ii 31; IV 33, 241, 303;
V 364 and *n*; VI 152, 157; other
ref., I 172*n*, 213; II 230; III.i
lxvii; VII 44; VIII 380; IX 181;
X 46, 362, 388
WORKS:
Cato Major (or *De senectute*), IX
272; X 330, 362; *De amic.*, III.i
131*n*; *De claris orator.*, VII 206;
De divinatione, III.i 23*n*; VIII
316; IX 371; X 239; *De domo sua*,
IX 35; *De fato*, III.i 140*n*; *De fin.*,
III.i 67*n*, 74*n*, 129*n*, 158*n*; *De
leg.*, III.i 110*n*; VII 384; IX 32,
218–19; *De nat. deorum*, III.i 24*n*,
37*n*, 103*n*, 110*n*; VII 287–8; IX
246, 344, 413; *De offic.*, III.i 62*n*,
64*n*, 97*n*, 113*n*, 116*n*; IV 32–3*n*;

De orat., VII 58; IX 272; X 46;
De redito, IX 35; *De repub.*, III.i
122*n*; IV 91; *Ep. to Atticus*, IX
344–5; *In Verrem*, X 62; *Orator*,
IX 26; his trans. and commen-
tary, IX 442; X 330; *Pro archia*,
VII 55; *Rhetorica ad Herennium*
(attrib.), I 240*n*, 241*n*, 278*n*;
Somn. Scip., III.i 149*n*; *Tusc. disp.*,
III.i 27*n*; IX 373; *Tusc. quaest.*,
VII 43, 338; VIII 3; IX 326
Cid, the, in AP poem, V 288 and *n*
Cimon, in *Dunciad*, V 69 and *n*, 275
Circaean, in AP poem, IV 245
Circe, in AP poem, IV 39
Circus, A Satyr on the Ring, II 400
Civil Polity (anon. tract), III.i 131*n*,
133*n*
Clagett, William (divine), III.i
35*n*, 50*n*
Clare College (Cambridge), V 362
Clarendon, Edward Hyde, 1st Earl
of, I 298*n*; III.i 137*n*; IV 241; V
125–6*n*, 344*n*
Clarissa, in *R. of the Locke*, II 107,
130, 135, 177, 199, 206, 378, 395
Clark, A. F. B., I 255*n*
Clark, G. N., I 301*n*
Clark, Rev. William, V 104*n*
Clarke, Alured (divine), III.i xvi *n*;
IV 322*n*, 359; V 350*n*; VI 391,
393–4*n*
Clarke, George (politician), VI
159*n*
Clarke, John (divine), III.i 95*n*, 98*n*
Clarke, John (publisher), III.i 51*n*,
81*n*
Clarke, M. L., VII lxxxviii *n*
Clarke, Samuel (divine), III.i 22*n*;
III.ii 144 and *n*; V 385*n*, 386–7*n*,
409*n*
Clarke, William (publisher), I viii,
60*n*; IV ix

Claude Lorrain, II 254*n*

Claudian (Claudius Claudianus), AP lines compared with, I 168*n*, 181*n*, 184*n*, 188*n*; II 319*n*; V 359*n*; other ref., II 172*n*; VI 20*n*, 418; VII xxxv

Clayton, Charlotte (later Lady Sundon), in AP poem, VI 181, 184*n*

Clayton, Thomas (composer), VI 35*n*

Cleanthes, Hymn of, III.i 79*n*

Cleland, William, Biog., V 434; "Letter to the Publisher", V xix *n*, xxv, 11–19, 251, 461; VI 339*n*; AP poem to, VI xvii, 321, 322*n*; other ref., III.ii xxvii; V 169*n*

Clement XII, Pope, III.ii 28*n*

Clement of Alexandria, VII 335

Cleopatra, in AP poem, VI 66, 67; other ref., III.ii 21*n*

Cleveland, Barbara (Villiers), Countess of Castlemaine and Duchess of (earlier Mrs Palmer), I 298*n*; IV 74–5*n*, 82*n*, 83; V 376*n*

Clifford, Hugh, 2nd Baron Chudleigh, I 31*n*

Clift, D. H., III.i vi

Clio, in AP poem, I 412

Cliveden House (Bucks.), III.ii 118 and *n*

Cloacina, in *Dunciad*, V 108 and *n*, 300

Clodio, in AP poems, III.ii 13*n*, 14, 30 and *n*, 33; IV 126

Clodius, in AP poem, IV 321

Cloe, in AP poems, III.ii 40 ff., 63*n*, 63–4; VI 377

Clutterbuck, Thomas (divine), III.i 123*n*, 133*n*

Cluverius (Philipp Clüver), IX 311

Clytemnestra, in AP poem, II 76

Coates, Dorothy, VI xix

Cobb, Samuel (poet and critic), I 226; II 6

Cobham, Richard Temple, Viscount, Biog., III.ii 15*n*; IV 389; *Ep. I* (first *Moral Essay*), addressed to, III.ii 3–38; VI 344; in other AP poems, III.ii 144; IV 165, 320, 333 and *n*; VI 368; AP corres., III.ii xlii, 34*n*, 38*n*; other ref., III.i 21*n*; III.ii 20*n*; IV xxxii

Cochin, Charles Nicolas, VIII xii

Cocytus, in AP poem, I 415, 427

Codrington, C., I 267*n*

Codrus, in AP poems, IV 101 and *n*; V 117 and *n*, 302; VI 15, 16

Coeffeteau, Nicolas (moralist), III.i 63*n*, 66*n*, 69*n*, 75*n*, 87*n*, 88*n*, 89*n*, 105*n*

Coke, Roger, I 191*n*

Colbert, Jean-Baptiste, I 298*n*

Cole [Colne] River, in AP poem, I 183 and *n*

Cole, G. D. H., I 178*n*, 184*n*, 187*n*

Cole, William, annotates *Dunciad*, I viii; IV ix; marginalia cited, III.ii 51*n*, 100*n*, 168; his transcript of *Verses on a Grotto*, VI 384*n*

Colepepper, Sir William (gambler), in AP poem, III.ii 90 and *n*

Coleridge, S. T., II 353*n*; III.i lxvi *n*, lxvii; IV 199*n*; VII xlii and *n*, 4

Colin, in AP poem, I 75

Colines, Simon de (printer), in AP poem, VI 82, 84*n*

Collection of Poems, a miscellany, VII cx, cxlii–cxliii and *n*

Collier, Jeremy (divine and essayist), I 291*n*, 304*n*; II 268*n*; III.i 61*n*, 67*n*, 134*n*, 153*n*

Collier, William, I 200

Collingbourne, William, IV 19*n*

Collins, Anthony (deist), III.i xxiv
n; III.ii 23*n*; V 144*n*

Collins, J. C. (critic), I 239*n*, 243*n*

Collins, William, II 230

Colne River. See Cole

Columbus, AP called "Columbus
of the human mind", III.i xvi;
in *E. on Man*, III.i 102

Columella, Lucius Junius Modera-
tus (agriculturalist), VIII 245;
X 62, 342

Commentator, V 448

Common Sense, or *The Englishman's
Journal*, III.i xvi *n*; V 448

Compleat Key to the Non-Juror, V 378*n*

Compleat Sportsman, III.i 14*n*

Compton. See Wilmington

Concanen, Matthew, Biog., V 434–
5; his *Supplement to the Profound*, I
61*n*, 212, 213*n*, 322*n*; II 127*n*,
341*n*; as "dunce", III.ii 128,
178 f., 179*n*, 180 and *n*; misc.
writing attacking AP, V 209,
210, 211, 435; his *Compleat Collection of all the Verses* cited, V xliii *n*,
21*n*, 39*n*, 40*n*, 76*n*, 117*n*, 184*n*,
231*n*, 233*n*; in *Dunciad*, V 112,
113–14*n*, 134*n*, 137 and *n*, 153*n*,
301 and *n*, 310 and *n*; other ref.,
V xlvi, 103*n*, 281*n*, 312*n*, 448*n*,
453 f.; VI 325*n*; X xii

Confucius, in AP poem, II 261
and *n*

Congleton, J. E., I 15*n*, 16*n*, 18*n*,
19*n*

Congreve, William, Biog., IV 355;
his writing of Imitations, IV
xxviii *n*; in AP poems, IV 105,
106*n*, 218–19*n*, 219; V 91, 110
and *n*, 301 and *n*; other ref., I 14,
37, 38, 59*n*, 80*n*, 357*n*; II 354*n*,
355*n*; III.ii 48*n*, 56*n*; V 62*n*,

114*n*, 200; VI 173 and *n*, 177*n*,
226*n*, 247*n*, 284

WORKS:

Love for Love, II 170*n*; *Mourning
Bride*, II 275*n*; III.i 55*n*; V 185
and *n*, 335; *Mourning Muse of
Alexis*, I 68*n*, 82*n*, 89*n*, 91*n*, 179*n*;
III.ii 49*n*; *Of Improving the Present
Time* (to Cobham), III.ii xxxviii;
Of Pleasing (to Sir R. Temple),
III.i 86*n*; *Old Bachelor*, I 308*n*; II
143*n*, 158*n*; *Prologue to the Queen*,
I 165*n*; *Semele*, I 77*n*; V 186*n*;
Tears of Amaryllis for Amyntas, I
62*n*, 72*n*, 79*n*; *To Sir Godfrey
Kneller*, III.i 70*n*; *Way of the
World*, II 98; III.ii 36*n*, 53*n*, 92*n*
Trans. of *Iliad*: VII cix *n*, cx,
cxxxix, cxl-cxli; text selections
of trans., X 542–9; *Lamentation
over Hector*, VIII 575; AP dedication of his *Iliad* to, VII cix; VIII
579; AP acknowledgements and
indebtedness to, VII cix *n*, clix,
23; X 443, 495, 500

Coningsby, Thomas, Earl, in AP
poems, III.ii 124 and *n*; VI 195,
196*n*, 297, 298*n*

Connelly, K. A., III.i vi

Convocation, in *Dunciad*, V 404
and *n*

Conway, R. L., III.i vi

Conway, R. S., I 101; II 195*n*

Conybeare, Dr John, V 368*n*

Cook, Albert, VII ccvi *n*

Cooke, Thomas, Biog., IV 355; V
435; as "dunce", III.ii 136*n*; V
xlv; attacks AP, IV 99*n*; V xii *n*,
65*n*, 112–13*n*, 208 and *n*, 209*n*,
211*n*; as translator, IV 99*n*; V
83–4*n*, 113*n*; VI 450; attacks AP
knowledge of Greek, VII lxxxvi,
lxxxvii and *n*; his *Battle of the*

Poets, V xxvi, 41*n*, 65*n*, 75*n*, 112–13*n*, 145*n*, 186*n*, 208*n*, 455; VII lxxxvii and *n*; in AP poems, IV 106; V 112 and *n*, 161 and *n*, 301 and *n*; other ref., V xxiv *n*, 68*n*, 203*n*, 212*n*

Cooke, W. H., *Herefordshire,* III.ii 115*n*

Cooper. See Shaftesbury

Cooper's Hill, in AP poem, I 173 and *n*

Cooper, John, I 401*n*; II 293

Cooper, Mary (publisher), V xxxii *n*, 248, 464

Cooper, T. (publisher), V 248

Cope, Mrs (cousin of John Caryll), II 353; VI 323–4*n*

Copernicus, III.i lxvii, 45*n*

Corbet, Richard (divine), III.i 119*n*

Corbett, Charles, IX xiii

Corbett, Elizabeth, AP *Epitaph on,* VI 322–4

Corbett, Sir Richard, VI 324*n*

Corbett, Sir Uvedale, VI 323*n*

Corinna, in AP poems, V 105, 299; VI 316. See also Thomas, Elizabeth

Corinth, in AP poem, I 430 and *n*

Cornbury, Henry Hyde, Viscount, Biog., IV 368; in AP poems, IV xxxviii, 241, 240–1*n*, 332; V 376*n*; other ref., VI 374*n*

Corn-Cutter's Journal, III.i xvii *n*; V 311*n*

Corneille, Pierre, in AP poems, IV 219; V 290; VI 310; other ref., I 210, 285*n*; II 299; IV 216–17*n*; V 91*n*, 286*n*, 288*n*

Cornelius Gallus, VI 417

Cornell University, printings of *Iliad* in library, X 587–8, 590, 591–2

Cornford, F. M., III.i 21*n*, 59*n*

Cornish, Mrs, VI 317*n*

Cornus, in *Ep. to Arbuthnot,* IV 97 and *n*

Cornutus, Lucius Annaeus (ed. Persius), VII 233

Cornwall[–ish], in AP poems, III. ii 122 and *n*; IV 243 and *n*

Correggio (Antonio Allegri), in AP poem, VI 157, 159*n*

Coscus, in AP poems, IV 136, 139

Cosins [Cozens] (stays-maker), in AP poems, IV 85 and *n*; VI 22, 23*n*

Cotswold Hills, in AP poem, IV 183

Cotta, in *Ep. to Bathurst,* III.ii xlv *n*, 108 ff.; VII ccxxix, ccxlix

Cotterell, Colonel (James Dormer), IV 164*n*

Cotton, Charles, I 217; VII cxxiv

Country Journal, VI 295*n*

Courthope, W. J. See Elwin, Whitwell

Courtine, in *Ep. to Cobham,* III.ii 24*n*

Coverdale, Miles, III.i 42*n*

Cowley, Abraham, in AP poems, I 173 and *n*, 174 and *n*; IV 159, 201; his reputation, IV 200*n*, 201; AP imitations of, VI 12–15, 20*n*, 47–8; other ref., I 210, 215, 217, 272*n*, 317*n*; II 155*n*, 221*n*, 233, 324*n*; IV xxviii, xxix, 159; V 71*n*; VI 92*n*; VII xxxv, ccxxxv; X 62, 603

WORKS:

Brutus, III.i 130*n*; *Complaint,* II 253–4*n*; III.i 153*n*; *Davideis,* I 69*n*, 117*n*, 263*n*, 280*n*, 321*n*, 388*n*, 421–2*n*; II 144*n*, 147*n*, 154*n*, 162*n*, 176*n*, 179*n*, 191*n*, 195*n*, 204*n*, 284*n*, 337*n*, 341*n*, 348*n*, 364*n*, 368*n*, 409; III.i 108*n*, 122*n*;

III.ii 83–4n; V 66n, 331n; X 222, 501, 504; *Eccho*, I 92n; *For Hope*, III.i 89n; *Inconstancy*, I 249n, 259n; *Life and Fame*, I 289n; II 217; III.i 54n, 149n; *Of My Self*, VI 168n; *Of Nature*, V 469; *Of Obscurity*, II 269n; *Of Solitude*, II 267n; *Of Wit*, I 290n; *On the Death of Mr Crashaw*, I 262n; III.i 124n; *On the Queens Repairing Somerset House*, I 142, 179n, 194n; *Plagues of Aegypt*, III.i 96n; *Plantarum Liber Sextus*, I 179n; *Prophet*, X 512; *Resurrection*, I 277n; *Spring*, VI 455n; *To Dr Scarborough*, IV 105n; *To Mr Hobs*, I 312n; *To Sir William Davenant*, I 285n

Trans. (Horace, Virgil) and imitations, I 162n, 187n; II 212n, 222–3; III.i 155n; III.ii 22n; IV xxvii; V 130n; VI 4–5n

Cowper, John (the poet's father), III.ii 138n

Cowper, Judith (Mrs Madan), AP corres., II 7n, 220, 222; III.ii 70n; IV 105n; VI 226–7n, 247n, 308n, 443n; AP *Verses* to, VI 306; other ref., II 6n, 415

Cowper, William, 1st Earl, Biog., IV 356; in AP poems, IV 175; VI 392; other ref., V 395n

Cowper, William, 2nd Earl, Biog., V 435; in *Dunciad*, V 395–6 and n; other ref., V 398n

Cowper, William (the poet), in AP poem, IV 175; other ref., VII cxxv, cxxxiii and n

Cox, N., I 160n

Cox, Susanna (actress), IV 376

Coxe, W., *Life of Sir Robert Walpole*, IV 298n, 300n, 345, 367, 379, 385; *Anecdotes of Handel*, V 442

Coypel, Antoine, VII xiii

Cozens. See Cosins

Craftsman, III.ii 29n, 137n; IV xxxi–xxxii, 206n, 299n, 302n, 367, 377, 379; V 174n, 212, 277n, 313n, 357n, 411n, 432, 451

Craggs, Anne. See Nugent

Craggs, James, Biog., IV 356; AP corres., III.i 151n; IV 110n; VI 145n; in AP poems, IV 239 and n, 273, 316 and n; VI 131n, 204, 205–7n, 209–10, 211, 281–3; other ref., IV 97n, 289n; V 19n, 30n, 33n; VI 210n, 364, 465n

Craig, Hardin, III.i xlviii n

Craig, John (mathematician), V 386n

Crane, R. S., III.i xxviii n, 157n

Crane (river), AP coach upset in, VI 254n, 256n

Crantor (philosopher, 4th c. BC), VII li, lxxviii

Crashaw, Richard, AP comment on, I 271–2n; IV 203–4n; V 273n; AP debt to, II 301, 305, 311, 320n, 336n, 337n, 341n, 343n, 346n, 347n, 362; III.i 26n; VI 319n

Crates of Mallos, VIII 82, 349; IX 344

Crauford, D., *Ovidius Britannicus*, II 294–5 and n, 300, 303, 307, 309, 319n, 329n, 349n

Crawford, Charlotte E., III.ii 50n

Crawfurd, R., 32n, 138n

Creech, Thomas, trans. of Horace, I 172n, 180n, 284n; III.i 30n; IV xxix n, 54n, 60n, 174n, 175n, 181n, 236n, 237 and n, 283n, 287n, 291n; AP use of his Horace, IV xliii n; trans. of Juvenal, II 278n; of Lucretius, I 304–5n; of Rapin, I 15n, 23n, 27n; of Theocritus, I

89n; of Virgil, I 66n, 78n, 79n

Cremona, in AP poem, I 322 and n

Crete [–an], in AP poems, I 394 and n, 426, 470; II 76

Cressi, in AP poem, I 177

Cressy [Crecy], in AP poem, IV 287

Crispissa, in AP poem, II 166 and n

Critical Specimen, V 127n

Criticism on the Elegy written in a Country Church Yard, ed. John Young, III.ii xv n

Croker, John Wilson, editor of AP, I viii, 88n, 279n; II 88n, 145n, 146n, 167n, 191n, 399; III.i 140n; III.ii 91n, 100n, 144n, 174; IV ix, 55n, 122n, 215n, 285n, 303n, 309n, 315n, 326n, 334n, 337n, 351, 387; V 370n, 395n; VI 29n

Cromwell, Henry, AP corres., I 93n, 171n, 198–9, 205, 271n, 278n, 281n, 283n, 305n, 336n, 340–4 *passim*, 346n, 347–9, 351–2, 417n, 419n, 427n, 429n, 430n; II 7n, 36n, 85 f.; III.i 145n, 153n; V 273n, 451, 456; IV xlii, 5n, 35n. 103n, 203n, 283n; V 106n, 456; VI 4n, 52n, 61n, 65n, 72n, 76n, 102n, 229n, 230n, 332n, 409n, 446n; VII xxxvi; in AP poems, VI 24–9, 39–40

Cromwell, Lady Mary, I 299n

Cromwell, Oliver, in AP poems, III.i 155 and n; III.ii 27 and n

Cronin, G., and P. A. Doyle, VII cvii n

Crook, Japhet, Biog., IV 356; in AP poems, III.ii 95; IV 122, 306, 324

Cross, Wilbur, *Life of Fielding*, IV 315n

Crotopus, in AP poem, I 438 and n

Crousaz, J. P. de, Biog., V 435–6; attacks *E. on Man*, II xv; III.i xxv and n; VII xxviii

His critiques of *E. on Man*: their character, III.i xix–xx; English trans., III.i xx–xxi; Curll's use of, III.i xx; Warburton's reply to, III.i xxi–xxii, xxiii

In *Dunciad*, V 361 and n, 362n

Crowne, John (dramatist), in AP poem, VI 137, 139n; other ref., II 112; III.i 177n, 129n

Croxall, Samuel (divine and poet), *E. on Man* attributed to, III.i xv; other ref., X 504

Crux-Easton, in AP poem, VI 353, 354n

Ctesilochus (painter), VIII 360

Cudgel (by Hercules Vinegar, Esq.), V 153n

Cudworth, Ralph (Platonist), III.i 81n, 93n, 124n, 169; VIII 204

Culverwell, Nathanael (Platonist), III.i 65n, 76n

Cumberland, Richard (bishop and political philosopher), III.i 43n, 66n, 106n, 107n, 123n, 126n, 133n, 134n, 136–7n, 139n, 151n

Cumming (a captain), his comment on AP Homer, VII cvii

Cumont, F., III.i 27n

Cunningham, Alexander, AP knowledge of his *Horace*, IV xliii

Cunningham, R. N., II 205n

Cuper, Boydell (Cuper's Gardens), III.ii 183n

Cuperus, Gisbertus (antiquarian), VII xxxviii, lxxxi, 173

Cupid, in AP poems, I 72, 176, 395, 397, 404; II 136, 207; III.ii 148; V 374

Cupids, in AP poems, III.ii 148; VI 367

Curio, identity of, III.ii 108*n*, 135*n*; in AP poem, VI 204

Curll, Edmund, Biog., IV 356–7; V 436; uses Crousaz against AP, III.i xx; as publisher of abuse of AP, V 207 ff., 210; publishes Dacier addendum on AP, VII xliv and *n*; annotates AP poems, VI 28*n*, 29*n*, 319*n*; value of his AP texts, VI 28*n*, 90*n*, 183*n*; attributes poems to AP, VI 105*n*, 112*n*, 144*n*, 163–4*n*, 165*n*; ed. of AP letters, VII xxvii; AP takes revenge on, VI 236*n*; VII xxvi; in AP poems, IV 100, 103*n*, 125 and *n*; V 64 and *n*, 74*n*, 97 and *n*, 104 ff. and *n*, 115*n*, 118–19*n*, 121–2, 152*n*, 153*n*, 165 and *n*, 166*n*, 171*n*, 196*n*, 199*n*, 203*n*, 273, 296, 298 ff., 328, 411*n*; VI 236 and *n*; other ref., II xiii, xiv, 9 and *n*, 325*n*; IV 206*n*; V x, xxii, xlvi, 33*n*, 39*n*, 91*n*, 248*n*, 433, 435, 441, 448, 450 f.; VI 100*n*, 174*n*, 292*n*, 421*n*, 446*n*; X xiii
WORKS:
Female Dunciad, V 24*n*, 210*n*; *Court Poems*, IV xv, 121*n*; *The Curliad*, V 210, cited *passim*; *Key to the Dunciad*, IV 111*n*; V xxiv, 210, cited *passim*; *Miscellanea*, IV 103*n*

Curll, Henry, Biog., V 436; in AP poem, V 304; other ref., V 121*n*

Currie, H. MacL., VII xxiii

Curtius, Marcus, in AP poems, III.i 79 and *n*; V 86, 285; other ref., III.i lxii

Cutler, Sir John, in AP poems, III.ii 108*n*, 119 and *n*, 120; VII ccxxxv; other ref., III.ii 116*n*

Cutts, John (poet), I 217, 324*n*

Cutts, John, 1st Baron C. of Gowran, II 375

Cyclop[-s], in AP poems, I 366, 370, 372 and *n*, 423

Cyllenius, in AP poems, I 427 and *n*

Cynthaeus of Chios (Homer scholar, 6th c. BC), VII 52, 59

Cynthia, in AP poems, I 122, 168, 377, 398, 430, 432; II 132, 183; III.ii 50; IV 153; V 165, 177, 328, 332; VI 153

Cynthus, in AP poems, I 67 and *n*, 165 and *n*, 444 and *n*

Cypria (lost epic, *c* 8th c. BC), VII 343

Cyprian, in AP poem, II 271

Cyrrha, in AP poem, I 414 and *n*

Cythaeron, in AP poems, I 416 and *n*, 429; II 259

Cytheraea, in AP poems, VI 11, 233

D

Dacian, in AP poem, I 410 and *n*
Dacier, André, editor of Aristotle's
Poetics, I 210; VII xl and *n*, 54,
89, 127, 331–2, 340; VIII 2, 64,
181, 318, 341, 349, 353, 358, 361;
IX 119, 279–80, 334–5; X 10, 14,
205, 214, 217–18, 233, 236,
271, 330, 378; trans. Plutarch's
Lives, II 236, 268*n*; his *Life of
Pythagoras*, II 260*n*, 263*n*; VIII
491; trans. Epictetus, X 39, 235
Dacier, Anne Lefèvre, discusses
marble relief, VII xii; trans. into
English, xiii (see also Ozell);
verbal parallels with AP Homer,
xv *n*; editions of her trans., xvii–
xviii *n*; AP use of, xl and *n*, xli,
xlv, lxxxi, cxxvi; X 575; 2nd ed.
attacks AP, VII xliii–xliv; her
Preface, xlvii *n*; trans. in "Prince
of Poets" tradition, lxxi; her
view of Homer *v* modern view,
lxxv; sources of her Homer comment, lxxvii; quarrel with de la
Motte, lxxviii–lxxix, lxxx; comparative study of a passage, xciv
and *n*, xcv, xcvii and *n*; a com-
parison with other trans., clix,
clx; AP attacks, xcvii; *Re-
marques*, xc, cv and *n*; ethical
interpretation of Homer, cii; use
of Eustathius, cv, cvi; facts about
her Homer, cix, cxi; AP com-

ment on her remarks, ccxx, ccxxi
Other ref. to her trans. of and
commentary on Homer:
V 120*n*, 121*n*, 450
VII xxxviii, xxxix–xl, l, li and *n*,
lxxxiv, c, cxv *n*, cxxvii, 14, 41–2,
55, 79, 83, 87, 97, 100, 104, 109,
112, 121, 125, 127–8, 135–6,
152–3, 166, 168, 181, 193, 195,
199–201, 210, 215, 217–18, 221,
227, 232–3, 235–6, 238, 242, 247,
249, 266, 273–4, 279, 282, 286,
304, 310–11, 313–14, 317, 319,
323, 327–8, 334, 340, 345, 350,
355–6, 360, 385, 388, 390, 400–2,
408, 422, 429, 432, 435, 438–9,
442, 446–9, 455, 462–3, 465–6,
468, 470
VIII 14, 22, 28, 36–7, 45, 50, 59,
72, 77, 86, 94–6, 98, 104, 106,
108, 113, 120, 127–8, 143, 145–6,
150, 157, 159, 175, 183, 194–8,
209, 224, 230, 240–1, 253, 266,
278, 284, 287, 290, 292, 296, 298,
301, 307–8, 310, 317–19, 332–5,
338, 351, 354, 372, 376–7, 382,
384–5, 387, 390, 394–5, 397, 403,
410, 414, 418, 427, 433, 444, 447,
456–7, 461, 465, 467, 476, 483,
488, 504, 507, 514, 522–3, 526,
528, 543, 555, 560
IX 28, 30–2, 34–5, 39, 41, 44, 48,
50, 54, 60–1, 64, 68–9, 76, 79, 81,

88, 95, 101–5, 107–8, 112, 115–
16, 119, 123, 133, 138, 142–3,
145, 147, 152, 155, 161–2, 164–5,
167, 173, 177, 180, 190, 196,
199–200, 205, 208, 214, 225–6,
228, 237, 242–4, 246, 253, 256–9,
264–5, 269, 272, 276–7, 279, 281,
284, 286, 290, 296, 300, 302, 306,
309–10, 317, 323, 327, 338–40,
344–5, 351–3, 355, 359, 361, 364,
378, 403, 405, 407, 410, 413, 424,
429, 437–9, 448, 451, 453, 457–8
X 17, 23, 27–8, 37, 40, 54–5, 58–
9, 71, 79, 86, 89, 94, 108, 110,
112, 121–2, 127, 135, 142, 144,
150–1, 167, 171, 177, 183, 186–7,
194, 196–7, 202–4, 206, 208,
210–13, 216–19, 224, 228, 232–3,
236–7, 244, 246, 252, 255, 260,
263, 276–9, 288, 293–4, 303,
312–13, 323, 325–6, 330–1, 338,
340, 342, 346, 348–9, 351, 361,
367–8, 370–3, 378, 384, 392–5,
397, 419, 427, 442, 445–56, 494–
5, 578–9
*Des Causes de la Corruption du
Goust*, VII 319; VIII 197
Iliad parallels to AP trans., X
500–6, 579–80; *Iliad* text selection, X 519–21
Odyssey parallels to AP trans., X
508–11
Daffy, Rev. Thomas, V 395*n*
Dagenham Beach (Essex), III.ii
156*n*
Daily Advertiser, III.i xx *n*, xxi *n*
Daily Courant, I xiv, 205*n*; II 104*n*;
    V 81*n*, 114*n*, 310*n*, 311*n*, 430,
    441, 443; VI 419*n*; VII xxxvii *n*
Daily Gazetteer, IV xxxviii–xxxix;
    V 285*n*, 287*n*, 303*n*, 311*n*, 399*n*,
    428, 434, 448, 451; VI 365*n*, 396*n*
Daily Journal, III.i xvi *n*, xvii *n*,

xviii *n*; III.ii xxvii; V xvii, xx *n*,
    xxii, xxiii, 33*n*, 34*n*, 45*n*, 67*n*,
    101*n*, 102*n*, 103*n*, 134*n*, 208 f.,
    211, 212*n*, 233*n*, 235, 444, 448 f.,
    456, 458; VI 432*n*; VII xxxvii *n*
Daily Post, V 293*n*, 444; VI 322*n*;
    VII xliii *n*
Daily Post-Boy, III.ii xxvii; VI
    319*n*, 342*n*
Dalilah [Delilah], in AP poem, II
    75
Dallaway, James, note in Walpole's
    Anecdotes of Painting, III.ii 113*n*;
    ed. Lady M. W. Montagu, VI
    212*n*
Dalrymple. See Stair
Dalrymple, David, Lord Hailes,
    anecdotes by, III.ii 57*n*, 98*n*
Dalrymple, Hugh, II 8
Damian, in AP poems, II 31, 34,
    39, 41, 44
Damon, in AP poems, I 59, 63 ff.;
    II 152; IV 107
Dampier, William, III.i 110*n*
Danaus, in AP poems, I 429 and *n*,
    436
Dancastle, Thomas, friend of AP,
    VI 194*n*; VII xxxvii
Dane [–ish], in AP poems, I 157,
    184
Daniel, G. (poet), V 81*n*
Daniel, Samuel (poet), II 216*n*,
    294, 303; III.i 13*n*, 81*n*, 84*n*, 86*n*,
    147*n*
Dante Alighieri, his use of Virgil, I
    101; philosophy of renunciation,
    III.i lxxi, 50*n*; in AP poems, IV
    43; other ref., II 220; VII clxxix,
    clxxxvi
Daphne, in AP poems, I 88 ff., 89,
    90, 91, 92, 93, 94, 95, 394; VI 47
Daphnis, in AP poems, I 59–70
    passim, 62 ff., 69, 70

Dapperwit, in AP poems, II 135, 205

Darbishire, Helen, VII cxxx n

Darby, H. C., I 153n

Darent, in AP poems, I 184 and n

Dares Phrygius, VII lxxxi, 33

Darius, King of Persia, in AP poem, II 69; other ref., VII 60

Darlow, T. H., II 402

Dartineuf, Charles, Biog., IV 357; in AP poems, IV 9, 171; other ref., III.ii 25n, 35n

Dartmouth, Edward Legge, 1st Earl of, IV 285n

D'Aubignac, François Hédelin, Abbé, VII lxxvi

D'Auverquerque. See Grantham

Davenant (journalist), in AP poem, VI 259, 264n

Davenant, William, Preface to Gondibert, I 211, 219, 255n, 258n, 272n; II 106n, 217, 221n, 234n, 287n, 322n; Gondibert, II 155n, 265n, 341n; other works, II 185n, 216n, 264n, 277n, 340n; III.i 15n; IV 208n

Davenport, A., II 160–1n

David, in AP poems, I 101; II 48; VI 290, 291

David II of Scotland, I 177n

Davidson, W. L., III.i xxxv n

Davies, Sir John (poet), III.i 69n

Davies, John, of Hereford (poet), III.i xlix, 94n

Davies, Miles (bibliographer), VI 197 and n

Davies, Thomas (bookseller), Life of Garrick, V xliii, 293n

Davis, Eliza Jeffries, II 159n; IV 62n, 172n

Davis, Herbert, I 315n; VI xix

Dawes, William (poet), III.i 115n, 151n, 158n

Dawley Farm (anon. poem), IV 17n

Dawley Farm (Uxbridge), VII xxvii

Dawson, C. M., III.i 151n

Dawson, Giles E., VI xix

Deane, C. V., I 53

Deane, Thomas, I 330n

Dearing, Vinton A., article on Atossa, III.ii xxxvi n, 41n, 159n; article on Prince of Wales's set of AP Works, VI 345n, 404n

Death, A Poem In Two Books (anon.), III.i 31n

De Beer, Esmond, V 467, 470

Deborah, in AP poem, VI 290, 291

Decebalus (Dacian general), I 410n

Decius Mus, III.i lxii, 79 and n

Defoe, Benjamin Norton, Biog., V 437; in AP poems, V 128, 148, 307, 317; other ref., V xxvi, 71n

Defoe, Daniel, Biog., V 437; his Tour, I 178n, 184n, 187n, 188n; III.ii 152n; Complete English Tradesman, II 149n, 152n, 176n, 366; as object of AP satire, V xxxix, xlii, xlvi, 72n, 148n, 447, 457; VI 59; Mother Ross, V 136n; in AP poems, V 71 and n, 117 and n, 148 and n, 276 and n, 302, 317 and n; other ref., II 10n, 11, 118, 396; V 428

De Geer, Charles, Baron, V 401

Dejanire, in AP poem, II 75

De Kéroualle. See Portsmouth

Dekker, Thomas, III.i 112n

Delacour, J., II 413, 415

Delaney, Dr Patrick (Swift's friend), III.ii xxxviii

Delany (earlier Mrs Pendarves), Mrs Mary (Granville), VI 338n, 396n

De la Touche, Mme, V 370n

De La Warr, John West, 1st Earl,

Biog., IV 393; in AP poems, IV 305 and *n*, 335 and *n*

Delia, in AP poems, I 65 ff., 80 ff.; VI 45. See also Delorain, Mary Howard, Countess of

Delian, in AP poem, I 386

Delilah. See Dalilah

Delorain[–e], Francis Scott, 2nd Earl of, Biog., IV 384; other ref., IV 285*n*

Delorain, Mary Howard, Countess of, Biog., IV 367; as Delia in AP poems, IV 12*n*, 13, 314*n*, 340; other ref., III.ii 178*n*

Delos, in AP poem, I 444 and *n*

Delphi, in AP poem, I 386

De Lyra. See Lyra

Demetrius Chalcondylas, X 441

Demetrius of Phalerum (4th c. BC), VII 150, 163; VIII 433; IX 333

Democritus, in AP poem, IV 223; other ref., III.i 11*n*, 86; V 193*n*, 407*n*

De-moivre. See Moivre, de

Demosthenes, VII 287; IX 68, 238; X 388

Deneau, D. P., V 470

Denham, Sir John, in AP poems, I 173, 174, 270 and *n*, 280 and *n*, 449; AP acknowledgement to, VII cix; other ref., I 281*n*; II 222; VIII 96, 261; X 34

WORKS:

Cooper's Hill, I 67*n*, 127, 132–5, 149*n*, 151*n*, 156*n*, 160*n*, 164*n*, 170*n*, 173 and *n*, 175*n*, 176*n*, 178*n*, 182*n*, 185*n*, 190*n*, 322*n*; II 210*n*, 281*n*, 283*n*, 327*n*; III.i 122*n*, 123*n*; V 122*n*, 166*n*; *The Destruction of Troy*, I 158*n*, 180*n*; II 191*n*; IV xxvii and *n*, xxviii; *Friendship and Single Life*, III.i 110*n*; *Of Justice*, III.i 112*n*; *Of*

Old Age, III.i 86*n*, 158*n*; *Of Prudence*, II 322*n*; III.i 11*n*; IV 114*n*; *On Mr John Fletcher's Works*, IV 110*n*; VI 144–5*n*; *Out of an Epigram of Martial*, I 267*n*; *Passion of Dido for Aeneas*, I 86*n*; *The Progress of Learning*, I 244*n*, 317*n*; IV 120*n*; V 401*n*; *Sophy*, III.i 117*n*; *To Edward Howard*, II 363*n* Translations: *Aeneid*, VII cviii; X 501; *Iliad*, I 357–8, 449, 450*n*; II 199*n*; VII cx, cxxvi, cxxix, cxxxvi; X 541; AP debt to trans., VII cix, cxxix; X 495; parallels to AP trans., X 498

Dennis, John, Biog., IV 357; V 437–8; his attacks on AP and AP reaction to them, I 264*n*, 293*n*, 295*n*, 307*n*, 482–4; II 392 ff.; IV 107 and *n*, 115, 123 and *n*; V x, xii *n*; VI 80; VII xxv; on AP trans. Homer, VII xlii, lxxxvi, cii; on Homer authorship, VII lxxvi; in AP poems, I 270 and *n*, 306 and *n*; IV 229; V 72 and *n*, 128, 134–5 and *n*, 167 and *n*, 277 and *n*, 307, 328 and *n*; VI 26, 29*n*, 142, 144*n*, 188, 189*n*, 283 and *n*, 328, 331–2*n*, 355–7 and *n*; other ref., I 18; IV xxvii *n*, 200*n*; V xvi, xlvi, 12*n*, 18*n*, 53, 82*n*, 114*n*, 125*n*, 135*n*, 139*n*, 153*n*, 167*n*, 197 and *n*, 199–200, 210, 415–18, 447, 467, 468

WORKS:

Appius and Virginia, I 199, 306*n*; V 127*n*; VI 356*n*; *The Char. and Conduct of Sir John Edgar*, V 150*n*; *The Grounds of Criticism in Poetry*, I 224–7, 231–2, 270*n*; *Iphigenia*, I 307*n*; Letters in *Daily Journal*, V xvii, 67*n*, 138*n*, 209, 235; Pref. to *Miscellanies*, I 317*n*; *Operas*

after the Italian Manner, V 190n;
Part of the Te Deum Paraphr., III.i
15n; *Pope Alexander's Supremacy*,
V xx n, xxii n, xxviii n, 212, 432;
criticism of (including *Reflections
upon*) *Essay on Criticism*, I 205–7,
212, 218–21, 235, 241n, 243n,
245n, 247n, 249n, 254n, 258n,
260n, 276n, 293n, 295n, 298n,
299n, 305n, 312–13n, 314n; V
13n, 24n, 25n, 38n, 44n, 73n, 207;
VI 332n; AP reply to him, VI 80;
Remarks upon the Dunciad, V xxii n,
xxvii, xli, 42n, 75n, 186n, 198,
199–200, 211; *Remarks upon
Homer*, V 27n, 44 and n, 45, 67n,
70n, 73–4n, 75n, 151n, 208, 231n,
233n, 235, 290n, 322n; *Remarks
upon Mr Pope's Translation of
Homer*, VI 189n; *Remarks on
Prince Arthur*, V 15n, 20 and n,
131–2n, 151n; *Remarks on The
Rape of the Lock*, II 90n, 104, 110n,
119, 122n, 123, 157n; V 39n, 44n,
110n, 169–70n, 208 and n, 231n,
235 and n; AP reply to, II 392–9;
The Stage Defended, V 115n, 147n,
170n; *A True Character*, V 16n,
20n, 25n, 38n, 39n, 42–3n, 45n,
74n, 115n, 132n, 197, 208, 231n,
233n, 235, 437; VI 331n
De Piles, Roger, I 240n, 252n, 256n,
258n, 273n, 320n
Deptford (London), in AP poem,
VI 44
De Quincey, Thomas, I 208
De Rabutin, Roger, II 297
De Rambouillet family, in AP
poem, VI 64, 65n
Derham, William (divine and
natural philosopher), III.i 110n,
111n; V 409n
Derwentwater, James Radcliffe,

3rd Earl of, scandal of his estates,
III.ii 99n
Desaguliers, J. T., Newtonian, *E.
on Man* attributed to, III.i xv;
other ref., III.i 14n, 18n, 60n,
116n
Desaulnais (Disney), Henry,
Colonel, VI 321n
De Scales peerage case, II 372, 373n
Descartes, René, I 220; II 382n;
III.i 48n, 131n, 148n; V 386n,
387n, 409n; VII xlix
De Sévigné, Marie, Marquise, II
297, 379
Desfontaines, P. F. G., II 105n
Des Maiseaux, Pierre, trans. St
Evremond, III.i 65n, 67n
Desprez, Louis, AP knowledge of
his *Horace*, IV xliii
Destruction of Oechalia (work attri-
buted to Homer), VII 53
Deucalion, in AP poem, I 402
Deutsch, O. E., I 77n
Devaux, Monsieur (cook), VI 254n
De Vega, Lopez, in AP poem, VI
178, 180n
De Villars, Abbé de Montfaucon,
Comte de Gabalis, II 123, 142 f.,
148n, 150n, 157n, 163n, 164n,
378 ff., 397
Devil Tavern (in London), in AP
poem, V 294 and n; other ref.,
VI 402n
Devonshire, William Cavendish,
1st Duke of, I 201, 302n, 303n;
IV 180n; V 117n, 446
Devonshire, William Cavendish,
2nd Duke of, I 303n; IV 180n
Devonshire, William Cavendish,
3rd Duke of, Biog., IV 352–3;
other ref., IV 180n, 181n; V 400n
Diana, in AP poems, I 67 and n, 76,
165 and n, 168, 436; II 166

Diaper, Rev. William (poet), II 6*n*; IV xxviii *n*; V 137*n*

Dickinson, Edmund (metaphysician), III.i 46*n*

Dictys of Crete, VII lxxxi, 33, 198, 343; IX 390, 414, 416; X 22–3

Didius (Roman emperor), in AP poem, III.ii 102 and *n*

Dido, in AP poems, II 134, 199, 272 (Eliza)

Didymus (commentator on Homer, 1st c. BC), VII 187, 202; VIII 22, 112, 144, 253; IX 269, 344, 406; X 345–6, 354

Digby, Edward (brother of Robert), VI 315*n*

Digby, Mary (sister of Robert), AP *Epitaph* on, VI 313–14, 315–16*n*; doubtful epitaph, VI 447*n*

Digby, The Hon. Robert, AP corres., III.i 86*n*; VII xxxvi–xxxvii, xliii *n*, ccxxiii *n*; in AP poems, III.i 138 and *n*; VI 313–14, 315–16*n*; other ref., III.i 156*n*

Digby, William, 5th Baron, Biog., IV 357; in AP poem, IV 326 and *n*; other ref., III.i 138*n*

Dilke, Charles Wentworth (critic), I viii, 199, 355*n*; II 244*n*, 353*n*, 355*n*, 375*n*, 408; III.ii 8, 62*n*, 103*n*, 107*n*, 121*n*, 145*n*, 160; IV ix, xxxvi *n*, 289*n*, 357; V 410*n*; VI 81*n*, 323*n*, 411*n*

Dillon. See Roscommon

Dimier, Louis, VIII xii

Dimock, George, VII ccxi *n*

Dinarchus (sculptor), X 600

Diodorus of Sicily (historian, 1st c. BC), I 179*n*; II 191*n*, 231, 232, 262*n* ff.; VII cliv *n*, 32, 46–7, 114, 323, 457; VIII 166, 261, 363; IX 114, 120, 133, 145, 239, 309,

315, 337–9, 345, 371; X 162, 182, 202, 228, 359

Diogenes the Cynic, VII 15; X 430

Diogenes Laertius (author of compendium of philosophy), II 260; III.i 112*n*, 139*n*; VII 41, 48, 53; VIII 240; IX 161; X 91

Diognetus (ruler of Athens, *c* 900 BC), VII 43

Diomed, in AP poem, I 449

Dion Cassius, III.ii 120*n*

Dione, in AP poem, I 427 and *n*

Dionysidorus (Alexandrian grammarian, school of Aristarchus), IX 213

Dionysius of Halicarnassus, in AP poem, I 314 and *n*; AP use of, VII xl; interpretation of Homer, VII xc, cvi; in AP Preface, VII 11, and MS Preface, X 422; other ref., I 260*n*; VII 90, 131, 134–5, 139–41, 144, 146, 148, 176, 195, 432–3, 435, 461, 470; VIII 65, 356, 384, 409, 427, 494, 542; IX 215, 219, 320, 367, 398, 422; X 33–4, 100, 134

Dionysius Periegetes (author of description of known world, *c* 300 AD), IX 226, 338; X 60

Dionysius Thrax (grammarian, 2nd/1st c. BC), VII 58

Dirce, in AP poem, I 412 and *n*

Diseases of Bath, anon., V 396*n*

Disney. See Desaulnais

Disney, Walter Elias, VII cxxiv

D'Israeli, Isaac, III.i 24*n*, 45*n*

Ditton, Humphrey (mathematician), VI 415*n*

Dives, Charlotte (later wife of Samuel, Baron Masham), VI 341, 342*n*

Di Vus, Andreas, X 441

Dob, A. (name under which pirated ed. of *Dunciad* was pub.), V xxix, 3 and *n*, 462

Dobell, P. J., VI xix, 438*n*, 447*n*

Dobrée, Bonamy, IV 339; VI xix

Dobson, Austin, on Dr Mead, III.ii 136*n*; on Stowe, III.ii 143*n*; other ref., II ix

Dobson, E. J., *English Pronunciation*, III.ii 19*n*, 35*n*

Dobson, W. (translator), V 352*n*, 429

Dodd, Anne, Biog., V 438; other ref., III.i xxi; V xvii ff., xxiv *n*, xxvi *n*, xxviii, 50*n*

Dodd, Nathaniel, V xviii, 438

Dodington, George Bubb, later Baron Melcombe (in AP poems as Bubo, Bufo), Biog., IV 357–8; AP use of his couplet, III.ii 29*n*; IV 322 and *n*; original of Bubo, III.ii 138*n*; ridiculed in *Key to Popery*, III.ii 178*n*, 184*n*, 186*n*; in AP poems, III.ii 138 and *n*, 182*n*; IV xxiv, 112–16 and *n*, 184*n*, 185, 298 and *n*, 303 and *n*, 334 and *n*; V 99*n*; other ref., III.ii 91*n*; IV xix, 285*n*; V 126*n*, 181*n*, 350*n*, 453–4; VI 163*n*

Dodsley, Robert, II 231; III.ii 89*n*; IV xxxix; V 249, 453; VI 354*n*, 356*n*, 385*n*, 387*n*, 388*n*

Domitian, I 410*n*, 411*n*

Donne, John, AP imitations and knowledge of, III.i xv *n*, 82*n*; IV xli–xliii, 3, 34–5*n*, 340; VI 25, 28*n*; AP *Satires of*, IV 23–49, 129–45; AP versifications of, VI 17*n*, 28*n*, 113; in AP poem, VI 25; other ref., I 156*n*, 245*n*, 307*n*; II 159*n*, 170*n*, 284*n*, 294, 300, 301, 340*n*, 341*n*, 365*n*; III.i lxxiv, 16*n*, 26*n*, 41*n*, 64*n*, 74*n*, 76*n*, 82*n*, 92*n*, 109*n*, 131*n*, 164*n*; V 117*n*, 292*n*; VI 115; VII 4

Doran, John, *Annals of the Stage*, IV 223*n*

Dorchester, Evelyn Pierrepont, Marquess of, I 38

Dorimant, in AP poem, IV 285 and *n*; other ref., III.ii 138*n*, 178

Doris, in AP poem, I 80 ff.

Dormer, General James, III.ii 25*n*

Dormer, T. Cottrell, VI 155*n*

Dorset, Charles Sackville, 6th Earl of, AP imitations of, VI 15–17, 48–51; AP *Epitaph on*, VI 334–6; other ref., I 244*n*, 298*n*; II 149*n*; V 133*n*

Dorset, Lionel Sackville, 1st Duke of, Biog., IV 382–3; other ref., IV 335*n*; VI 335*n*

Dorset, Thomas Sackville, 1st Earl of, in AP poem, VI 335, 336*n*

Douglas. See Queensberry

Douglas, Charles. See Selkirk

Douglas, James, Biog., V 438; in AP poems, V 380, 380–1*n*; VI 259, 264*n*; other ref., V 364*n*

Douglas-Home, Sir Alexander, X xii

Dover, in AP poem, IV 141

Dover, Thomas, Biog., IV 358; in AP poem, IV 241

Doyle, P. A. See Cronin, G.

Drake, James, I 304*n*

Drayton, Michael, I 132, 157*n*, 163*n*, 176*n*, 183*n*, 184*n*, 187*n*; II 45*n*, 106, 227, 294, 303, 308, 309, 383; III.i xlviii, 122*n*

Drennon, Herbert, III.i xxxviii *n*

Drew, Sarah. See Hewet

Druids, in AP poem, II 264

Drummond, Mary, Biog., IV 358–9; other ref., IV 308*n*

Drummond, William, of Hawthornden, I 83n, 265n, 266n; II 328n; III.i 27n

Drury Lane (London), in AP poems, III.i 82; IV 99 and n, 139; V 99 and n, 179, 293, 297, 333; VI 26, 39, 40n, 165

Drury-Lane Monster, VI 179n

Dryads, in AP poem, I 89

Dryden, John, Biog., IV 359; his part in "neo-classical" literary theory, I 210–12, 222–3, 226, 231; views on trans., IV xxvii–xxviii; VII clxxxiv; elements in trans. AP rejects, VII cxxvi; *Parallel of the Characters of Dryden and Pope*, I 359–60; V 230–5; AP epitaph on, VI 209n, 237, 238n; AP inscription on his tomb, VI 209n; in other AP poems, I 284 and n, 290, 293, 309 and n; IV 15 and n, 105, 113 and n, 175, 213, 217, 218n, 219; VI 27, 29n, 59, 156, 208, 369, 379, 450; tradition of dramatic speech, VII lxx n; AP acknowledgement to, VII cix n; AP bust of, IX xiii; in AP MS Preface, X 439; other ref., I 37n, 281n, 284n, 291n, 317n, 320n, 361, 484; II xii, 53n, 108, 153n, 182n, 199n, 237, 379, 380, 382; III.i lxxvii n; III.ii 155n; IV 226n, 345, 355, 361, 363, 383, 392; V xlv, xlvi n, 8n, 41, 105n, 114n, 299n, 429, 456; VI 35n, 169n, 292n; VII xxv, cxliii, ccxxxv; X 475

WORKS:

Absalom and Achitophel, I 186n, 292n, 324n, 325n; II 177n, 199n, 283n, 327n, 330n, 363n, 366n; III.i 14n, 43n, 76n, 105n, 117n, 128n, 147n; III.ii 15n, 60n, 109n,

112n, 118n; IV 279n, 314n; V 72n, 133n, 454; VII clii, ccxvii–ccxviii; X 501, 505, 511, 512; *Albion and Albanius*, I 142 and n; II 162n, 165n, 410; *Alexander's Feast*, I 283n, 284n; II 30n, 208n, 266n; VII cliv, clv; X 504, 505, 509, 511, 512; *All for Love* and Epilogue, I 239n; II 299n; III.i 88n, 129n; V 167n; *Annus Mirabilis*, I 150n, 181n, 190n, 192n, 251n, 280n, 402n; III.i 111n; *Astraea Redux*, I 246n, 298n; II 279n; *Aureng–Zebe*, including Prologue and Epilogue, I 121n, 257n, 286n, 308n; II 325n, 345n; III.i 14n, 83n, 141n; IV 12n, 220n, 385; VII lii; *Britannia Rediviva*, I 118n; *Circe*, Prologue to, I 326n; *Cleomenes*, II 345–6n; *Conquest of Granada*, including Prologue and Epilogue, I 242n, 308n; II 277n, 364n; III.i 73n, 163n; *Dedication of the Aeneis*, I 26n; V 471; VII cix, 156; IX 187, 298, 378, 428; X 34, 69, 115; *Don Sebastian*, I 66n, 114n; II 193n, 320n, 335n, 346n; III.i 112n, 130n, 158n; *Eleonora*, I 267n; II 253n; III.i 20n; *Epitaph on Sir Palmes Fairborne's Tomb*, II 364n; *Essay of Heroic Plays*, VII ccv n; *Hind and the Panther*, I 242n, 243n; II 147n f., 151n, 256n, 333n, 343n; III.i 49n, 73n, 82n, 115n; V 315n, 466n, 470; VI 369, 371n; *Husband his own Cuckold*, Epilogue, IV 108n; *Indian Emperor*, V 148n; IX 389; X 61; *King Arthur*, II 164n, 263n, 363n, 411; *Love Triumphant*, Prologue, I 316n; *Loyal Brother*, Prologue and Epilogue, I 290n; *MacFlecknoe*, I 263n, 290n; II

112*n*, 159*n*, 161*n*, 169*n*, 172*n*, 217*n*, 364*n*; V xxxviii f., 66*n*, 67*n*, 81*n*, 96*n*, 97*n*, 99*n*, 106*n*, 141*n*, 278*n*, 294*n*, 454, 471; *Medal*, I 242*n*, 249*n*; III.i 67*n*; *Man of Mode*, Epilogue, I 242*n*; *Marriage A-La-Mode*, II 207*n*; *Miscellanies*, Tonson-Dryden. See Tonson; *Oedipus*, and Prologue, I 314*n*; II 209*n*; III.i 51*n*; *Of Dramatic Poesy*, VII lxxiii and *n*; *Of the Pythagorean Philosophy*, X 500; *On the Death of Amyntas*, I 91*n*; II 279*n*; *Parallel of Poetry and Painting*, IV 218*n*; [*Pilgrim* by Fletcher], Prologue and Epilogue to, I 298*n*; IV 6*n*; V 131*n*; VI 175*n*; Prefaces, I 32*n*; VII lii *n*, xc, civ, cv *n*, 352; *Prologue, To the University of Oxford*, I 295*n*; *Religio Laici*, I 262*n*, 301*n*, 320*n*, 326*n*; III.i lxxviii–lxx, 12*n*, 17*n*, 30*n*, 46*n*, 115*n*, 125*n*; *Secret Love*, I 308*n*; *Secular Masque*, II 24*n*; *Song to a Fair Young Lady*, II 159*n*; *State of Innocence*, I 169*n*, 265*n*; II 208*n*, 275*n*, 321*n*, 342*n*; III.i 69*n*; 86*n*; IV 170*n*; [*Tempest*, Shakespeare], Prologue, I 255*n*, 316*n*; *Threnodia Augustalis*, I 181*n*, 297*n*, 319*n*; III.i 27*n*; *To Mr Congreve*, II 19*n*; *To Mr Granville*, II 145*n*, 195*n*; *To my Honour'd Kinsman, John Driden*, I 150*n*, 161*n*, 171*n*; III.i 156*n*; III.ii 140*n*; *To the Pious Memory of . . . Mrs Anne Killigrew*, I 122*n*; *Ode to Mrs Anne Killigrew*, VI 316*n*; *To Sir Godfrey Kneller*, I 267*n*, 293*n*, 319*n*; II 324*n*; IV 207*n*; V 157*n*; *To Mr Oldham*, I 322*n*; *To her Grace the Duchess of Ormond*, II 363*n*; III.i 26*n*; *To the Earl of*

Roscommon, I 318*n*, 324*n*; II 266*n*; [*Troilus and Cressida*], Prologue, V 141*n*; *Tyrannick Love*, including Prologue and Epilogue, I 266*n*, 269*n*; II 149*n*, 301*n*, 328*n*, 335*n*, 337*n*, 342*n*; *Verses to her Highness the Duchess*, I 61*n*; *Wild Gallant*, II 188*n*

Prose works, I 26*n*, 31*n*, 32*n*, 81*n*, 239*n*, 241*n*, 243*n*, 244*n*, 246*n*, 247*n*, 249*n*, 250*n*, 253*n*, 256*n*, 257*n*, 259*n*, 260*n*, 261*n*, 266*n*, 267*n*, 269*n*, 272*n*, 274*n*, 276*n*, 278*n*, 281*n*, 282*n*, 283*n*, 284*n*, 285*n*, 287*n*, 291*n*, 292*n*, 293*n*, 297*n*, 304*n*, 311*n*, 313*n*, 315*n*, 321*n*, 322*n*, 323*n*, 324*n*, 334, 335*n*, 343, 344*n*, 349, 357, 360*n*, 395*n*
II 3 and *n*, 5 and *n*, 9 and *n*, 109*n*, 165*n*, 167*n*, 200*n*, 223, 243 and *n*, 258*n*, 268*n*, 271*n*, 277*n*, 293, 297*n*, 300 and *n*, 310 and *n*, 357*n*, 363*n*, 380*n*, 381*n*
III.i 14*n*, 70*n*, 140*n*, 147*n*
IV xxvii–xxviii, 199*n*, 202*n*, 218*n*, 389, 392
Translations:
Boccaccio, *Cym. and Iph.*, II 25*n*, 203*n*, 335*n*; III.i 77*n*; *Sigism. and Guisc.*, I 119*n*, 159*n*, 160*n*; II 32*n*, 33*n*, 367*n*; III.i 114*n*; *Theod. and Honor.*, I 60*n*, 71*n*; II 332*n*; III.i 118*n*; X 503, 510
Boileau, *L'Art Poétique* (with Sir William Soames), I 246*n*, 247*n*, 250*n*, 252*n*, 257*n*, 260*n*, 264*n*, 267*n*, 280*n*, 282*n*, 292*n*, 296*n*, 305*n*, 310*n*, 311*n*, 326*n*; III.i 165*n*
Chaucer (including adaptations), *Character of A Good Parson*, I 245*n*; X 511; *Cock and the Fox*, I 63*n*; II 15*n*, 20*n*, 30*n*, 38*n*, 41*n*, 42*n*, 253*n*, 338*n*; III.i 42*n*;

D

Flower and the Leaf, II 21*n*, 41*n*, 44*n*, 149*n*, 188*n*, 215, 253*n*, 277*n*; *Pal. and Arc.*, I 62*n*, 120*n*, 313*n*; II 15*n*, 25*n*, 27*n*, 34*n*, 35*n*, 38*n*, 39*n*, 51*n*, 52*n*, 162*n*, 200*n*, 256*n*, 257*n*, 281*n*, 289*n*, 322*n*, 344*n*; III.i 47*n*, 92*n*, 144*n*; VII lix, cxxxi; X 149, 501, 502, 505, 509, 511; *Wife of Bath Her Tale*, II 16*n*, 24*n*, 34*n*, 37*n*, 42*n*, 45*n*, 46*n*, 53*n*; III.i 146*n*; IV 100*n*; other ref., II 3–7, 36*n*, 37*n*

Dufresnoy, *De arte graphica*, I 164*n*; VI 156, 159*n*

Homer, *Iliad* and AP debt to, I 189*n*, 441*n*, 469*n*; II 17*n*, 42*n*, 43*n*; VII xli *n*, lxxxix, xcii, cii, cviii, cix *n*, cx, cxv and *n*, cxxxv, cxxxvii, cxxxix, cxl, cxli–cxlii, clix; X 494, 495, 496, 497, 501, 504, 508, 510, 575–6, 603–4; *Odyssey*, VII cxxv; other ref., I 356–7, 359–60; VII 22, 87–8, 116, 121, 124–5, 153, 349

Horace, I 66*n*

Juvenal, I 179*n*; II 18*n*, 155*n*, 257*n*, 365*n*; III.i 72*n*, 92*n*; IV 96*n*, 339; V 117*n*, 310*n*; X 505

Lucretius, II 188*n*, 344*n*; III.i 32*n*, 26*n*, 69*n*, 86*n*, 99*n*; VII lvii, lviii *n*; IX 420; X 502, 504, 505, 510

Ovid, I 74*n*, 86*n*, 153*n*, 160*n*, 166*n*, 167*n*, 168*n*, 169*n*, 184*n*, 268*n*, 332–6, 339, 343–4, 349, 365–73*n*, 388*n*, 390*n*, 396*n*, 399*n*; II 16*n*, 31*n*, 39*n*, 42*n*, 145*n*, 155*n*, 156*n*, 162*n*, 168*n*, 169*n*, 187*n*, 254*n* f., 258*n*, 277*n*, 285*n*, 286*n*, 306 f., 307*n*, 322*n*, 323*n*, 325*n*, 328*n*, 332*n*, 338*n*, 340*n*, 345*n*, 348*n*, 365*n*; III.i 13*n*, 21*n*, 24*n*, 29*n*, 30*n*, 93*n*, 108*n*, 109*n*, 110*n*,

140*n*; V 135*n*, 144*n*, 288*n*; X 275, 324, 501, 511, 512

Persius, I 241*n*, 243*n*, 244*n*, 313*n*, 326*n*; II 17*n*, 160*n*; III.i 30*n*, 83*n*; IV 299*n*

Theocritus, I 75*n*

Virgil, I 16, 17*n*, 24*n*, 26*n*, 27*n*, 30*n*, 31*n*, 32*n*, 44, 49*n*, 59*n*, 60*n*, 63*n*, 64*n*, 65*n*, 66*n*, 69*n*, 72*n*, 73*n*, 74*n*, 75*n*, 76*n*, 77*n*, 78*n*, 79*n*, 80*n*, 82*n*, 83*n*, 84*n*, 85*n*, 86*n*, 87*n*, 89*n*, 90*n*, 91*n*, 93*n*, 94*n*, 95*n*, 112*n*, 114*n*, 115*n*, 118*n*, 120*n*, 121*n*, 135, 148*n*, 150*n*, 154*n*, 159*n*, 160*n*, 162*n*, 163*n*, 165*n*, 166*n*, 167*n*, 169*n*, 172*n*, 173*n*, 174*n*, 177*n*, 180*n*, 181*n*, 184*n*, 186*n*, 190*n*, 192*n*, 194*n*, 245*n*, 248*n*, 253*n*, 254*n*, 259*n*, 263*n*, 279*n*, 283*n*, 291*n*, 296*n*, 310*n*, 324*n*, 352, 377*n*, 378*n*, 387*n*, 388*n*, 401*n*, 403*n*, 409*n*, 410*n*, 414*n*, 416*n*, 417*n*, 420*n*, 421*n*, 422*n*, 426*n*, 428*n*, 430*n*, 431*n*, 432*n*, 433*n*, 435*n*, 436*n*, 437*n*, 442*n*, 445*n*, 450*n*, 451*n*, 452*n*, 457*n*, 458*n*, 459*n*, 461*n*, 462*n*, 466*n*, 467*n*, 472*n*; II 10, 113*n*, 146*n*, 150*n*, 151*n*, 152*n*, 156*n*, 157*n*, 161*n*, 162*n*, 163*n*, 167*n*, 171*n*, 174*n*, 175*n*, 177*n*, 178*n*, 179*n*, 180*n*, 181*n*, 183*n*, 191*n*, 193*n*, 195*n*, 196*n*, 198*n*, 199*n*, 200*n*, 203*n* f., 206*n*, 208*n*, 210*n*, 212*n*, 253*n*, 255*n*, 257*n*, 258*n*, 262*n*, 268*n*, 270*n* f., 271, 277*n*, 279*n*, 280*n*, 283*n*, 319*n*, 321*n*, 328*n*, 332*n*, 333*n*, 345*n*, 365*n*, 366*n*, 408*n*; III.i 41*n*, 94*n*, 96*n*, 104*n*, 108*n*, 129*n*, 135*n*; III.ii 73*n*, 91*n*, 93*n*, 156*n*; IV 18*n*, 174*n*, 386, 389, 392; V 61*n*, 64*n*, 71*n*, 85*n*, 87*n*, 89*n*, 98*n*, 107*n*, 121*n*, 139*n*,

141*n*, 151*n*, 160*n*, 167*n*, 168*n*,
186*n*, 351*n*; VI 380*n*, 385*n*; VII
xv *n*, cvii, cviii and *n*, cix and *n*,
cxii–cxiii *n*, cxxix–cxxx and *n*,
cxxx–cxxxii, cxxxv, cxliv and *n*,
cliv, clv, clvi and *n*, ccviii–ccix,
ccxxxvi, 272–3; VIII 264; IX
94, 280, 353; X 9, 188–9, 231,
250, 302, 305, 312, 347, 349, 494,
495, 501, 502, 504, 505, 510, 511;
Aeneid parallels to AP *Iliad* trans.,
501–6, to AP *Odyssey* trans., 508–
12
Dryope, in AP poem, I 385, 388 and *n*
Du Bartas, Guillaume de Salluste,
III.i 13*n*, 15*n*, 20*n*, 60*n*, 67*n*,
103*n*, 112*n*
Du Bellay, Joachim, IV 320*n*
Du Boccage, Marie Anne (Le
Page) Fiquet, II 229*n*
Du Bosc, C., II 140
Duck, Stephen, Biog., IV 359; in
AP poems, IV 175; VI 327,
331*n*; other ref., III.ii 114*n*; IV
225*n*; V 413*n*, 415*n*; VI 394*n*
Duckett, George, Biog., V 438–9;
in AP poems, V 169, 329; VI
301, 304*n*; other ref., IV 121*n*;
V 16*n*, 126*n*, 163*n*, 168*n*, 170*n*,
207, 210, 212, 432; VI 100*n*, 135*n*
Duck-Lane, in AP poem, I 289
and *n*
Dufresnoy, Charles Alphonse
(painter and poet), in AP poem,
VI 156, 159*n*; other ref., II 238
Du Fresnoy, Nicolas Lenglet, I 164*n*
Du Guernier, L., II 140
Duilius, in AP poem, II 73 and *n*
Duke, Richard (poet), I 93*n*; IV
xxviii *n*
Duke Street (London), VI 237*n*
Duke University, VII xvi
Duncan, G. M., I 256*n*

Dunciad Dissected, V 24, 32, 210,
231*n*, 456
Dunciad, Female. See Curll
Duncombe, Sir Charles (banker),
III.ii 37*n*; IV 69*n*
Dunk. See Halifax
Dunkirk (French port), in AP
poem, IV 39 and *n*
Duns Scotus, John, VII lxxviii
Dunton, John, Biog., V 439; in AP
poems, V 117, 302; VI 173, 175*n*;
other ref., V xlv *n*, 73*n*, 93*n*
Dupin, Louis Ellies-, VII xl and *n*,
42, 177
Duport, James (author of *Homeri
Gnomologia*), VII xl and *n*, 9;
VIII 204; X 419, 442
Dupplin, Thomas Hay, Viscount
(later 9th Earl of Kinnoul), IV
xxv, 115*n*
Durastanti, Margaritta (singer),
VI 440*n*
Dürer, Albrecht, in AP poem, IV
45 and *n*
Du Resnel, J. F. du B., trans. AP
E. on Criticism, I 208; trans. AP *E.
on Man*, III.i xviii–xix, xx *n*, xxii
D'Urfey, Thomas, Biog., V 439; in
AP poems, I 309 and *n*; V 161
and *n*, 326; VI 85–90, 101–2,
173; AP imitates line from his
song, V 346*n*; other ref., I 218;
II 187*n*; V xlv, 45*n*, 135*n*, 167*n*,
328*n*, 354*n*
Durrant, C. S., II 373*n*
Du Suëil, Augustin (binder), III.ii
150
Dutch[–man, –men], in AP poems,
V 154, 316, 323, 361; VI 49
Dyce, Alexander (editor), VI 462*n*
Dyke, Daniel, III.i 73*n*, 81*n*
Dyson, H. V. D., IV 196*n*, 228*n*
Dyve. See Dives

E

Eastbury House (Dorset), III.ii 139*n*, 188*n*

Easthampstead (Berks.), in AP poem, VI 169, 170*n*

Ebor, in AP poem, IV 335

EC. See Elwin

Eccles, John, I 77*n*

Echo, in AP poem, I 92

Eckersall, James, II 245*n*

Eddy, Donald D., X 587

Eden, in AP poems, I 148; II 337

Edinburgh Magazine, VI 459*n*

Education, modern, V 355 ff.

Edward ["Old E.'s Armour"], in AP poem, IV 223

Edward III, in AP poems, I 135, 142, 175*n*, 177 and *n*, 178*n*; IV 195 and *n*

Edward IV, in AP poems, I 142, 177*n*, 179 and *n*; III.ii 105; VI 114

Edward the Black Prince, I 177*n*, 178*n*; X 430

Edward Longshanks, X 430

Edwards ["of all our E. talk"], in AP poem, IV 33

Edwards, Thomas, *Canons of Criticism*, V xxxvii *n*, 398*n*

Edwards, T. R., V 466

Effingham, Henry Howard, 6th Earl of, II 371

"Egerton, William" [pseud.], (Curll hack), III.ii 36*n*

Egmont, John Perceval, 1st Earl of, *Diary* cited, IV xxxiv, xxxv, 37*n*, 39*n*, 42*n*, 141*n*, 195*n*, 210*n*, 298*n*, 304*n*, 313*n*, 322*n*, 332*n*, 336*n*, 344, 345, 346, 349, 350, 353, 363, 376, 377, 381, 384, 387; V 381*n*, 404*n*, 430, 432, 446, 458; VI 432*n*

Egypt [Ægypt, –ian], in AP poems, I 425 and *n*; II 262; III.i 21; V 68, 175, 275, 330; VI 66, 88

Ehnmark, Erland, VII ccvii *n*

Ehrenpreis, I., I 315*n*

Eliah [Elijah], in AP poem, VI 199

Eliot, T. S., III.i lxix; VII ccxix *n*

Elis, in AP poem, I 470

Eliza, in AP poems, II 272. See also next entry; Haywood, Eliza

Elizabeth I, in AP poems, [Bess], IV 29; [Eliza], VI 290, 291; other ref., I 189*n*

Elizabeth, Czarina, III.ii 28*n*

Ellis, Havelock, II 91*n*

Ellis, John, Biog., IV 359; in AP poem, IV 83; other ref., III.ii 117*n*

Ellys, Sir Richard, IV 289*n*

Eloisa, historical information, II 411–16; in AP poems, II 74, 319, 320, 328, 341, 344, 346

Elton, Oliver, II 216*n*

Elwin, W., and W. J. Courthope (editors of AP), cited as EC, I 7*n*, 13*n*, 61*n*, 63*n*, 65*n*–67*n*, 69*n*, 71*n*–

76n, 80n, 82n, 84n, 85n, 89n, 90n, 91n, 93n, 103n, 112n, 116n, 120n, 125n, 150n 151n, 153n, 154n, 156n, 158n, 159n, 161n, 162n, 165n–7n, 169n, 170n, 172n, 173n, 178n, 180n, 182n–5n, 187n–90n, 193n, 194n, 197n, 198n, 208n, 218n, 239n, 240n, 242n–4n, 247n, 252n–4n, 258n–60n, 262n, 264n, 267n, 269n, 273n–5n, 279n, 280n, 284n, 286n, 287n, 289n, 290n, 292n, 294n–6n, 304n, 306n, 308n, 313n, 325n, 326n, 340n, 379n, 385n, 389n, 399n, 411n, 412n, 414n, 416n, 419n, 420n, 423n, 426n, 430n–3n, 435n, 438n–40n, 445n
III.i 11n, 13n, 14n, 24n, 32n, 44n, 54n, 55n, 58n, 62n, 64n, 77n, 79n, 83n, 88n, 96n, 99n–101n, 105n, 108n, 110n, 112n–14n, 120n, 128n, 131n, 134n, 135n, 138n, 140n, 145n, 146n, 151n, 153n–5n, 158n, 159n, 164n
IV 6n, 97n, 108n, 112n, 114n, 115n, 141n, 178n, 179n, 218n, 245n, 314n, 333n, 336n, 337n
V xxxi, xxxvi, 62n, 72n, 113n, 127n, 128n, 135n, 141n, 144n–6n, 154n, 157n, 159n, 209, 277n, 355n, 358n, 362n, 370n f., 377n, 386n, 392n f., 400n ff., 453
VII xxxvi n, cxciv n, cxcvii n, ccxli n
Elwin's notes, I viii, 102, 208, 340; II 84, 87n, 88n, 204n, 207n, 230 ff., 268n, 287n, 288n, 311, 342n, 355n, 368n, 379n, 382, 393n, 406; III.i xxiv, xxv; IV ix–x; VI 29n, 76n, 84n, 112n, 158n, 163n, 394n
Courthope's notes and Life of AP, I viii, 340; II xii, 90, 311; III.ii

8, 22n, 23n, 47n, 70n, 105n, 106n, 121n, 144n, 160, 168; IV x, xlv, 93–4n; VI 112n, 158n, 163n, 213n, 232n, 298n, 419n; VII xxv, xxxv n, xlii n
Elysium [Elysian, Elyzian], in AP poems, I 76; II 187; V 150, 320, 382; VI 33, 39, 64
Elzevier, Louis (printer), in AP poem, VI 83, 84n
Embankment (London), IV 62–3n
Empedocles, III.i 139n; VIII 348
Empson, William, article on wit, I 211n, 218n; Seven Types of Ambiguity, III.i 12n; III.ii xxvi n
Emylius Porta, X 441
Endymion, in AP poems, I 394, 398
England [English], in AP poems, III.ii 113; IV 35, 177, 199, 304, 309; V 172; VI 85, 178, 320
Englishman [–men], in AP poems, IV 209; VI 290
Englefield, Anthony, early patron of AP, III.ii 47n
Englefield, Edward, I 99
Ennius, Quintus (Roman poet, translator, 3rd/2nd c. BC), X 232
Enoch, in AP poem, VI 399
Ensor, George (critic), III.i xxx n
Eobanus Hessus. See Hessus
Epaminondas, in AP poem, II 267 and n; other ref., V 62n
Ephorus of Cyme (historian, 5th/4th c. BC), VII 45; X 201–2
Epicles, in AP poem, I 453
Epictetus, III.i xxviii, xxxv; III.ii 52n; VIII 58; IX 32; X 39, 235, 303
Epicureanism, III.i xl, lxvii, lxix
Epicurus, Lucretius' address to, III.i xxiii; in AP poem, VI 151; other ref., III.i 15n, 40n; X 239–40

Epigoni (lost work attributed to Homer), VII 54

Epimenides (religious teacher of Crete, 7th?/6th? c. BC), X 55–6

Epsom, in AP poem, VI 26

Erasinus, in AP poem, I 431 and *n*

Erasmus, Desiderius, AP defence of, I 204–5; in AP poems, I 318 and *n*; IV 10*n*, 11; other ref., V 103*n*; X 252

WORKS:

Adagia, I 292*n*; *Ciceron.*, III.i 87*n*; *De pueris instit.*, III.i l; *Enchirid. Mil. Christ.*, III.i 42*n*; *Praise of Folly*, III.i 37*n*, 53*n*, 73*n*, 85*n*, 90*n*, 142*n*

Eratosthenes of Cyrene (literary critic, 3rd/2nd c. BC), VII 76, 431; VIII 285; IX 143, 283

Eridanus, in AP poems, V 122, 304

Eringo, in AP poem, II 32 and *n*

Erinna, in AP poem, VI 306

Eryphile, in AP poem, II 76

Esdras, in AP poem, IV 135

Esher (Surrey), in AP poem, IV 316 and *n*

E'sham, in AP poem, IV 181

Esprit, Jacques (moralist), III.i 34*n*, 35*n*, 50*n*, 59*n*, 89*n*, 112*n*, 147*n*; III.ii 16*n*, 20*n*

Essais Politicke and Morall, by D. T., III.i 73*n*

Essay on the Dunciad, V 42*n*, 133*n*, 143*n*, 210

Essay on the Taste and Writings of the present times, anon., V 211

Estcourt, Richard, II 205*n*

Estienne, Robert (printer), in AP poem, VI 83, 85*n*

Etheocles, in AP poem, I 419

Etherege, George, II 143*n*; IV 44*n*, 285*n*; V 469; VII cxliii

Ethiopian. See Aethiopian

Eton College, in AP poems, V 191, 336, 355

Euclid, in AP poem, V 369

Euclio, in AP poem, III.ii 37

Eudoxus of Cnidus, I 64*n*

Eugene, Prince of Savoy, in AP poem, III.i 150 and *n*; other ref., I 40

Euler, Leonhard (natural philosopher), III.i 56*n*

Euphorion of Chalcis (poet and philosopher, 3rd/2nd c. BC), VII 447; IX 399

Euphrates, in AP poem, VI 203

Euripides, *Aegeus*, X 167; *Alcestis*, VII 165; *Cyclops*, IX 324–5; X 187; *Hecuba*, VIII 414; *Hippolytus*, VIII 275; IX 230; *Ion*, VIII 253; *Iphigenia in Tauris*, VII 342; X 331; *Orestes*, VII 441; *Rhesus*, VIII 496; *Trojan Women*, VIII 136; other ref., I 250*n*; V 256; VII lvii

Europa, in AP poems, I 409 and *n*, 420; VI 224

Europe, in AP poems, III.ii 26, 29; IV 39, 337; V 373–4; VI 82, 274

European Magazine, II 33*n*, 345*n*; VI 393*n*, 449*n*

Eurota, in AP poem, I 417 and *n*

Eurus, in AP poem, I 421 and *n*

Eurydice, in AP poem, VI 33, 34

Eusden, Laurence, Biog., IV 359; V 186–7*n*; in AP poems, IV 231; V 72, 186, 276, 291; other ref., II 154*n*, 157*n*, 167*n*, 186*n*; IV 97*n*; V xlv, 68*n*, 71*n*, 135*n* f., 139*n*, 149*n*, 266, 350*n*, 456; VI 100*n*, 305*n*, 330*n*

Eustathius (Bishop of Thessalonica,

commentator on Homer, 12th c. AD), V 48*n*, 431

VII xxxviii, xxxix, xl, lxxvii, lxxxi, lxxxiv, xcix, c, cii, cv, cvi, clxix, cxcvii *n*, 28, 53, 61, 83, 85–90, 93, 100–2, 108–9, 112, 114, 119, 121, 123–4, 128–9, 154, 160, 169, 173, 183, 187, 192, 200, 213, 217, 229, 237–8, 247, 265, 268–9, 272, 278–80, 282, 285, 288, 290, 293–4, 297, 307, 309, 312–16, 318–19, 329, 331, 339–40, 358, 363–5, 368–70, 372, 374–5, 379–81, 383, 386–8, 396–7, 399–400, 403, 405, 409–14, 420, 422–5, 428, 431–2, 434, 436, 438–44, 446–8, 453, 455, 457, 459, 461, 465–7, 469–71, 473

VIII 1–20, 22–4, 24–6, 28–31, 35–8, 41–8, 50, 54–5, 60, 62–4, 67–70, 73–4, 76, 78, 82, 85–6, 88, 90–2, 94–101, 106, 108, 113, 119, 121, 123, 128–9, 133, 135–6, 139–41, 143–6, 150–1, 157–8, 160–4, 169, 171, 173, 176, 178–9, 181, 184–5, 187, 189, 194–6, 200–1, 203, 205, 207, 211–15, 219, 222, 227, 228–30, 237, 239, 243–4, 246, 248, 255–6, 258–60, 262, 294, 266, 271, 275, 282–3, 287, 290, 292–6, 298–300, 304–6, 315, 319–20, 322–5, 328, 330, 332, 337–8, 346–7, 350–1, 359, 384, 391–4, 396, 398–9, 401–2, 405–6, 408–10, 414, 416, 421–2, 426–8, 432, 439–40, 442, 445–6, 449, 451, 454–5, 457, 460–1, 463, 465–9, 472–7, 480–2, 487, 495, 498, 500, 502–5, 507–9, 512, 519–17, 522–3, 527–8, 531, 536–7, 542, 544–5, 547–51, 554, 558–60, 564–6, 569–71, 578

IX 26–31, 33, 35, 37, 39, 41–6, 49–54, 56–7, 60–1, 64–7, 69–71, 74–6, 78–84, 86, 88, 90–9, 102, 104–10, 112–16, 119–20, 123–6, 128, 130, 132, 134–8, 142, 145, 151–2, 155–7, 160, 162, 165–6, 168, 171–7, 179, 183, 185, 189, 193–4, 196, 200, 202, 204–7, 209–10, 213–14, 216, 218–19, 221, 224, 226–8, 230, 233–5, 237–43, 248–50, 253–7, 261–2, 264–9, 272, 274, 276–9, 284–8, 291, 293, 295–6, 300–5, 307, 309, 311–12, 314, 317, 319, 323–4, 326–7, 329, 333, 337–8, 340–1, 343–4, 346, 348–50, 352–3, 357, 361, 364, 366, 368, 370–2, 377, 381, 383, 387–97, 399–402, 404, 406–7, 410–11, 415, 417, 419–20, 422–5, 429, 432, 434–40, 446, 450–1, 453, 458

X 2, 4, 7, 11–12, 16, 21, 27–8, 37–9, 43–4, 47–8, 52–5, 58–9, 61, 64, 73, 77–9, 87–94, 98, 103, 107–8, 110, 115–17, 120, 122, 125, 127–9, 134, 137–8, 140–4, 147, 149, 151, 154, 157–9, 162–3, 167–8, 171, 175, 179, 183–5, 187–8, 192–5, 197–8, 202, 204, 206, 208, 213, 216–20, 223, 225, 228, 230, 237–9, 241–2, 246, 248, 252–3, 254–6, 260, 265–6, 268, 272, 277–82, 286–8, 290–6, 301–3, 308–11, 313, 318–19, 322, 324–5, 327, 329–30, 332, 338, 348, 354–5, 357, 360, 363–4, 366–7, 373, 376, 392, 394, 396, 442, 445, 454

Evander, in AP poem, VI 369

Evans, Abel, Biog., V 439; in AP poems, V 109 and *n*, 301 and *n*; imitated by AP, V 369*n*; other ref., V 102*n*; VI 286*n*, 412*n*

Evans, A. W., *Warburton and the*

Warburtonians, III.i xxvii *n*; V 268*n*, 353*n*, 449

Eve, in AP poems, II 17; IV 118, 119; VI 259

Evelyn, John, in AP poem, VI 340, 341*n*; other ref., I 174*n*; II 6, 257*n*; III.ii 118*n*

Evening Journal, V 165*n*

Evening Post, II 325*n*, 378 f.; V xxiv *n*, 97*n*, 169*n*, 212*n*, 438, 459; VI 304*n*

Ewart, W., III.i 11*n*

Examen Miscellaneum, III.i 86*n*, 89*n*

Examen Poeticum, VII cx

Examiner, V 39*n*

Excise Bill (1733), III.ii 101*n*; IV 64*n*, 133

Explicator, III.i 12*n*

F

Faber, G. C., VI 180*n*, 291*n*, 346*n*, 347*n*, 410*n*, 415*n*, 443*n*, 447*n*

Fabretti, Raffaelle (antiquarian), VII 54

Fabricius, Johann Albert, VII 66

Fagles, Robert, VII xv, xvi

Fairchild, H. N., III.i lxxiii, 47*n*

Fairclough, H. R., I 136

Fairfax, Edward, II 333*n*

Fairholt, F. W., IV 301*n*

Falkland, Lucius Cary, 2nd Viscount, in AP poem, III.i 137 and *n*

Falmouth, Hugh Boscawen, 1st Viscount, III.ii 188*n*

Fane, Charlotte (daughter of Nicholas Rowe), in AP poem, VI 400, 401*n*

Fannia, in AP poem, III.ii 49 and *n*

Fanny, Lord. See Hervey

Farinelli (castrato), IV 286*n*, 360

Farmer, Richard, V 167*n*

Farnese collections, IX xiii

Farquhar, George (dramatist), in AP poem, IV 219 and *n*

Farrell, Barbara, VII xxiii

Faulkner, George (Dublin printer), III.ii xlvi *n*, xlix, 4*n*, 40, 76, 128

Faunus, in AP poem, I 365 and *n*

Faustus, Dr (pantomime), in AP poem, V 185 and *n*, 335 and *n*; other ref., V 176*n*

Favonio, in AP poem, IV 302

Fazakerley, N., V 461

Feith, Everard, VII 209

Fell, John (divine), III.i 123*n*

Felltham, Owen (essayist), III.i 50*n*

Felton, Henry, II 166*n*

Female Dunciad. See Curll

Fénelon, François de Salignac de La Mothe-, *Télémaque*, II 104, 109; VII lviii and *n*, 22; X 385; AP associates his religious opinions with, III.i xxii; *Demonstration of the Existence of God*, III.i 111*n*; defence of Homer, VII lxxii

Fenton, Elijah, his poetry, I 77*n*, 93*n*; IV xxviii *n*; play, V 187*n*; trans. *Sappho to Phaon*, II 293*n*, 302*n*, 333*n*; AP corres., III.ii xvi *n*; in AP poems, VI 173, 318, 319*n*
As AP collaborator and his trans. from *Odyssey*, III.ii xvi*n*; V 32*n*, 431; VII xxxix *n*, xliii, xliv–xlv, xlvi, lxxxiv *n*, cxii and *n*, cxxii *n*, cxciii and *n*, cxciv–cxcv, cci, ccix and *n*; ccx; IX xii; X 506–7, 508, 509, 511, 574, 597, 599; faults of trans., VII lxviii, cxcv and *n*, cxcvi; 1st p. his trans. *Od. IV* illus., IX xii
Trans. Longinus, VIII 285; trans. Oppian, VIII 390; his portrait, X xiii; Broome's tribute

to, X 378; other ref., VI 448*n*; X 585

Fenton, Lavinia (actress), V 190*n*

Fermor, Arabella, II viii, 81 ff., 394; VI 108*n*, 160*n*; VII ccxliv *n*

Fermor, Henrietta. See Pomfret

Fermor, "Mrs" (Abbess), II 99

Fermor (family), II 81 ff., 371 ff., 395

Ferrers, Selina (Finch) Shirley, Countess, VI 386*n*

Ferret, John (Burlington's agent), III.ii xxxi *n*

Ferretius, J. B., *Musae Lapidariae*, VI 249*n*

Festeau, Paul (teacher of French), IV 165*n*

Festus, Sextus Pompeius (grammarian, late 2nd c. AD), V 361*n*

Fielding, Henry, III.i 14*n*; III.ii xxxiv, 102*n*; IV 344, 371, 392; V xxxv and *n*, 347*n*, 434, 452, 464; VII ccxxxi; X 589

Fig's Academy, in AP poem, IV 42*n*, 43

"Filthy", gloss on AP use of, III.ii 92

Finch. See Winchilsea

Finley, M. I., VII ccvii *n*

Fitzgerald, Lady Elizabeth, I 176*n*

Fitzgerald, Roy G., VI xix, 340*n*

Fitzroy. See Grafton

Fitzwilliams, Mary (later Mary (Fitzwilliams) Herbert, Countess of Pembroke), in AP poem, VI 342, 343*n*

Flaccus, in AP poem, V 85

Flamen, in AP poem, V 142, 314

Flamsteed, John (natural philosopher), III.i 56*n*

Flanders, in AP poem, VI 63

Flatman, Thomas (poet), I 217*n*; II 217*n*, 288*n*; VI 95*n*

Flavia, in AP poems, II 128, 161; III.ii 51 and *n*, 52, 57; VI 378

Flavio, in AP poem, IV 291

Flecknoe, Richard (poet), in AP poems, V 96, 296; other ref., V xxxviii, xlv, 49*n*

Fleet-ditch, in AP poems, V 133 ff., 308 ff.

Fleetwood, Charles, Biog., V 439–40; in AP poem, V 375

Fleetwood, John (theatrical manager), VI 395*n*

Fleetwood, William (divine), III.i 158*n*, 159*n*, 163*n*, 164*n*

Flestrin, Quinbus, in AP poem, VI 279

Fletcher, E. G., II 386 f.

Fletcher, John (dramatist), in AP poems, IV 200*n*, 201; V 91, 279, 284, 290; other ref., I 298*n*; III.i 88*n*, 94*n*, 151*n*

Fleury, André Hercule de, Cardinal, Biog., IV 360; in AP poems, VI 11, 301, 302*n*; other ref., III.ii 89*n*; IV xx, 299*n*, 306*n*

Flimnap, in AP poem, VI 277

Flora, in AP poems, I 151; VI 273

Florio, in AP poem, II 152

Florio, J., II 161*n*, 269*n*

Flower, Barbara, VI xix

Flower, Robin, VI xix

Fludd, Robert, II 378

Flying-Post, V 118*n*, 126*n*, 148*n*, 153*n*, 184*n*, 209, 211, 212*n*, 450, 458 ff.; VI 303*n*

Flying-Post; Or, The Weekly Medley, V xxviii *n*, 102*n*, 163*n*, 165*n*, 184*n*, 198, 273*n*, 450 f., 453

Foerster, D. M., VII lxxviii *n*

Fog's Journal, V 312*n*, 345*n*, 448; VI 453–4*n*

Foley, Paul, IV 141*n*

Foley, Thomas, M.P., III.ii 37*n*

Folkes, Martin (antiquarian), V 427

Fontenelle, Bernard Le Bovier de, I 15, 16, 17, 18, 19, 23n, 27 and n, 28n, 29n, 31n, 48, 49; II 209n, 210n, 237, 265n, 268n, 381 f.; III.i 16n, 38n, 44n, 55n, 62n, 67n

Fop. See Suffolk, Henrietta Howard, Countess of

Fopling, Sir, in AP poems, II 135, 205; IV 45; V 282

Forbes, C., III.i 146n

Ford, Charles, II 243n, 246n; V 62n; VII ccxxiii n

Forman, Charles (translator), III.i xx n

Fortescue, William, Biog., IV 360; AP corres., III.i 64n; IV xv n, xvii, xviii, 4n, 321n; V 19n; 401n; intermediary between AP and Walpole, IV xviii; other ref., IV 6n; VI 198n; VII xiii; X 606

Foster, J., *Registers of Gray's Inn* II 376n

Foster, James, Biog., IV 360–1; in AP poem, IV 307

Foster, M., III.i 71n

Fouler (poet), in AP poem, VI 25, 29n

Fountaine, Sir Andrew, III.ii 135n; V 376n f., 427, 452

Fourmont, Etienne, VII lxxix and n

Fowler, Edward (bishop), III.i 124n

Fowler, W. W., I 101

Fox. See Holland; Ilchester

Fox, Sir Stephen (statesman), III.ii 181n

Foxe, John, *Book of Martyrs*, in AP poems, III.ii 55 and n; VI 287, 288n

Foxton, Thomas, Biog., V 440; in AP poem, V 164; other ref., V 210

Fracastorius, Hieronymus, V 9n

Fraguier, Claude-François, VII xxxix and n; VIII 324, 343, 364; IX 30, 377–8, 418

France, in AP poems, I 178; II 36; III.ii 89, 124; IV 207, 211, 217, 219; V 91, 290, 370, 402; VI 64, 85, 173, 178, 311; its Homer denigrators in 17th c., VII lxxii; French, in AP poems, I 285; II 128, 161; IV 165 and n, 245; V 371, 397; VI 49, 97, 123, 133, 173, 356; Frenchman, in AP poems, IV 35, 165

Frederick, Prince of Wales, Biog., IV 361; his set of AP *Works*, III.ii xxxvi n, 41n, 159, 161; VI 345n, 404n; association with the Opposition, IV xxxiii–xxxv, 306n, 352; with AP, IV xl–xli, 287n, 318 and n; VI 370n, 372; in AP poems, IV 242n, 243, 337 and n; VI 369; other ref., III.ii 119n; IV 306, 316; V 371–2n, 402n, 442; VI 342n, 343n, 392n

Free Briton, V 311n f., 428

Freeman (curate of St Botolph's, Aldersgate), VI 449n

Free-masons, in AP poem, V 398 f.; other ref., V 473

Freind, Robert, Biog., V 440; in AP poem, V 364 and n; other ref., IV 203n, 303n; V 102n, 361n; VI 364n

French Academy (Rome), VIII xii

Frere, John Hookham, on Cliveden, III.ii 118n

Friedman, A., V 473

"Frightful", gloss on, III.ii 36n

Fromondus (Libert Froidmont), VIII 266

Frontinus, Sixtus Julius, VII 72, 237

Frost, William, III.i vi; VII xv, xxii, cxviii *n*, cxxv *n*, ccxxxvii *n*

Frowde, Philip, in AP poems, VI 128, 131*n*, 173, 176*n*

Fufidia, in AP poems, IV 77

Fuller, T., *Worthies of England*, IV 340

Fulvia, in AP poem, III.ii 96; VI 316

Fungoso, in AP poem, I 275 and *n*

Fury, in AP poem, I 414

G

Gage, Joseph (adventurer), in AP poem, III.ii 103 and n

Gagey, E. McA., II 205n

Galanthis, in AP poem, I 385 and n

Galatea, in AP poem, I 369 and n

Gale, Roger (antiquarian), V 427

Galen, X 232, 248

Galileo, in AP poems, II 137, 211 and n; other ref., III.i lxvii; VII cxxxiv

Gallias of Agrigentum, VII 323-4

Gallus, Gaius Cornelius (poet, 1st c. BC), II 192n, 289n

Gammer Gurton's Needle, in AP poem, IV 202n, 203

Ganges, in AP poems, I 186 and n, 443

Garasse, François (Jesuit), III.i 75n

Gardening, landscape, AP poem on, III.ii xxi f., xxiv f.; theories, including AP, III.ii 141-2n; other ref. to AP interest in, III.ii xxiv; IV 17-19, 65-7, 183n. See also AP Works, *Guardian*

Gardner, Daniel, II viii

Gardner, James (translator of Rapin), III.ii xxiv n

Garrod, H. W., VI 249n

Garth, Sir Samuel, Biog., IV 361; *Dispensary*, I 72n, 85n, 89n, 251n, 267n, 279n, 281n, 282n, 288n,

309, 324n, 416n, 458n; II 43n, 108, 112 ff., 116 ff., 150n, 161n, 164n, 169n, 170n, 182n, 204n, 288n, 364n, 378, 384n; III.i 12n, 32n, 35n, 69n, 88n; V 62n, 66n, 67n, 79n, 80n, 113n; VII X 504; in AP poems, I 41, 44, 71, 72 and n, 309 and n; IV 105; V 114 and n, 302 and n; VI 129, 172; AP predecessor in mock-epic, V xxxviii, 114n; other ref., I 38, 59n; V 27 f.; VI 131n, 175n, 177n; VII 23

Gastrell, Francis, bishop, III.i 20n, 65n, 70n, 162n

Gaul, in AP poems, IV 195; V 157, 324; VI 151

Gawthorpe Hall (Yorks.), III.ii 108n

Gay, John, Biog., IV 361-2; attacked, V 45n, 91n, 138n, 164n, 165n, 445; member Scriblerus Club, VI 115, 116n, 117n, 118n; his treatment by Giles Jacob, VI 191n; death and monument, VI 351n; AP corres., II 7; III.i 13n; III.ii 58n, 145n; IV 126n, 355, 359; VI 145n, 179n, 247n; VII xlii n, cxciv n, ccxxiii n; corres., with Fortescue, VI 198n; with Swift, VI 254n, 296n, 345n; in AP poems, IV 114, 255; V 109n, 111, 189 and n, 301, 336; VI 116,

117, 118, 126, 130, 173, 182, 196, 232; AP verses to, VI 225–7, 433*n*; AP epitaphs on, IV 114; VI 295–7, 309*n*, 349–52; other ref., I 18, 307*n*; II xii, xiii, xiv, 6, 198*n*, 243, 246*n*; III.ii xxvii, 66*n*, 150*n*, 174; IV 121*n*; V xxv, xxxiv, 45 and *n*, 100*n*, 105*n*, 165*n*, 239*n*, 342*n*; VI 126, 130*n*, 173, 195*n*, 196*n*, 197*n*, 265*n*, 287*n*, 437*n*, 444*n*, 445*n*, 465*n*; VII xvii *n*, xxv, xxvii; X 606

AP collaborator with, VI 45*n*, 115–18*n*, 179–80*n*, 196–7, 201*n*, 216–17*n*, 234*n*, 267*n*, 414*n*, 448*n*
His hand in, VI *The Alley*, 45*n*; *Epitaph on P. P. Clerk of this Parish*, 234*n*; *Receipt to make Soup*, 254–5; *Three Hours after Marriage*, 179–80*n*, 286*n*; *Verses on Gulliver's Travels*, 267*n*
WORKS:
Acis and Galatea, VI 216–17*n*; *Achilles*, Prologue to, VI 457; *The Beggar's Opera*, V 190*n*; VI 448*n*; *The Captives*, Epilogue to, VI 438; *Council of Horses*, III.i 96*n*, 97*n*; *Ep. to Burlington*, III.ii 180*n*; *Ep. to Snow*, III.ii 95*n*; *Fables*, IV 18*n*; V 189–90*n*; *The Fan*, II 98*n*, 115 and *n*, 184*n*, 194*n*; VI 411*n*; VII clvi and *n*; X 501, 503; *Journey to Exeter*, VI 291*n*; *Polly*, VI 296*n*; *The Shepherd's Week*, V 190*n*, 213*n*; VI 412; *The Sick Man and the Angel*, III.i 26*n*; *Thoughts on Eternity*, III.i 27*n*; *Toilette*, II 200*n*; *To William Pulteney*, V 130*n*; *Trivia*, II 105*n*; IV 117*n*, 290*n*; V 80*n*, 108*n*, 129*n*, 148*n*, 190*n*; VI 265*n*, 338*n*; *Welcome from Greece*, II 91*n*; III.ii 172–3; IV xv, 105*n*, 350,

372, 374, 379; V 62*n*, 162*n*, 170*n*, 439; VI 131*n*, 132*n*, 184*n*; VII ccxxv, 25*n*; attributed poems, VI 291*n*, 347*n*, 370*n*, 410*n*, 415*n*, 439*n*, 443*n*, 447*n*
"Gay, Joseph" (phantom poet), in AP poem, V 111 and *n*, 301; other ref., V 100*n*, 103*n*, 164*n*, 208, 431
Gelli, G.-B., *Circe*, III.i 58*n*, 78*n*, 87*n*, 98*n*, 100*n*, 110*n*, 111*n*, 115*n*
Gellius, Aulus. See Aulus Gellius
Genest, John, *Account of Eng. Stage*, IV 222*n*
Geneva, in AP poem, VI 133
Genseric, in AP poems, V 157 and *n*, 324
Gentleman's Magazine, II 4, 200*n*, 315*n*, 320*n*, 343*n*, 347*n*, 375; III.i xvi *n*, 71*n*, 148*n*, 155*n*; III.ii 114*n*; V xxxv *n*, 263*n*, 268*n*, 292*n*, 312*n*, 345*n*, and Biog. App. *passim*; VI 77*n*, 294*n*, 352*n*, 381*n*, 384*n*, 389*n*, 395*n*, 399*n*, 457*n*
Geoffrey of Monmouth, VI 193*n*
George, Sir, in AP poems. See Oxendon
George I, I 208; V 45*n*, 289*n*, 306*n*, 368*n*, 441
George II, Biog., IV 362; quarrels with the Prince of Wales, IV xxxiii–xxxiv; character, IV xxxvii–xxxviii, 191*n*; taste, IV 7, 112, 286*n*, 287; accent, IV 30*n*; preference for Hanover, IV 194–5*n*, 337*n*; celebrations at his coronation, IV 222*n*; treatment of George I's will, IV 306*n*; opinion of Tyrconnel, IV 351; of AP, IV 362; in AP poems, III.ii 110; IV 7 and *n*, 112, 30*n*, 31, 33, 122, 194–231 *passim*, 279, 286*n*, 287, 298 and *n*, 299, 306 and *n*;

V 292 and n; VI 327, 342, 392, 394n; other ref., V xxiii, xxviii, xxxii n, 45n, 60n, 61n, 71n, 184n, 268n, 293n, 341n, 360n, 368n, 374n, 395n, 442, 453; VII ccxxxiii, ccxxxix, ccxlix

George, Dorothy, II 118n, 152n; IV 307n

Geraldine, in AP poem, I 176 and n

Gerard, Alexander, *Essay on Taste*, IV 219n

Gerbelii, Nicolai (writer on Greek geography), VII 177

German[-s], in AP poems, I 179; IV 139, 243; V 50, 361

Gerrard Street (London), in AP poem, VI 186

Gibbon, Edward, VII li and n, cv

Gibbons, Grinling (sculptor), IV 207n

Gibbs, James (arthitect), III.ii 143n, 183; V 116n

Gibson, Edmund, Bishop of London, Biog., IV 362; in AP poems, IV 79; V 174, 175n, 330; other ref., II 264n; IV 197n, 382; V 263, 404n, 459

Gibson, John, on Buckingham's death, III.ii 117n

Giffen, Hubert van, VII 193

Gilbert, John, Dean of Exeter, later Archbishop of York, Biog., V 440; in AP poem, V 404; other ref., IV 303n, 322n; V 368n; VI 393n

Gilbert, Sir, in AP poem, V 307

Gildon, Charles, Biog., IV 362-3; V 92-3, 440-1; in AP poems, IV 107 and n; V 92, 167, 291, 328; VI 123, 124n, 142, 190, 283; other ref., I 240n, 252n, 269n, 306n, 323n; II 90n, 179n, 300, 379n; IV 215n, 343n, 348; V ix, x,

xvi, 20n, 25n, 38n, 42 and n, 45n, 115n, 131n, 167n, 188n, 197, 198, 207, 208, 444; VI 285n, 442n; VII lxxvi, lxxxv

Giles, J. A., I 156n

Gillett, E. H., III.i xxxv n

Gilliver, Lawton, in AP poems, VI 326, 329n; AP publisher, III.ii xlix and n; V xviii–xix, xxvi n, xxvii–xxviii, xxxiv, 460–4

Gilpin, William, on Stowe, III.ii 143n, 144n

Gilson, Etienne, I 221n

Gin-drinking, in AP poems, IV 307 and n, 324

Giulio Romano, VIII 369

Glanvill, Joseph, II 209n, 381; III.i 44n, 65n, 66n, 124n

Glasgow, D., II 146n

Glaucus, in AP poems, I 449, 450, 453, 454, 460, 461

Glencus, in AP poem, IV 122n

Gloucester, William, Prince of Denmark and 5th Duke of, II 399

Glumdalclitch, in AP poem, VI 270, 279

Glumglum, in AP poem, VI 279

Godalming (Surrey), in AP poem, VI 259, 264n

Goddard, Jeanne, VII xxiii

Goddard, Jonathan (professor of physic), V 395n

Godeau, Antoine, I 210

Godley, A. D., VII lxxxv n

Godliman, in AP poem, VI 259

Godolphin, Henrietta, Countess of, VI 160n

Godolphin, Sidney, 1st Earl of, III.ii 26n; VII cviii

Goethe, Johann Wolfgang von, philosophy of renunciation, III.i lxxi–lxxii

Goldsmith, Oliver, II 155*n*; IV 220*n*; VI 361*n*; X 509

Goltzius, Hubert, VII 258*n*

Gombrich, E. H., VII lxii

Gongora, Luis, V 340*n*

Gonson, Sir John, Biog., IV 363; in AP poems, IV 29, 47; other ref., IV 375

Goode, Barnham, Biog., V 441; in AP poems, V 163, 327; other ref., III.ii 184; V 199, 447

Goodman, Cardell (actor), in AP poem, V 331; other ref., V 288*n*, 297*n*

Goodman, Godfrey, bishop, III.i 45*n*

Goodrich (Herefordshire), VI 251–2*n*

Gordon, Alexander (antiquary), V 449

Gordon, Thomas, Biog., V 441; other ref., V 134*n*, 390*n* f.

Gorgon[-s], in AP poems, III.ii 117, V 177, 331; VI 25

Gormogons, in AP poem, V 399 and *n*

Goropius Becanus (Jean Becan), IX 315

Gosfield (Essex), VI 364, 365*n*

Gosse, Edmund, II 295

Gossett family (waxwork modellers), IV 42*n*

Gotch, J. A., II 227*n*

Goths, in AP poems, I 318; V 157, 324

Gould, Robert (poet), II 183*n*, 189*n*, 340*n*; III.i 12*n*, 54*n*, 55*n*, 62*n*, 84*n*, 88*n*, 128*n*, 149*n*, 151*n*, 155*n*

Government of the Passions, III.i 68*n*, 77*n*, 78*n*

Gower, See Leveson-Gower

Gower, John, AP opinion of, II 7

Gracchus, in AP poems, II 73 and *n*

Gracchus, Tiberius, in AP poem, VI 26

Graevius, J. G., II 237*n*, 266*n*; VI 249*n*; VII xl and *n*, 35

Grafton, Charles Fitzroy, 2nd Duke of, in AP poem, VI 450, 451*n*; other ref., V 126*n*, 252*n*, 350*n*, 376*n*, 455

Graham. See Montrose

Gramont Memoirs, IV 82–3*n*

Grange, James Erskine, Lord, IV 76*n*

Granger, J., *Biog. Hist. England*, VI 396*n*

Grant, Sir Archibald, M.P., III.ii 99*n*

Grant, M. H., VII xiii

Grantham, Thomas, trans. *Iliad*, VII cx, cxii, cxxv, cxlii; X 495; parallels to AP trans., X 496, 540

Grantham, Henry D'Auverquerque, 1st Earl of, in AP poem, VI 341, 342*n*

Granville. See Lansdowne

Grattius "Faliscus" [Gratius], VII 417

Graves, Richard (poet), IV 308*n*; VI 386*n*, 398*n*, 402*n*, 412*n*, 461*n*

Gray, Thomas, anecdotes from, III.ii 26*n*, 47*n*; acquires AP copy of Dryden's *Virgil*, III.ii 91*n*; *Letters*, III.ii 90*n*, 123*n*; IV 231*n*, 372, 373; V xxxii *n*; other ref., II 230, 304; VI 340*n*

WORKS:

"The Candidate", VII clxiii; *Distant Prospect of Eton*, X 503, 511; *Elegy*, II 408; VII clx; "Lord Holland's Seat", VII clxiii; *Ode for Music*, X 502; "Ode on the Spring", II 163*n*

Greece [–ian], in AP poems, I 32, 250, 270, 324, 412 and *n*, 418, 450, 461, 472; II 256, 272; IV 197; V 78, 91, 280, 290; VI 79, 97, 101, 107

Greek[–s], in AP poems, I 283, 449, 453, 455 and *n*, 457; V 363, 365, 380; VI 83, 88, 123, 204

Green, Matthew (poet), III.ii 25*n*

Greene, Joseph, V 267*n*

Greene, Dr Maurice, II 357 f.; VI 36*n*

Greenfield, in AP poem, VI 26

Greenland, in AP poem, III.i 82

Greenslade, Basil, V 466

Greenwich (London), in AP poem, IV 289

Gregorians, in AP poem, V 399

Gregory, David, Canon of Christ Church, V 368*n*

Gregory, Pope, V 158*n*

Greville, Sir Fulke, 1st Baron Brooke, III.i 31*n*, 61*n*, 73*n*, 112*n*, 116*n*, 117*n*, 118*n*, 120*n*, 121*n*, 122*n*, 125*n*

Grew, Nehemiah (botanist and moralist), III.i 86*n*, 139*n*

Grey, de. See Kent, Duke of

Grey, Zachary, II 191*n*, 341*n*; III.ii 112*n*

Gribelin, Samuel, II viii, 244

Grierson, H. J. C., IV 35*n*, 143*n*; VII 4*n*

Griffin, Miss, in AP poems, VI 180, 181*n*, 184*n*, 185, 187*n*

Griffin, Benjamin (actor), V 207*n*

Griffith, R. H., I xiii, 126*n*, 207*n*, 223*n*, 228*n*, 234–5, 249*n*; II xi, 14, 56, 103*n*, 140, 141, 237, 242, 244*n*, 245 ff., 314 f., 324*n*, 353*n*, 357*n*, 359*n*; III.i vi, 42*n*; III.ii xxiv *n*; IV xliv, 17*n*, 92*n*, 303*n*, 371; V xvi *n*, xix *n*, xxii *n*, xxiv *n*,

xxix *n*, xxxii *n*, 60*n*, 114*n*, 169*n*, 217*n*, 248 f., 462, 464; VI 106*n*, 421*n*, 454*n*; VII xvi, cxi, cxii, ccl and *n*; X 589, 590

Grildrig, in AP poems, VI 270, 271, 273, 279

Grimston, William (Luckyn), in AP poem, IV 68–9*n*, 69

Gripus, in AP poem, III.i 154 and *n*

Grolier Club of New York, VII xlvi *n*; X 587, 588

Gronovius, Jacobus, VII xl and *n*, 55

Grosvenor family, in AP poem, IV 184*n*, 185

Grote, George, VII lxxiv

Grotius, *Annotata in Vetus Testamentum*, IX 183; X 86

Grove, R. (divine), III.i 159*n*, 164*n*

Grubbs, H. A., III.i 151*n*

Grube, G. M. A., VII ccviii *n*

Grubstreet, in AP poems, IV 103, 124; V 65, 94, 110, 160, 185, 274, 292, 301, 326, 335

Grub Street Journal, II 6; IV 103*n*, 121*n*, 124–5*n*, 359, 375; V xxvi *n*, xxix, 72*n*, 88*n*, 90*n*, 100*n*, 139*n*, 165*n*, 174*n*, 212*n*, 359*n*, 381*n*, 400*n*, 412*n*, 436; VI 310*n*, 324–32*n*, 339*n*, 355*n*, 450–2*n*, 455*n*, 456*n*, 457*n*

Grubstreet-state, in AP poem, V 85

Grumbler, in AP poem, V 168–9*n*, 170, 329; other ref., V 168*n*, 169*n*

Grundy, C. R. II 176*n*

Grushow, Ira, VII xxiv

Guardian, contributions by Tickell, I 17, 42; by AP, I 251*n*; II 103; III.i 24*n*, 29*n*; VI 28*n*; VII xxv (for Nos. 40, 61, 78, and 173 by AP, see AP, Works, *Guardian*); by Steele, VI 102*n*; by Addison and others, VI 112*n*, 139*n*; other ref.,

E

I 14; II 152n, 178n, 184n, 189n, 323n; III.i 16n, 22n, 75n, 86n, 99n, 112n, 131n, 162n, 163n, 164n; V 39n, 346n; VI 207n, 411n

Guarini, Giovanni Battista, VI 150n, 155n

Guelfi, Giovanni Baptista (sculptor), III.ii 145n

Guido Reni, in AP poem, VI 157, 159n; other ref., VIII 370

Guildford, in AP poem, VI 260

Guinnet, R., VI 412n

Guise, Sir John (sculptor and landowner), in AP poem, VI 218–24; other ref., III.ii 172n

Gumley. See Pulteney

Gustavus Adolphus (Gustavus II, King of Sweden), VII 299

Guthkelch, A. C., I 149n

Guthry, Ordinary of Newgate, in AP poem, IV 313 and n

H

Habert, Philippe, II 216*n*

Habington, William (poet), III.i 68*n*, 117*n*

Hackney (Middlesex), in AP poem, III.ii 25

Hadrian (Roman emperor), VII 35, 43; AP version of his *Animula vagula*, VI 91–5

Haemus, in AP poem, VI 34

Hagstrum, Jean H., III.ii 48*n*

Hakewill, G., II 260*n*

Hale, Dr Richard, Biog., IV 364; in AP poem, IV 291 and *n*

Hale, Stephen (minister of Teddington), IV 364

Hales or Hale, Stephen (physiologist), in AP poem, III.ii 66 and *n*; other ref., III.ii 18*n*

Hales, John (divine), III.i 132*n*, 134*n*

Halifax, Charles Montagu, 1st Earl of, Biog., IV 373; in AP poems, IV xxiv, 112–13, 317 and *n*; VI 123, 124*n*, 129, 131*n*; his poems imitated, V 119*n*, 198, 405*n*; AP acknowledgement in Preface, VII 24; other ref., I 38, 59*n*, 179*n*; II 156*n*; V 305*n*, 350*n*; VI 117*n*

Halifax, George Montagu-Dunk, 2nd Earl of, IV 164*n*, 181*n*

Halifax, George Savile, 1st Marquis of, III.i 35*n*, 57*n*, 146*n*

Hall, Arthur, his trans. of Homer, VII lxxxviii *n*, cx, cxii, cxv, cxxiv–cxxv and *n*, cxxxv, cxlii; AP use of trans., X 495; AP parallels in *Iliad*, X 496, 497, 498; text selections of his trans. of *Iliad* from French, X 539–40

Hall, Edward, *Chronicles*, IV 34, 35 and *n*

Hall, Henry, I 281*n*

Hall, Jacob (rope-dancer), in AP poem, IV 82*n*, 83

Hall, Joseph (bishop and writer), II 128*n*; III.i 36*n*, 108*n*, 147*n*, 164*n*

Halley, Edmund (astronomer), III.i 56*n*

Halliday, B., VI 447*n*

Halsband, Robert, V 467

Hamilton, Anthony, AP corres., I 208; his *Mémoires de Grammont*, III.ii 119*n*; other ref., III.ii xliii n

Hamilton, Elizabeth (Gerard), Duchess of, as Sylvia, VI 287*n*; other ref., III.ii 54*n*

Hamilton, Newburgh, I 77*n*

Hamm, V. M., I 263*n*

Hammelman, H. A., VI xix

Hammond, Anthony, friend of Chandos, III.ii xliii n

Hammond, James, Biog., V 441; other ref., V 37*n*

Ham pie, a recipe for, IV 8n

Hampstead (London), VI 317n

Hampton, in AP poems, II 129, 132, 169, 191

Hampton Court, in AP poems, II 133, 196; description of, II 169 ff., 396, 399; tapestry at, II 396; IV 48–9n

Handasyde, Elizabeth, I 65n, 77n, 176n

Handel, Georg Friedrich, Biog., V 441–2; *Semele*, I 77n; at Cannons chapel, III.ii 151n; *Esther*, III.ii 151n; V 348n; VI 217n, 423–35; effect on London music, V 190n, 346n ff., 444; VI 440; music for *Acis and Galatea*, VI 216–17n; acquaintance with AP, VI 216n; AP as collaborator, VI 432–4n; in AP poems, V 348 and n; VI 447

Hanmer, Sir Thomas, Biog., V 442; in AP poem, V 351 f. and n; other ref., III.ii xxxviii; V 268n, 280n; VI 118, 119n

Hannes, Edward, V 189n

Hannibal, I 172n, 266n

Hanson, L., *Government and the Press*, cited V 134n and Biog. App., V 428 ff. *passim*

Harcourt, Simon, 1st Viscount (1661–1727), in AP poem, V 395; VI 242; his criticism of AP epitaph on his son, VI 244n; other ref., V 31, 153n; VI 198n, 234n; VII 24

Harcourt, Hon. Simon (1684–1720), AP epitaph on, VI 242, 243–4n; other ref., II 231, 281n, 288n; V 35, 35–6n; VII 24

Harcourt, Simon, 1st Earl (1714–77), Biog., V 442; in AP poem, V 395, 395–6n

Harcourt, William Edward, 2nd Viscount, IX xii

Harding, Davis P., VII cxliv

Hardwicke, Philip Yorke, 1st Earl of, Biog., IV 394; in AP poem, IV 335 and n; other ref., III.ii 100n; IV xx n, 364; VI 384n. See also Yorke, Philip Chesney

Hardy, Thomas, II 166n f.

Hare, Francis, Bishop of Chichester, Biog., IV 364; V 442–3; ed. Terence, IV 77n; in AP poems, IV 335 and n; V 174, 174–5n, 330; other ref., IV 284n, 379; V 311n, 459

Hargraves, C. P., II 391n

Harington, Sir J., II 209n

Harison, William, II 3, 9n

Harlan, Earl, X 585

Harley. See Oxford

Harnach, Adolph, III.i xli n

Harpax, in AP poems, III.ii xlv, 97; IV 8n, 9

Harpsfield, Nicholas (theologian), V 80n

Harries [pl. Harry], in AP poem, IV 33

Harrington, John, VII cviii

Harris, G., *Life of Lord Hardwicke*, III.ii 89n; IV xx n, 327n

Harris, I. [John?], VII xii–xiii

Harris [John?], in AP corres., VII xiii

Harris, John, Bishop of Llandaff, Biog., IV 364; in AP poem, IV 308 and n

Harrison, Harry, VII xxiii

Harry, Sir (unidentified), in AP poems, IV 333

Harte, Walter, Biog., V 443; other ref., II 293n; V 36, 137n

Hartford, Frances Seymour, Countess of, VI 384n, 386n, 389n

Hartington, William Cavendish, 4th Duke of Devonshire and Marquis of, V 400 and n
Hartshorn, the use of, IV 6n
Hartwell, K. E., III.i 39n
Harvard, Houghton Library, X 590, 591
Harvequini's, in AP poem, VI 367
Harvey, Mr (author of an epigram), VI 448n
Harvey, William, II 115
Hastings. See Huntingdon
Haterius, Quintus (1st c. BC), I 215
Hatton (clockmaker), VI 237n
Hatton, E., II 159n
Hautgout, in AP poem, III.ii 57
Havens, G. R., III.i 71n
Havens, Raymond D., X 494, 495, 501, 502, 503, 504, 505, 509, 510, 511, 512, 585
Hawkins, Sir John, Life of Johnson, IV 378; History of Music, IV 360; other ref., VI 413n
Hawksmoor, Nicholas (architect), Hist. Account of London Bridge, IV 62n, 63n; other ref., IV 390
Hawley, Francis, 2nd Baron H. of Duncannon, III.ii 90n
Hawley, Lt-Gen. Henry, III.ii 90n
Hayley, William, II viii
Haym, Nicol (composer), III.ii 151n
Haymarket Theatre, VI 356n
Hays (gamester), in AP poem, 397 and n
Hayward, A., Art of Dining, IV 56n
Haywood, Eliza, Biog., V 443; in AP poems, V 52, 119 and n, 162 and n, 303; other ref., III.ii 178n; IV xvii; V xlvi, 13n, 208
Hazard, Paul, III.i xliv n
Hazen, A. T., III.i xxi n
Hazlitt, William, II 119n

Hearne, Thomas, Biog., V 443; in AP poems, III.ii 135 and n; V 171, 329; other ref., III.ii 113n; IV 390; V xlvi, 59, 170n ff.; VII lxxiii
Heathcote, E. D., Account of Families of Heathcote, III.ii 99n; IV 365
Heathcote, Sir Gilbert, Biog., IV 365; in AP poems, III.ii 99; IV 181; V 129, 307; in Master Key to Popery, III.ii 182 and n
Hebrew[–s], in AP poems, II 18, 30, 48; VI 88
Hebrus, in AP poem, VI 33
Hecataeus (historian, 6th/5th c. BC), VII 77
Hector, in AP poems, I 449, 455, 456, 457; II 271 and n
Hectors, in AP poem, IV 11 and n
Heidegger, John James, Biog., V 443–4; in AP poems, V 92, 290
Heins, D., X xii
Heinsius, Daniel (critic), his Horace used by AP, IV xliii; in AP poems, VI 25, 28n; other ref., I 24n
Helen [Hellen], in AP poems, I 380; III.ii 66; VI 27, 107, 158
Heliodorus (author of Aethiopica), VII 28, 40, 100, 313
Hell-fire Club, VI 343n
Helluo, in AP poems, III.ii 35, 57
Helsztynski, S., II 105n, 416n
Hemsley (Helmsley, Yorkshire), in AP poem, IV 69 and n
Henley, John, Biog., IV 365; V 173–4n, 444; in AP poems, IV 29, 102 and n, 302; V 96 and n, 142 and n, 173–5, 173–4n, 285, 296, 315, 318, 330 and n; other ref., IV 269n, 363n; V xiii, xxvi, xxix. See also Hyp Doctor

Hennepin, Louis (voyager), III.i 27n, 28n

Hennessy, G., *Nov. Repertorium*, IV 62n

Henry I of England, I 158n

Henry V of England, in AP poem, IV 195

Henry VI of England, in AP poem, I 179 and n; other ref., I 142, 177n

Henry VII of England, I 78n, 157n

Henry VIII of England, in AP poem, VI 195; other ref., I 132, 156n, 175n, 177n, 180n

Henry and Minerva, A Poem, V 379n

Hepp, Noemi, VII lxxix n

Heptapection Goat (work attributed to Homer), VII 54

Heraclides Ponticus (philosopher and writer, 4th c. BC), VII 41; VIII 194, 344, 347

Heraclitus, his metaphor of harmony-from-discord, III.i xxxiv f., xxxvii, xlviii–xlix, liv–lv, lxii; in AP poem, IV 44n, 45; other ref., III.i 59n; VIII 347, 349

Herbert, Edward, 1st Baron H. of Cherbury, III.i 117n, 124n

Herbert, George, II 306n; III.i lxxiv, 43n, 65n, 128n, 151n

Herbert, Mary, Countess of Pembroke. See Fitzwilliams

Herbert, Lady Mary (adventuress), III.ii 103–4n

Herbert, Thomas, II 260n

Hercules, in AP poems, I 385; VI 212

Herder, Johann Gottfried von, III.i xxvii

Hereditary Right Exemplified, V 118n

Hermes, in AP poems, II 135, 202; V 192, 380, 407

Hermias [Hermeias] (tyrant of Atarneus, 4th c. BC), VII 72

Hermitage (Richmond Park), in AP poem, III.ii 144 and n

Hermolaus Barbarus. See Barbarus

Hermolytus (author of a work on tactics), VIII 113

Hermus, in AP poem, I 185 and n

Herod, in AP poem, IV 47

Herodotus, II 232, 260n, 262n ff.; V 379n; VII cvi, 7n, 15, 37, 39–40, 44, 47, 53–4, 75, 179, 184–5, 309–10, 313, 324, 343, 377, 446; VIII 64–5, 100, 195–6, 252, 355, 405; IX 64, 66, 90, 113, 124, 134, 145, 307, 315, 338, 379–80, 440, 453; X 33, 37, 52, 73, 341, 395, 415, 430, 452

Herrick, Robert, II 368n, 383; III.i 53n

Hertford, Lady, II 306n

Hervey, John, 1st Baron H. of Ickworth, Biog., IV 365–6; his *Memoirs*, III.i 154n; III.ii 23n, 56n, 65n, 66n, 101n; IV xxxiv, 68n, 119n, 191n, 195n, 299n, 304n, 332n, 335n, 336n, 345, 351, 354, 357, 358, 360, 364, 369, 371, 372, 375, 376, 379, 380, 389, 393, 394; V 400n, 402n; VI 184n, 343n; collaborates with Lady M. W. Montagu, IV xvii; Latin epitaph on the Queen, IV 303, 303–4n; *Ep. from a Nobleman*, IV xix–xx, 95, 121n, 203n; *Verses to an Imitator of Horace*, IV 118n, 125n, 340; *Letter to Mr Cibber*, V xxxii n, 41n; *Some Remarks on the Minute Philosopher*, V 370n; *Ep. to a Doctor of Divinity*, VI 355n
Relations with AP, III.ii xxxi, 91n, 147n, 163, 178n; IV xv,

xvii, xix–xx, 95, 121n, 125n; V
xxxii n, 212 and n
In AP poems, as "Adonis", III.ii
91; VI 357; as "Lord Fanny",
III.ii 178, 181, 184; IV xv, 4 and
n, 5, 40n, 41, 61, 75, 83, 107, 297,
301; VI 369; as "Sporus", IV
xix, xxii, 93n, 117–20, 122, 339;
as "Narcissus", V 351 and n;
"Fibster", VI 355; "Harvequini", VI 367; in other poems,
IV 77 and n, 125 and n, 303 and
n, 335 and n; V 93n, 291 and n,
292n; VI 173, 174n, 176n, 355
and n
Other ref., III.i 159n; V 416n,
430; VI 130n
Hervey, Mary (Lepell), Lady, in
AP poems, IV 77 and n; VI 180,
184n, 185, 186, 187n, 201; other
ref., IV 365
Hesiod, Addison quotes, I 32n;
Virgil borrows from, I 137
WORKS:
Fragment, VIII 252; *Shield of
Heracles* (opened by Catalogue
of Women), VIII 353; IX 399;
Theogony, V 61n; VII 312; VIII
397; IX 105, 272, 347, 353; X 7;
Works and Days, VII 15, 34–5;
VIII 112–13; IX 243, 270, 459;
X 103, 152, 186, 208; description
of Tartarus, X 601–2; other ref.,
VII 29; VIII 537
Hesperia[–n], in AP poems, II
259; VI 68
Hessus, Helius Eobanus, trans.
Iliad, VII lxxxiii, 158; X 441
Hester [Esther], in AP poem, II
18, 30
Hesychius of Alexandria (lexi-
cographer, 5th? c. AD), VII 200;
IX 115, 173, 415, 451; X 28, 102,

127, 144, 147, 167, 173, 184–5,
205, 208, 210, 294, 303
Hesychius Milesius (author of
Greek lexicon, 6th c. AD), X 91
Hewet, John, and Sarah Drew
(lovers of Stanton Harcourt), VI
198n
Hewson, L., II 391n
Heydon, John, II 378
Heysham, Mrs, in AP poem, IV 89;
other ref., IV 366
Heywood, John (dramatist), in AP
poem, IV 201 and n; V 70 and n,
276
Heywood, Thomas, II 293n; V
70n f.
Hiatus, AP avoidance of, III.ii
159
Hibernia[–n], in AP poems, V 93,
190, 336, 348
Hickes, George (divine), III.i
123n, 133n
Hide-Park Circus, in AP poems, II
133, 193. See also Hyde-Park-
Corner
Hierocles, III.i 136n
Higgons, Elizabeth, I 175n
Highet, Gilbert, trans. Jaeger,
Paideia, III.i lxiv n, 121n; VII
ccvii n
Hill, Aaron, Biog., V 444–5; his
poetry, III.i 12n, 31n, 89n, 98n,
102n; AP corres., III.ii xxvii n,
xxxix, xl n, 21n, 128n, 131n, 151n,
152n, 173; IV xxiv, 14–15n,
105n, 127n, 339; V 180n, 440;
VI 333n; in AP poems, V 136
and n; other ref., I 284n; IV
205n; V xliv, 167n, 209n, 277n,
430, 440, 447 ff., 452; VI 294n,
458n
Hill, G. Birbeck, I 130n, 208n; VII
lxxxviii n

Hillhouse, J. T., IV 125*n*, 359; VI
  127*n*, 325*n*, 457*n*
Hills, H., II 402
Hillsborough, Mary Hill, Vis-
  countess, Biog., IV 366; in AP
  poem, IV 79
Hinchinbroke, Edward Richard,
  Viscount, VI 131*n*
Hinks, R. P., VII xiv
Hinton St George, John Poulett,
  Viscount (later 1st Earl Poulett),
  Biog., IV 379; in AP poem, IV
  335 and *n*
Hipparchus (astronomer, 2nd c.
  BC), VII 75
Hippia, in AP poem, III.ii 96 and *n*
Hippias of Elis (5th/4th c. BC), VII
  127
Hippocrates, I 246*n*; III.i 110*n*;
  VII 78, 89; VIII 70; IX 196,
  457; X 89
Hippomedon, in AP poem, I 412*n*,
  413
Historical Register, III.ii 87*n*, 98*n*,
  100*n*, 104*n*
*History of the Present State of the
  British Islands*, III.ii 70*n*
History of the Works of the Learned,
  III.i xxi
Hittite, in AP poem, VI 373
Hoadly, Benjamin, Biog., IV 366;
  V 445; in AP poems, IV 31 and
  n, 335 and *n*; other ref., V 134*n*,
  142*n*, 145*n*, 311*n*, 315*n*
Ho-am-ti, Emperor of China, V
  156*n*
Hoare, family, VI 249*n*; VII ccxxvi
  n
Hobbes, Thomas, on wit, I 215–16;
  Answer to Davenant, I 275*n*, 288*n*;
  Leviathan, II 397; the relation of
  his philosophic position to *E. on
  Man*, III.i xxxix, xl, lxvii, lxix–

lxx; *Paradise Lost* perhaps a reply
  to, III.i lxx; other ref., I 220; II
  221*n*; III.i xlii, 50*n*, 54*n*, 72*n*, 77–
  8*n*, 107*n*; V 285*n*, 386*n*, 387*n*,
  388*n*
Trans. of Homer: on relative
  merits of Homer and Virgil, VII
  lxxiii; Preface to *Odysses*, VII
  lxxiii and *n*; facts about his trans.,
  VII cix, cxi; AP debt to, VII
  lxxxv, cxii, cxxxvi, clii; characteristics of trans., VII cxxi–
  cxxiv; his trans. compared with
  others, VII cxv and *n*, cxxiii,
  cxlviii, clx, clxi; *Iliad* parallels to
  AP trans., X 496–500, 579–81;
  text selections *Iliad*, X 518–19;
  parallels to AP *Odyssey*, X 506,
  507, 508; other ref. to his trans.,
  I 353, 356, 451*n*, 455*n*, 466*n*; V
  108*n*, 378*n*; VII xxxix, xlix,
  lxxxiv, cxxix, cxlix and *n*, cl *n*,
  clviii, 21–2, 154, 166, 201, 223,
  248, 280, 311, 345, 408; VIII
  127, 178, 184, 199, 202; IX 141,
  194; X 36, 97, 313, 440, 494, 495,
  575, 576–7, 578, 584
Hockley Hole [Hockley-in-the-
  Hole] (London), in AP poems,
  IV 9 and *n*; V 286 and *n*, 294;
  other ref., V 207*n*
Hodges, John C., I 77*n*; III.ii 56*n*
Hoffman, William, *Cyclopedia of
  Card Games*, II 383*n*, 389–90
Hogarth, William, II viii; III.ii
  lvii f., 129; IV 220*n*, 363; V 294*n*
Holahan, Michael, VII xxiv
Holdecombe (musician), VI 223*n*
Holden, G., II 92*n*, 155*n*, 163*n*,
  170*n*, 179*n*, 211*n*, 372, 399
Holinshed, Raphael, *Chronicles*, in
  AP poem, IV 35 and *n*
Holland, in AP poem, VI 195

Holland, George, X 575 n

Holland, Henry Fox, 1st Baron, Biog., IV 361; in AP poems, IV 303 and n, 323 and n, 335 and n; other ref., IV xx n, 9n; VI 357n

Holland, Philemon (translator), III.i 102n; in AP poems, V 80, 281

Hollins [Hollings], Dr John, IV 6n

Holme, R., II 154n

Holyday, Barten (translator), III.i 98n

Homer, AP bust of, II 239n; IX xiii; other representations, VII xii, xiv, 46, 54–5; AP view of, I 228, 254n, 281n; II 109n, 239, 270n; IV xxix; V 254, 256, 340n; in AP poems, I 253, 255, 261 and n, 292, 312 and n, 314 and n, 449, 465, 484; II 135, 188, 202, 270 and n, 271; IV 67 and n, 104, 169 and n, 175, 228n, 229, 263; V 378; VI 83, 107, 129; AP use of his epithets in Dunciad, V 68n, 120n; as support for 18th c. traditions of belief, VII clxxxiv; Augustan recognition of greatness, VII clxxxv; AP MSS, X 409; Renaissance and 18th c. trans. of, X 578; Horace's comments on, X 600; other ref., I 149n, 218, 249n, 253n, 257n, 262n, 292n, 312n, 313n; II 189n, 231, 398; III.i xvi, lxiv; V 106n, 205; VI 20; X 601, 605. For Essay on, see Parnell

Iliad, influence on Dunciad (for direct use of AP trans. in Dunciad, see AP Works), V 104n, 108n, 111n, 121n, 140n, 153n, 378n; Bentley's view of authorship, VII lxxvi; list of English translators,

VII cix–cxi; its special position in literature, VII clxxxv–clxxxvi; cited in Parnell essay, VII 26, 31, 33–4, 49, 53, 54, 58, 60–1, 68–9, 71, 73, 76, 80; other ref., I 180n, 185n, 244n; II 106, 108, 133n, 135n, 188n, 191n, 195n, 196n, 200n, 203n, 206n, 207n, 208n, 239, 398; V 406n

Odyssey, ref. to in Dunciad, V xxxviii, 55, 295, 371n, 394n, 403n; cited in Parnell essay, VII 33–4, 49, 52, 54, 58, 61, 66, 70, 73, 76, 78; other ref., I 334; II 106, 196n, 200n, 203n, 307n; V 142n

Translations of Homer are listed under translators' names

Homer scholarship, VII: state of in AP day, lxii, lxxvii, lxxx–lxxxi, lxxxv, cxxvi–cxxix; "Prince of Poets" tradition, lxxi–lxxii; taste becomes standard of judgement in, lxxii–lxxiii; Homer–Virgil controversy and relevance to AP, lxxii–lxxiii, lxxvi; in Renaissance, lxxii, xc, cxvii, cxviii n, cxlviii; English critical tradition, lxxiii, lxxviii; modern critical tradition, lxxiv–lxxvi, lxxviii, xcix, ci, and relevance to AP trans., clxiii, clxxiv, compared to Augustan and 19th c., clxxxiii–clxxxv; theory of composite authorship, lxxiv, lxxvi; critical tradition in study of epic, lxxv–lxxvi; Ancient v Modern controversy, lxxviii–lxxx, xcvii, cv; the ethical interpretation, xc; in Restoration period, cxxi; special position of Iliad in literature, clxxxv–clxxxvi; romantic view, clxxxvii

Homeric Hymns, VII lxxxii, 34, 44, 49, 52; IX 218, 265; X 127

Homerides, an attack on AP, V 168n, 207, 459

Hooke, Nathaniel (historian), transcribes *The Universal Prayer*, VI 149n

Hooker, E. N., I 206n, 207n, 213n, 214n, 217n, 218n, 219n, 220n, 221n, 222n, 225n, 232n, 241n, 245n, 247n, 249n, 254n, 258n, 270n, 276n, 290n, 293n, 295n, 298n, 299n, 305n, 307n, 313n, 314n, 317n; II 398; VII lxxxvi n, cvii, cxiii n

Hooker, Richard, *Eccles. Pol.*, III.i xliv, xlviii, li, liv, 20n, 21n, 25n, 53n, 54n, 63n, 66n, 72n, 103n, 114n, 116n, 120n

Hope, W. H. St John, I 177n, 178n, 180n

Hopkins, Charles, I 78n, 136, 148n, 185n, 187n, 188n, 279n; II 196n, 200n, 284n, 343n, 345n; X 502

Hopkins, G. M., "particularity" of his poetry, III.i lxxviii

Hopkins, John (miser), in AP poems, III.ii 95 and n, 116, 116–17n

Hopkins, John, in AP poems, IV 214–15n, 215; translator of Psalms, IV 111n; V ix

Hopkins, Samuel, III.ii 95n

Horace (Quintus Horatius Flaccus), influence of phrase "ut pictura poesis", I 241n; use of "curiosa felicitas", I 256n; use of "splendide mendax", I 257n; use of "insanire cum ratione", I 259n; the Horatian epistle, I 269n; III.ii xvi, xxxvii f.; AP imitations [TE IV contains the poems known as *Imitations of*

Horace, with the original Horatian poems printed opposite the English versions; see AP Works]; AP adaptation for "Epistle to Augustus", II 230; AP imitations of, IV xxx, 3, 191–2, 211n, 215n; AP text of, IV xliii; other AP imitations, VI 79, 80n, 338–40, 390, 391, 392n, 394n

In AP poems, I 313–14, 314n, 323 and n, 483; II 273 and n; IV 104 and n, 112 and n, 175, 297 and n, 298, 299n; V 82, 85 and n, 363 and n, 365; VI 376, 450

His view of Homer, VII lxxi, lxxviii; AP debt to, VII ciii; 18th c. preoccupation with, VII clxxxiv; epic implications in, VII ccxxxi; tonal differences in AP from original poems, VII ccxxxii and n

Other ref., I 15, 316n; II 230; V 364n; VII lxxvii, ccxxxv, ccxl, 48; IX 11, 244; X 600

WORKS:

Ars poetica, I 223–4, 244n, 253n, 260n, 261n, 267n, 269n, 274n, 276n, 284n, 287n, 293n, 307n, 310n, 311n, 313n, 320n, 324n, 326n; II 259n, 278n; III.i 88n, 113n; III.ii 142n; IV 98n; V 105n, 177n, 259 and n, 396n; VI 17n; VII lxxi and n, 64, 84; VIII 284, 336, 518, 545; IX 4, 24, 26, 29, 71, 74, 175, 255, 336, 345, 356, 459; X 11, 14, 69, 142, 205, 331, 369, 382–3

Carmen saeculare, V 154

Epistles, I 172n, 287n; II 146n, 273n, 337n; III.i 21n, 113n, 129n, 132n, 134n; III.ii 128n; IV 104n, 189; V 81n, 322n, 361n, 371n, 377n; VI 17n, 394n; VII lxxviii

and *n*, 51, 67, 73, 383, 557; IX
xiii, 26, 28, 39, 41, 44, 157, 278,
327, 353, 359, 445; X 3, 177, 342,
382-3, 500
  Odes (includes *Epodes*; *Carmine*),
I 66*n*, 83*n*, 171*n*, 180*n*, 185*n*,
193*n*, 243*n*, 321*n*; II 92*n*, 180*n*,
182*n*, 212*n*, 273*n*, 366*n*; III.i 23*n*,
30*n*, 56*n*, 65*n*, 134*n*, 156*n*; III.ii
155*n*; IV 96*n*, 101*n*, 211*n*; V 86*n*,
130*n*, 366*n*, 372*n*; VI 80*n*; VII
190; VIII 544; IX 153, 179, 273,
344, 353; X 203, 239, 274, 501,
511
  Satires (includes *Sermones*), I
318*n*; II 391*n*; III.i 165*n*; III.ii
1, 25*n*; IV 23, 104*n*, 105*n*, 116*n*,
297*n*; V 65*n*, 71-89, 190*n*; VI
338, 392*n*; VII ccxxix-ccxxx;
IX 4, 286, 378, 421, 432; X 150,
182, 252, 306
Hornbeak, Katherine, III.i vi
Horneck, Philip, Biog., V 445; in
AP poems, V 162, 163*n*, 327;
other ref., VI 132*n*, 134*n*
Hoskins, John (poet), VI 115*n*
Hotham, Lady Mildred, VI 323*n*
Hough, John, Biog., IV 367; in AP
poems, IV 326 and *n*; VI 399,
400*n*
Houghton, Arthur A., Jr, VI xii,
13*n*, 38*n*, 39*n*, 477
Houghton Hall (Norfolk), III.ii
137*n*, 186
Hounslow-heath (Middlesex), in
AP poem, IV 67
Houyhnhnm, in AP poem, VI 274,
275, 279
Howard, Hon. Edward (poet), in
AP poems, V 92, 93*n*, 291; other
ref., VI 452*n*
Howard, J. J., II 82*n*, 372*n*, 376*n*
Howard, John (surgeon), VI 262*n*

Howard, Robert, I 285*n*, 287*n*;
III.i 141*n*; VII cviii
Howards, the, in AP poem, III.i
147
Howe, Sophia (court lady), in AP
poem, VI 201, 202*n*
Howell, James, II 193*n*, 296
Hoyle, Edmond, *Treatise on Quad-
rille*, III.ii 92*n*
Hubbard, J. H. (publisher), V
248
Hudson, H. H., I 216*n*, 272*n*,
290*n*
Huetius (Pierre Daniel Huet), X
116
Hughes, John, I 20*n*, 283*n*, 291*n*; II
8, 295 ff.; III.i 15*n*, 25*n*, 38*n*,
55*n*, 62*n*, 67*n*, 89*n*, 148*n*; IV
xxviii *n*, 41*n*, 347; V 8*n*, 137*n*; X
606
Huggins, John, Biog., IV 367; in
AP poem, IV 298 and *n*
Hulett, James (engraver), VI 396*n*
Hull, Barbara, VII xv *n*
Hulme, T. E., III.i xxxviii
Hume, David, II 358; III.i xlii
Hume, Patrick (first editor of
Milton), III.i 53*n*, 110*n*, 114*n*
Humphreys, David, *Antiquity Ex-
plained*, VI 249*n*
Humphreys, Samuel, *Cannons. A
Poem*, III.ii 147*n*; librettist, VI
433*n*, 454*n*
Hungerford, in AP poems, V 131,
308
Hungerford, John (lawyer), V 8*n*,
92*n*, 131*n*
Huns, in AP poems, V 157, 324
Hunt, W. H., II 376*n*
Hunter, G. K., information sup-
plied by, III.ii 15*n*, 50*n*, 111*n*,
112*n*
Hunter, W., X 589

Huntingdon, Selina Hastings, Countess of, VI 459n

Huntington Library (Calif.), annotated copy of AP *Works*, III.ii 100n; VII xxii

Hurd, Richard, bishop, II 87n; III.i 26n, 27n, 31n, 122n, 124n, 151n, 155n; III.ii xiv n, xix n, 100n; IV 308n; V 313n

Hussey, Christopher, on William Kent, III.ii 141n

Hussey, Richard, VII li n

Hutcheson, Francis, III.i xl, 22n, 67n, 69n, 83n, 88n, 130n, 139n

Hutcheson, Thomas, on the Man of Ross, III.ii 114n

Hutchinson, F. E., V 460, 469, 470

Hutton, William Holden, II 399

Hybla, in AP poem, I 67 and n

Hyde-Park-Corner, in AP poems, IV 179. See also Hide-Park Circus

Hyginus (mythographer, 2nd? c. AD), IX 390

Hylas, in AP poems, I 80 ff.; V 140, 314

Hymen, in AP poems, II 30; VI 63, 153, 154

I

Iamblicus (neo-Platonist philosopher, 3rd/4th c. AD), VIII 290

Ibbot, Benjamin, poet, VI 227n

Iber[–ian], in AP poems, I 186 and n; IV 17

Ibn al-Tufail, Abū Bakr, Abū Ja'far, III.i 58n

Ibycus (poet, 6th c. BC), VIII 136

Icarus, in AP poem, V 403

Ida, in AP poems, I 462; VI 185

Idalia, in AP poem, I 67 and n

Idomeneus, in AP poem, I 470

Idume, in AP poem, I 121 and n

Ilchester, Stephen Fox, 1st Earl of, Biog., IV 361; in AP poems, IV 9 and n, 335; other ref., IV xx

Ilchester, Giles Stephen Holland Fox-Strangways, 6th Earl of, *Lord Hervey and his Friends*, IV 339, 370; VI 357n; other ref., VI xix

Iliad: entries occur under Homer and names of translators. See especially AP entry, Works

Iliads, in AP poems, I 449, 457

Ilias Minor [*Ilias Parva*] (part of a non-Homeric, non-Hesiodic epic cycle, c 9th/6th c. BC), VII 53

Ilion, in AP poems, I 444, 458, 472; V 88, 289

Imitation, theory and practice of, IV xxvi–xxx

Inachian[–s], in AP poems, I 413 and n, 440 and n

India[–n, –ns], in AP poems, I 151, 192 and n; II 129, 156, 170; IV 237, 241; VI 229, 276

India [Indies], in AP poem, IV 283

Indus, in AP poem, II 323

Innis, Louis, II 83 and n, 91n

Innocent Inconstant (anon. poem), III.i 76n

Iole, in AP poem, I 385

Ion of Chios, (5th/4th c. BC), VIII 285

Ireland, in AP poems, IV 213; VI 184n, 251, 398

Irelond, in AP poem, VI 41

Irving, W. H., VI 447n

Irwin, Anne, Lady (courtier), III.ii xxxviii n, 121n

Isaiah, in AP poem, I 112 and n. See also Bible, O.T.

Isham, Z. (divine), III.i 162n

Isis, in AP poems, I 73, 183 and n, 425 and n; IV 173; V 191, 336, 360–1, 399

Islington (London), VI 317n

Ismenos, in AP poem, I 412 and n

Isocrates, VII 58; IX 361

Israel, in AP poems, II 18; VI 264

Issachar, in AP poem, VI 179

Ister [the Danube], in AP poems, I 186 and n, 410 and n

J

Jack, in AP poem, IV 77

Jack, Ian, V 470, 471; VII xxiii

Jackson, A., VI 401*n*

Jackson, Gabrielle B., VII xxiv

Jackson, John, *History of the Scottish Stage*, V 177*n*

Jackson, Thomas, VII xxiv

Jacob, Giles, Biog., V 445–6; compiler of *The Poetical Register*, V xxiii *n*, 9, 44*n*, 74*n*, 164, 198 and *n*, 199 and *n*, 441, 452; VI 421; VII cxlii *n*; in AP poems, V 164 and *n*, 327; VI 190, 191*n*; *Lives of the Poets* quoted V *passim*; other ref., V 452, 469

Jacobs, J., II 296*n*

Jacob, in AP poem, II 18

Jaeger, Werner, III.i lxiv, 121*n*; VII ccvii and *n*

James, Old, in AP poem, V 146 and *n*

James I, in AP poems, V 358, 358–9*n*; other ref., I 137, 289*n*; V 471

James II, in AP poems, IV 15 and *n*; other ref., I 141–2, 117*n*, 194*n*, 205, 300*n*, 302*n*

James, H. R., trans. Boethius, III.i 135*n*

James, William, III.i lxviii

Jansen, Sir Henry, Biog., IV 368; in AP poems, IV 141 and *n*; V 375; other ref., III.ii 91*n*; IV 15*n*

Jansen, Sir Theodore (financier), III.ii xlvi *n*; V 430

January, in AP poems, II 13, 18, 25, 38, 41

Japan, in AP poems, II 130, 175

Japhet. See Crook, Japhet

Jaunssen, in AP poem, III.ii 28

Jean le Bon, I 177*n*

Jebb, R. C., II 232*n*; III.i 24*n*; VII lxxvi *n*

Jefferies (adulterer), in AP poem, IV 79, 89; other ref. IV 366

Jehovah, in AP poem, VI 145

Jehu, I 165*n*

Jekyll, Sir Joseph, Biog., IV 368–9; in AP poems, IV 300 and *n*, 335 and *n*; other ref., IV 301*n*, 393

Jenkin, in AP poem, II 62, 63

Jenkins. See Spain

Jenkins, Iredell, III.i lxv

Jenny, in AP poems, IV 79; VI 261

Jeremy [Jeremiah], in AP poem, VI 290. See also Bible, O.T.

Jerningham, Edward, II 415

Jerome. See St Jerome

Jerusalem, in AP poem, II 68

Jervas, Charles, his portrait of AP, I xiv; VIII xii; friend and teacher of AP, II xii, 237–8; III.ii 50*n*; VI 110*n*; studies in Italy, VI 159*n*; in love, VI 160*n*; trans. *Don Quixote*, III.ii 153*n*; VI 176*n*; AP corres., I xiv; IV

317n, 361; VI 130n, 209n; VII ccxxiii n; in AP poems, VI 108, 109n, 128, 173; *Ep. to*, III.ii 58n; VI 109n, 156–8; other ref., VII xii

Jesse, in AP poem, I 113 and n

Jessides, in AP poem, VI 373

Jesu, in AP poem, IV 47

Jesus, in AP poem, VI 104

Jew[–s], in AP poems, II 18, 47 and n, 127, 159; V 157, 324

Joab, in AP poem, II 29

Job, in AP poems, II 65; III.ii 122; VI 290–1. See also Bible, O.T.

Job, Sir, in AP poems, IV 289 and n

Jocasta, in AP poems, I 413, 443

John, in AP poem, VI 42

John, Duke, in AP poem, VI 220

John, King, in AP poem, V 289

John of Salisbury, V 158n

Johnson, Charles, Biog., V 446; in AP poems, V 91 and n; VI 129, 131n, 140, 141n, 284, 286n; other ref., IV 109n; V 164n, 433

Johnson, Samuel, on AP, from *Lives*, I 50, 92n, 130n, 208, 265n; II 99, 110n, 123n, 349n, 355–6, 355n, 356n, 393n, 395; III.i 26n; III.ii xxviii, 65n, 116n, 131n, 170 f., 172n; V 156n, 202n, 304n; VI 387n; on other poets, from *Lives*, II 224, 304, 413; IV xxiv, xxvi, 109n, 225n, 279n, 352n, 376; V xxvi n, 14n, 187n, and Biog. App. *passim* (429 ff.); VI 311n, 322n; *Dictionary* cited, I 326n; II 150n, 151n, 152n, 153n, 166n, 168n, 185n, 188n, 189n, 192n, 197n, 201n, 203n, 253n; III.i 43n; V 98n, 162n; his *Shakespeare*, II 205n, 231; his trans. of Crousaz, III.i xix n, xx n, xxi n; his opinion

of philosophy in *E. on Man*, III.i xliii, 12n, 121n; on editing AP, III.ii 12n; *Rambler*, IV 104n; on AP Homer trans., VII xxxv n, xxxvii n, xlii and n, xliii n, cviii, cxciii–cxciv and n; on AP learning, VII lxxxiii–lxxxiv, lxxxv; other ref., IV 346, 360, 370; VI 150n, 299n; VII lxvii, lxxxviii; X 509, 606

Johnson, T., II 245

Johnson's England. See Turberville

Johnston, Arthur (translator), in AP poem, V 352

Johnston, James, of Twickenham (statesman), III.ii xxx, 28–9n; IV 122n; VI 45n

Jones, Inigo, in AP poems, III.ii 141, 155; V 189, 336; other ref., I 188n; II 227

Jones, John (anecdotist), III.ii 145n

Jones, (L?) (poet), V 102n

Jones, R. F., *The Seventeenth Century*, I 105n, 213n; *Lewis Theobald*, V xl n, 76n, 77n, 88n, 433n

Jonson, Ben, *Timber, or Discoveries*, I 211, 215, 248n, 288n; III.i 88n, 136n; IV 202n, 218n; V 279n; *Masque of Queens*, II 218n, 227, 231n; other works, I 77n, 161n, 253n, 272n, 275n; II 286n, 362n; III.i 71n, 148n, 151n, 154n; III.ii 84n; IV 340; V 156n, 363n, 469; as trans. of Horace, IV xxvi, xxvii, xxviii; in AP poems, IV 197 and n, 199 and n, 201, 229; V 127, 307; on relative merits of Homer and Virgil, VII lxxiii

Jordan (chamber pot), in AP poem, V 124 and n, 304

Jortin, John, I 301n, 302n; VII xxxix

Josephus, VII 47, 66; IX 315; X 323

Jourdain, Margaret, III.ii 141*n*, 143*n*

Jove, in AP poems, I 72, 170, 283 and *n*, 369 and *n*, 370, 411, 414, 420, 422, 423, 424, 425, 426 and *n*, 427, 433, 437, 444, 449, 454, 456, 458, 459, 461, 469 and *n*, 471, 473; II 44, 54, 134, 135, 199, 203, 206, 272; III.i 18; III.ii 83; IV 11, 293; V 61, 94, 107, 108, 121, 159, 178, 269, 294, 299, 300, 304, 325, 348; VI 9, 66, 85, 88, 106, 117, 145, 224, 230, 279, 336

Jovius, Paulus, V 97*n*, 412 f.

Judaea, in AP poem, VI 203

Judeth, in AP poem, II 18 and *n*

Julian, in AP poem, II 273

Julius II, Pope, I 320*n*

June, in AP poem, II 34 and *n*

Junia, in AP poem, VI 153

Juno, in AP poems, I 409 and *n*, 425 and *n*; V 120, 303

Jupiter, in AP poems, I 449, 457; II 59; VI 86–7

Justin, in AP poems, II 21, 23, 27

Justin Martyr, VII 63, 397; VIII 376; IX 239

Juvenal, in AP poem, VI 76; other ref., I 179*n*, 323*n*; II 156*n*, 180*n*, 182*n*, 240*n*, 278*n*, 365*n*; III.i 74*n*, 92*n*, 97*n*, 98*n*, 109*n*, 146*n*, 157*n*; III.ii 94*n*, 124*n*; V 17*n*, 117*n*, 174*n*; VII lxxvi, ciii, ccxl, 285; VIII 496; X 149, 260

K

Kaminski, Ludwik, II 105*n*

Kant, Immanuel, influenced by *E. on Man*, III.i xli

Karpf, A., II 411

Katt. See Cat

Keats, John, not a poet of "Magnificence", III.i lxxiv; poetic "world" of *Ode to a Nightingale* and poetic "world" of *E. on Man*, III.i lxxviii; other ref., II 156*n*, 186*n*, 222

Keightley, T., I 182*n*

Keith, Mrs R., II 396

Kelly, Edward, VII xxiii

Kelly, Lionel, VII xxiv

Kelsall, Henry (treasury clerk), III.ii 179*n*, 184*n*; V 147*n*

Kelsey (unidentified), in AP poem, V 147, 148*n*

Kempis, Thomas à, in AP poem, VI 5

Kendal, Ehrengard Melusina von der Schulenburg, Duchess of, V 392*n*

Kenefick, J. G., III.i vi; VII xxiii

Kennedy, James, cited V 452

Kennedy, W., II 285*n*

Kennet, in AP poem, I 183 and *n*

Kennett, Basil, I 322*n*

Kennett, White, Bishop of Peterborough, Biog., IV 369; V 446; in AP poems, V 174, 174–5*n*; other ref., I 201, 302*n*, 303*n*; IV 180*n*; V 117*n*, 125*n*, 350*n*, 466, 470

Kensington, in AP poem, VI 219

Kensington Gore (London), in AP poem, VI 222

Kensington Palace, II 399

Kent, Henry de Grey, 1st Duke of, Biog., IV 364; as Bug in AP poems, IV 284*n*, 285; V 392 and *n*; other ref., V 368

Kent, William, Biog., IV 369; as architect, III.ii 138*n*, 139*n*; IV 48*n*, 224*n*; V 189*n*; VI 395*n*; as landscape gardener, III.ii 141*n*, 143*n*; in AP poems, IV 316; VI 340; plates for *Odyssey*, VII xlv, ccxxiv; IX xiv; X xiii–xiv; illus., IX xii–xiii; other ref., VI 459*n*

Ker, John (of Kersland), V 97*n*, 104*n*

Ker, W. P., I 284*n*, 335*n*, 343*n*; VII ccv *n*, ccxlviii

Kerby-Miller, C., his edition of *Memoirs of Martinus Scriblerus*, VI 116–19*n*, 207*n*

Kermode, Frank, VI xx

Kersey, John, I 159*n*, 164*n*, 192*n*

Ketton-Cremer, R. W., *Horace Walpole*, III.ii 137*n*; other ref., VI xix

Kew, in AP poem, VI 372

Key to the Times (anon. pamphlet), V 98*n*

Killigrew, Thomas (courtier), III. ii 174

Kimball, Fiske, on Burlington as architect, III.ii 139n

King, Henry (bishop), his poems, III.i 13n, 94n

King, John, 2nd Baron K. of Ockham, V 395nf., 446

King, Peter, 1st Baron K. of Ockham, Biog., V 446; in AP poem?, V 395 and n

King, William (1650–1729), Archbishop of Dublin, *De orig. mal.* and *E. on Man*, III.i xxvii ff., xxxi, xxxii, xxxiii, xlvii, 44n, 45n, 95n, 98n

King, William (1663–1712), II 357n; III.i 24n; V xl; VI 410n, 412n

King, William (1685–1763, Principal of St Mary Hall, Oxford), V 440

Kingsford, C. L., I 310n

Kingston, Evelyn Pierrepont, 2nd Duke of, V 370nf.

Kinnoul. See Dupplin

Kinnoul, George Hay, 7th Earl of, Biog., IV 364–5; in AP poem, IV 244n, 245

Kinsley, James, VII cix n, cxxx n; X 494

Kip, Johannes, II 400; VII xiii

Kirchoff, Adolf, VII lxxiv

Kirkall, Elisha (engraver), in AP poems, V 120, 303

Kit-Cat Club, AP epigram on its toasts, VI 177 and n

Kliger, S., I 323n

Knapton, J. and P. (AP publishers), III.ii xiii; V 249

Kneller, Sir Godfrey, Biog., IV 369; AP poems to, II 237n; VI 212, 213n, 312–13; in AP poems, IV 166n, 167, 227 and n; VI 108, 249 and n; his portrait of Lady M. W. Montagu, VI 212n; portraits of AP illus., VIII xiii; IX xii; other ref., III.ii 37n; IV 347; VIII 370

Kneller, Susannah (Cawley), Lady, quarrel with AP, VI 249n, 313n; AP epitaph on, VI 249

Knight, Anne. See Nugent

Knight, C., II viii

Knight, Douglas M., III.i vi; VII xv, xvi, xxxvi n, li and n, liv, lxxxiv n, xc–xci, cxv n, cxviii n, cxxxiii n, ccx n; X 409n

Knight, G. Wilson, III.i lxi n

Knight, John, AP corres., III.i 86n; III.ii 69n, 143n; VI 282n, 317n; AP epitaph on, VI 364–5

Knight, Robert, Biog., V 446; in AP poem, V 397; other ref., IV 210n

Köhler, Karl, *History of Costume*, IV 301n

Kökeritz, Helge, III.i vi

Krapp, R. M., I 225n

Küster, Ludolph, Biog., V 446–7; in AP poem, V 365n, 366; other ref., V 458

Kurtz, John, VII xxiv

Kurz, Otto, VII ccxxvi n

Kyrle, John (the Man of Ross), III.ii 113 ff.; IV 318

L

Labelye, Charles (architect), III.ii 156*n*

Labeo, Attius (Homer translator, 1st c. AD), VII 62

La Bruyère, Jean de, I 240*n*, 268*n*, 284*n*; III.i 22*n*, 44*n*, 62*n*, 69*n*, 83*n*, 85*n*, 133*n*, 134*n*, 151*n*, 153*n*; III.ii 50*n*, 150*n*; V 206, 394*n*

La Chausse, M. A. de, II 237*n*

Lachman, Karl, VII lxxiv

Lactantius, V 255; VIII 205

Lacy, John, II 220*n*, 342*n*

"Laelius" (pseud. for Bolingbroke), III.i 11*n*, 129*n*; VII ccxxx

Laertius. See Diogenes Laertius

Lafitau, J. F. (voyager), III.i 28*n*, 58*n*

La Fontaine, Jean de, III.ii 35*n*

Laguerre, Louis (painter), in AP poem, III.ii 151 and *n*

Laird, John, III.i xxv *n*, xxxi *n*, xliii, 62*n*

Laius, in AP poem, I 424, 427

La Mancha, in AP poem, I 270 and *n*

Lamb, Charles, II 386; VII cxciv and *n*

Lambe, John (divine), III.i 163*n*

Lambeth (London), in AP poem, VI 44

Lambley, K., *The French Language in England*, IV 165*n*

Lamoignon, Guillaume de, II 115

La Mothe le Vayer, François de, X 7, 328–9

La Motte, Antoine Houdar de (critic of Homer), II 398; VII xxxix, xl and *n*, xli and *n*, cv, 14, 16, 101, 110, 210, 229, 238, 254, 260, 319, 408, 432, 446, 448, 450, 453, 455, 457, 459–60, 462; VIII 59, 64, 105, 168, 171, 197, 241, 317, 358–9, 394, 461, 567; X 393, 396, 419, 427, 431, 434, 447, 457. See also Dacier, Anne

Lancastere, Duke of, in AP poem, VI 218, 219, 220, 222

Landino, Cristoforo, I 321*n*

Landscape gardening. See Gardening

Lanesborough, James Lane, 2nd Viscount, III.ii 37*n*

Lang, Andrew, VII lxxiv

Langbaine, Gerard, *Account of Eng. Dram. Poets*, I 291*n*; II 250; IV 200*n*, 201*n*; V cited *passim*

Langley, Batty, on gardening, I 85*n*; III.ii 141*n*

Lansdowne, George Granville, 1st Baron, Biog., IV 363; on AP *Pastorals* and *Windsor Forest*, I 37, 38, 59*n*, 130; AP corres., I 130; VII xxxvi; in AP poems, I 65 and *n*, 148, 174, 175 and *n*, 193; IV 105; VI 158, 160*n*; acknowledgement in AP Preface, VII

24; other ref., I 68n, 77n, 81n, 141, 175n, 176n, 178n, 194n; II 262n; III.i 100n, 138n; IV 111n, 206n; V 114n, 364n; VI 176n; VII cxliii

Lardella, in AP poem, VI 26

Lares, in AP poem, V 378

Larissa, in AP poem, I 432 and n

La Rochefoucauld, François, Duc de, on wit, I 214, 216; AP intention to oppose his maxims, III.i xii n, 65n; III.ii 84n, 106n; AP opinion of, III.ii 106n; other ref., III.i 29n, 62n, 66n, 74n, 75n, 76n, 78n, 79n, 84n, 85n, 87n, 88n, 121n, 145n, 146n, 148n, 150n; III.ii 16n, 17n, 20n, 21n

Larwood, J., II 193n, 400

Lascaris, Andreas Johannes, I 319n

Latian, in AP poems, I 411; II 272; IV 245; VI 230

Latin, in AP poems, IV 304; V 374; VI 171

Latium, in AP poems, I 322; V 157, 324

Latona, in AP poems, II 135, 202

Lattimore, Richmond, VII cxciii; X 579

Lauderdale, Richard Maitland, 4th Earl of, trans. Aeneid, VII cviii, cix and n; X 505

Laureat (pamphlet), V 278n, 335n

Lauremberg, Johann (writer on Greek geography), VII 177

Laurus, in AP poem, V 149

La Valterie, Abbé de, VII xxxviii, xxxix, lxxxi, lxxxiv, xcii, 166; X 393, 441, 446

Law, Edmund, trans. King, De orig. mal., III.i xxvii n, xxix n

Law, E., Hist. of Hampton Court, IV 49n

Law, William (financier), III.ii 93n

Law, Rev. William, Biog., V 447; in AP poems, V 146, 147n, 317

Lawrence, W. J., IV 220n

Lawrence College (Appleton, Wisconsin), VII xv

Lay Monastery (periodical), III.i 77n, 83n, 84n

Layng, Henry (translator), III.i 58n; VII cxciv n

Lea, C. A., II 415

Leadam, Isaac S., Polit. Hist. Eng., IV 11n, 39n, 298n, 335n

Leather, Mary Steward, X 494

Leavis, F. R., II 358n; III.ii xxvi n

Lebanon, in AP poem, I 115 and n

Le Bossu, René (author of Traité du poëme épique), Iliad discussed in Traité, IX 5–8, 11–12, 14–22, 24; Odyssey discussed in Traité, IX 8–12, 15–22, 24; other ref., I 16n, 23n, 201n, 210, 211, 224, 251n, 352n, 359; II 109 ff., 116, 121n, 122 f., 394, 395, 397, 398; V 50n f., 77n, 254, 256; VII xl, xc, 22–3; VIII 2, 154, 373; IX xii, 3–24, 27, 30, 59, 61, 111, 170, 175, 186, 204, 252, 255, 260, 299, 336, 341, 384, 428; X 14, 69, 218

Lechmere, Elizabeth, Lady, III.ii 57n

Lechmere, Nicholas (attorney-general), in AP poem, VI 218–24 and n

Lecky, William E. H., History of England in the Eighteenth Century, IV 11n, 169n, 345, 362, 380, 387, 388

Leda, in AP poem, III.ii 49

Lediard, Thomas, Life of Marlborough, IV 74n

Lee, River, in AP poem, I 184 and n

Lee, Nathaniel, Biog., IV 370; in

AP poem, IV 15; other ref., III.i
35n, 67n
Leeds University, VII xv n
Lefèvre. See Dacier, Anne Lefèvre
Lefèvre, Tannegui (Mme Dacier's
father), I 47; X 210
Le Gal, Simonne, VII xxxvii n
Legislation, anti-Catholic, IV 67,
168–9n, 337n; enactments against
libel, IV 19n; licensing act
(1737), IV 44n, 301 and n, 313n;
V 343n f.
Le Grand, Antony (moralist), III.i
68n
Leibniz, Baron Gottfried Wilhelm
von, his system the main objective of Crousaz's attack on *E. on
Man*, III.i xix; *Essay* identified
with his system, III.i xx, xxi,
xxvi; associated with principle
of plentitude, III.i xxii; problem
of his influence on *Essay*, III.i
xxiii, xxvi f., xxxi, xli n; repudi-
ated by AP, III.i xxii; other ref.,
I 256n; III.i 94n; V 409n, 435
Leicester Fields (London), in AP
poem, VI 182, 184n
Leigh, Richard, II 201n
Leishman, J. B., II 295n
Lake. See Scarsdale
Lely, Sir Peter, in AP poem, IV 207
and n
Le Moyne, Pierre (moralist), III.i
68n
Leng, John (divine), III.i 39n, 101n
Le Nôtre, André, in AP poem,
III.ii 141, 144n
Lent, in AP poem, II 70
Leo X, Pope, in AP poems, I 319
and n; VI 67; other ref., I 320n;
V 412, 414
Leoni, Giacomo (architect), III.ii
144n

Lepell, Mary. See Hervey, Mary
(Lepell), Lady
Lerna (river) in AP poem, I 431–2
Le Sage, Alain René, II 379
Lesbia, in AP poem, III.ii 102 and
n
Lesbian, in AP poems, I 394, 396,
398, 404
Lessing, Gotthold Ephraim, his
and Mendelssohn's *Pope ein
Metaphysiker!*, III.i xli n; other
ref., II 239
L'Estrange, Roger, II 295n
Lethe, in AP poems, V 140, 151,
314, 321
Lethieullier, William (collector),
V 449
*Letters and Poems, Amorous and Gal-
lant*, II 300
Letters of Wit. See Bentivoglio
Lettuce, the use of, in AP poem, IV
5 and n
Leucadia, in AP poem, I 402
and n
Leucothoë, in AP poem, I 417
Leveson-Gower, John, 1st Earl,
Biog., IV 370; in AP poem, IV
333 and n
Levin, Harry, VII lii n
Lewis, in AP poem, IV 253
Lewis, C. S., II 69n; III.i xlviii n;
VII lxii–lxiii, cxxix
Lewis, David (editor of *Miscel-
laneous Poems*), III.ii 69n; V 116n;
VI 92n, 299n, 315n
Lewis, Erasmus, Biog., IV 370; in
AP poems, VI 116, 195, 196n;
other ref., IV 10n
Lewis, William (bookseller), V
xxiv, 212
Lewis, Wilmarth S., IV 148
Lewys, Sir John (landowner), III.ii
108n

Libanius (Greek sophist, 4th c. AD), VII 58

Libel, AP distinction from satire, III.ii xxxix f. See also Legislation

Licensing act. See Legislation

Liddel, Richard, Biog., IV 370; in AP poem, IV 88–9n, 89

Liebert, Herman, VII xxiii

Lilliput, in AP poem, VI 277, 278, 279

Lillo, George, III.i 54n; III.ii 122n

Lincoln (Lincolnshire), in AP poem, IV 183

Lincoln Fen, in AP poem, IV 181

Lincoln's-Inn, in AP poems, IV 261; V 179, 333

Lintot, Barnaby Bernard, Biog., IV 370–1; as AP publisher, I xiv, 9n, 125, 126n, 128, 165n, 205, 243n, 346, 361, 406n; II xii, 81, 92n 103n, 104n, 244; V xxviii n, 207; VI 35n, 131n, 138n, 189n; connection with AP Iliad, VII xii, xxxvi n, xxxvii n; IX xii; X 587–9; X 606; with AP Odyssey, VII xliii, xlv, xlvi; payment to Ozell, X 574; in AP poems, IV 100; V 64 and n, 103 and n, 105, 106, 107n, 109, 273, 298–300; VI 82–3, 84–5n, 129; Miscellany (ed. AP), VI 106n, 138n; VII xxv; AP poem on Miscellany, VI 82–3; other ref., II 6n; IV 111n; V 81n, 85n, 88n; VI 38n, 175n; VII xiii, ccl; VIII xiv; X 575n, 589

Lintot, Henry (son of Bernard), V xxxiv, 463; VII ccl

Lipsius, Justus, III.i 139n, 140n

Lipson, E., I 191n

Lisle, Edward (collector), V 449

Lisle, the Misses, in AP poem, VI 353, 354n

Litchfield, X 594

Littlebury, Isaac, trans. Herodotus, VII 324

Livy, II 210n; III.i 79n; V 158, 325; VIII 64, 390; IX 373, 454; X 33, 314

Loane, G. G., V 460, 466 ff.

Locke, John, separates wit from judgement, I 216–17, 217n, 245n; in AP poems, III.ii 51, 150; IV 280n, 281; V 175, 331, 361 and n; VI 48, 51n; on imagination, VII xlvii; other ref., II 148n, 149n, 200n; III.i xxiv, 38n, 43n, 98n, 107n, 114n, 116n, 117n, 120n; III.ii 16n; V 321n, 373n; VII xlix

Locke, Joshua (collector), V 449

Locker, Frederick, X 474

Loddon (river), in AP poem, I 183 and n; other ref., I 168n

Lodge, Richard, I 298n

Lodge, Thomas, III.i 36n, 158n

Lodona, in AP poem, I 165 and n

Loeb Classical Library, VII xvii, lii n, ccxxiv n; X 579

Loiseau, Jean, Cowley's Reputation, IV 200n

Lombard, Peter, I 288n

Lombardy, in AP poem, II 15

London and Wise (gardeners), III.ii 145n, 149n

London, in AP poems, III.ii 121; IV 171–3, 285; other ref., IV 14n, 15, 62n, 63 and n, 96, 99 and n, 107, 139; VI 26, 39, 40n, 44, 155n, 162, 164n, 172, 174n, 178, 182, 184n, 186, 197n, 222, 237n, 249, 317 and n, 356n, 402n, 449. See also individual entries of place names and buildings

London Belles (anon. poem), II 373

London Bridge, IV 63n

London Evening-Post, III.i xvi n,

xviii *n*, xxii; III.ii xxix *n*; V xxiii,
212*n*, 248, 400*n*, 430, 446; VI
339*n*, 351*n*, 396*n*
London Journal, III.i 155*n*, 162*n*; V
xlvii *n*, 47*n*, 103*n*, 118*n*, 128*n*,
134*n*, 146*n*, 165*n*, 212*n*, 311*n*,
437, 441, 445, 451, 455, 459; VI
243*n*, 244*n*, 262*n*; VII xliii *n*
London Magazine, VI 381*n*, 398*n*,
434*n*
Long, C., VI xx
Longinus (critic of Homer; author
of *On the Sublime*), in AP poems,
I 316 and *n*; other ref., I 208, 210,
211, 229, 247*n*, 248*n*, 255*n*, 257*n*,
258*n*, 260*n*, 261*n*, 314*n*, 323*n*,
483; II 106*n*, 172*n*, 203*n*, 271*n*,
398; III.i 109*n*; VII xl, ccxxii, 9,
53, 160, 233, 244, 287, 312, 356;
VIII 64–5, 105, 212, 224–5, 284,
316, 397, 437; IX 92, 160, 191,
221, 334, 336, 338, 356–8, 402,
418, 435, 454–5, 458–9; X 101,
131, 151, 187, 284, 382–6, 432,
599
Lord, George deF., VII cxvi *n*,
cxviii and *n*, ccvi *n*, ccxviii *n*,
ccxix *n*
Lorraine, Francis of, Grand Duke
of Tuscany, III.ii 186
Lort, Michael (antiquary), VI 150*n*
Lotis, in AP poem, I 387
Lotspeich, C. M., I 281*n*
Loughton (unidentified name in
EC MS), V 148*n*
Louis, in AP poems, II 137, 211;
IV 15, 319
Louis XI of France, III.ii 28*n*
Louis XIV of France, in AP poems,
IV 226*n*, 227; other ref., I 179*n*,
298*n*, 322*n*; II 109*n*; VII liii
Louis XV of France, III.ii 28*n*
Lewis the Bold, X 430

Lounsbury, T. R., II 4*n*, 11*n*; V 60*n*
Lovejoy, A. O., I 139*n*, 219*n*, 220*n*,
228*n*; III.i xxix *n*, xxxv *n*, xli *n*,
xlvi *n*, 105*n*, 108*n*
Lovell, A., II 378
Lover (periodical), V 354*n*
Lowde, James (moralist), III.ii
xxxvii
Lowell, Robert, VII ccviii and *n*
Lower, Richard, VIII 133
Lu, in AP poem, II 172
Lucan, I 61*n*, 79*n*, 172*n*, 245*n*; II
110, 144*n*, 147*n*, 153*n*, 164*n*,
172*n*, 178*n*, 196*n*, 203*n*, 221*n*,
260*n*, 264*n*, 356; III.i 32*n*, 45*n*;
V 468; VII xlviii, clxxxiii, 4,
179; VIII 434; IX 304; X 60,
412
Lucas, E. V., VII cxciv *n*
Lucian (author of *Dialogues*, 2nd c.
AD), II 183*n*, 221*n*, 237, 260*n*,
265*n*; III.i 94*n*, 96*n*; V 70*n*, 140*n*;
VII 45, 52, 201, 463; VIII 204,
290; IX 323, 386, 394, 396, 413,
417
Lucifer, in AP poem, VI 341
Lucilius, Gaius (Latin satirist, 2nd
c. BC), I 313*n*; III.i 11*n*; VII
ccxxix–ccxxx
Luckyn. See Grimston
Lucrece, in AP poem, III.i 146;
VI 108
Lucretia, in AP poems, II 47;
III.ii 57
Lucretius, some passages in *E. on
Man* said to be Lucretian, III.i
xvii *n*; his address to Epicurus
and AP hymn to the Saviour,
III.i xxiii; philosophy of renun-
ciation, III.i lxxi; in AP poems,
V 389 and *n*; *De rerum natura*, I
117*n*, 304*n*; II 188*n*, 344*n*; III.i
15*n*, 30*n*, 36*n*, 85*n*, 93*n*, 104*n*,

107*n*, 109*n*, 113*n*, 114*n*, 117*n*, 120*n*; IV 214*n*; VII lvii, clxxxiv, 284; VIII 168; IX 207, 241, 420; X 332, 502, 504, 505

Luctus Britannici (collection), IV 113*n*

Lucullus, L. Licinius, III.ii 34

Lud, in AP poem, V 142, 183, 315, 333

Ludwig, Frederic, VII xxiii

Lully, Jean Baptiste de, II 306*n*

Lumley. See Scarborough

Lutetia, in AP poems, V 139, 313

Luther, Martin, IV 140, 142, 143

Luxury at the table in AP poems, V 396 f., 402

Lybian, in AP poems, I 86, 283 and *n*, 443; II 266

Lycean, in AP poem, I 431 and *n*

Lycia[–n, –ns], in AP poems, I 444 and *n*, 449, 450, 452, 453, 455, 458, 459, 460, 462

Lycidas, in AP poem, I 88 ff.

Lycomede, in AP poem, I 453

Lycophron (poet, 4th c. BC), V 340*n*; VII 447; VIII 496; IX 66, 219, 379–80, 432; X 52, 90, 257, 339–40

Lycurgus of Sparta, VIII 43, 49–50, 56–7, 113

Lyly, John, II 265*n*

Lynch, K. M., article on Marlborough, III.ii 56*n*

Lyra, Nicholas de, in AP poems, V 80, 281

Lysias (author of forensic speeches, 5th/4th c. BC), IX 283

Lyttelton, George, 1st Baron, Biog., IV 371; in opposition to Walpole, IV xxxiii–xxxiv, xxxviii; secretary to the Prince of Wales, IV xl, 301 and *n*, 337*n*; *Persian Letters*, IV 9*n*, 367; *Dialogues*, IV 357; AP corres., IV xl–xli; VI 372*n*; in AP poems, IV 281, 320; VI 333–4*n*; other ref., III.i xxiv *n*, 159*n*; IV xxiv; VI 374*n*, 381*n*

M

Mabbott, T. O., VI xx, 206*n*, 207*n*

Macaulay, T. B., I 154*n*; II 227*n*; IV 11*n*, 141*n*, 386

McCarthy, David, X 575

McCarthy, Mary, trans. Weil, *Iliad*, VII ccvi *n*

Macclesfield, George Parker, 2nd Earl of, V 395*n* f., 451

Macclesfield, Thomas Parker, 1st Earl of, Biog., V 451; in AP poem, V 395

Macdonald, D. B., II 357*n*

Macdonald, Hugh, *John Dryden: A Bibliography*, V 70*n*

Mace, D. T., I 277*n*

Macedonia, in AP poem, III.i 148

Macer, in AP poem, VI 137

Machiavelli, Niccolo, in AP poem, VI 259; other ref., III.i lxvii, lxix; III.ii xx; V 262*n*

Mack, Florence, VII xxiv

Mack, Maynard, I xiii, 131*n*, 136*n*, 143*n*, 152*n*, 188*n*; III.ii xxxi *n*; IV xliv, 148, 162, 190, 266, 276, 340; V 471; VI xx, 359*n*, 362*n*; VII xv, ccxxiii *n*, ccxxiv *n*, ccxxvi *n*; X xiii, 495, 510, 589

Mackail, J. W., II 10; VII cxciv

Mackenna, Stephen, trans. Plotinus, III.i xxxii *n*, xxxiii *n*

M'Kenzie, Mary (maid of honour), IV 367

McKillop, A. D., III.i xxviii *n*, xlvii *n*, 32*n*, 63*n*, 93*n*, 125*n*

Macky, John, *Memoirs*, III.ii 91*n*

McLachlan, H. J., I 301*n*

Macleane, A. J., VII lxxviii and *n*, lxxx

Macmillan's Magazine, II 383*n*

Macrobius, trans. Homer, VII xxxviii, xl, lxxii, lxxxi; X 414; *Commentarii in somnium Scipionis*, VII 79, 127; X 359; *Saturnalia*, VII 6, 114, 119, 132, 163, 174–6, 244, 246–7, 266, 353, 396, 400, 422; VIII 40, 89, 150, 537; IX 133, 320, 362, 402, 444; X 5

MacSwiney, Owen, II 205*n*

Maeander (river), in AP poems, II 135, 205; V 122, 304, 323; VI 33

Maeonian, in AP poems, I 312; IV 229

Maeotis, in AP poems, V 324; VI 79

Maevius (critic of Horace and Virgil), in AP poems, I 243 and *n*; VI 16; other ref., I 250*n*, 262*n*

Maffei, Scipio, Biog., V 447; other ref., V 362*n*

Magdalen, in AP poem, III.ii 49

Magi, in AP poem, II 260

Maginn, William, VII xcvi

Magnus, O., II 263*n*, 264*n*, 411

Mahomet (prophet), in AP poems, V 157 and *n*, 378 and *n*

Mahomet (George I's servant), III.ii 66 and *n*

Mahound, in AP poem, IV 45

Mainwaring, Arthur, I 38, 59*n*; II 7*n*, 205*n*

Maitland, W., I 88*n*, 182*n*

Malalas, Johannes (author of world history, 5th/6th c. AD), VII 33

Malcolm, J. P., *Lond. Rediv.*, IV 62*n*

Malea, in AP poem, I 415 and *n*

Malebranche, Nicole, I 263*n*; III.i 33*n*; V 408; VI 48, 51*n*

Malherbe, François de (poet), AP trans. of, VI 71–2, 72*n*

Mall, in AP poems, II 137, 211; IV 79; VI 321; other ref., II 399–400

Mall (anon. poem), II 211*n*, 373 f.

Mallet, David, Biog., V 447; his *Verbal Criticism*, III.i 165*n*; IV 112*n*; V 83*n*; in AP poems, V 36*n*; AP corres., IV 164*n*; other ref., IV 94; V 199, 440; VI 311*n*

Malmesbury, William of, I 156*n*, 157*n*, 158*n*

Malone, Edmond (editor of Spence), material collected for projected ed. of AP, I viii; III.ii xvi *n*, 12*n*, 28*n*, 37*n*, 47*n*, 63*n*, 140*n*; notes on AP poems, IV ix *n*, 110*n*, 243*n*, 367, 376; V 60*n*, 100*n*; on MS of *1740*, IV 330; other ref., III.ii ix

Mandeville, Bernard, the relation of his philosophic position to AP, III.i xl; III.ii 84*n*, 153*n*; V 388*n*; in AP poems, V 317; relation to the modern temper, III.i lxvii, lxix; *Fable of the Bees*, III.i xxxviii *n*, 78*n*; III.ii 19*n*, 87*n*, 111*n*; V 391*n*; AP opinion of, III.ii 84*n*; other ref., VII ccxxviii

Manes, in AP poem, I 441 and *n*

Manilius, Marcus (author of *Astronomica*), III.i 26*n*, 46*n*, 71*n*; V 365; IX 344

Manillo, in AP poem, II 172

Manly, in AP poem, III.ii 24

Manley, Mary de la Riviere, II 181*n*; IV xvii, 74*n*

Mannock, William, I 330; VII xii, xxxvi *n*

Man of Ross. See Kyrle

Mansfield. See Murray

Mantua[–n], in AP poems, I 80, 254 and *n*, 322 and *n*; II 271

Mantuanus, Baptista, I 31 and *n*

Manutio, Aldo (printer), III.ii 150*n*

Manwaring, Elizabeth W., *Italian Landscape in Eighteenth Century*, II 254*n*; III.ii 141*n*

Mapes, Walter, I 152*n*

Mapledurham, VI 190*n*, 231*n*, 247*n*, 332*n*

Mar, Frances (Pierrepont) Erskine, Countess of, IV 76*n*

Marana, G. P., III.i 45*n*

Marcellus, Marcus, III.i 152 and *n*

Marchmont, Alexander Hume, 2nd Earl of, II 337*n*; IV xxxii, xxxv, 320*n*, 336 and *n*; VI 385*n*

Marchmont, Hugh Hume, 3rd Earl of (formerly Lord Polwarth), Biog., IV 367–8; an executor of AP estate, III.ii xi ff., 167; IV 330; AP corres., IV 305*n*, 326*n*, 394; VI 394*n*; in AP poems, IV 320 and *n*, 336 and *n*; VI 383, 385*n*; other ref., III.ii xiii *n*, xv–xvi; IV xxxiii

Marchmont, Patrick Hume, 1st Earl of, IV 320*n*

Marchmont Papers, IV xxxvi *n*, 304*n*

Marcus, in AP poem, VI 152

Marcus Aurelius. See Aurelius Antoninus

Margites (comic epic attributed to Homer), II 106; V xxxviii, 48–9*n*; VII 53

Marillier, H. C., *Tapestries at Hampton Court*, IV 49*n*

Marlborough, Henrietta Churchill, Duchess of, III.ii 55–6*n*, 57*n*, 58*n*

Marlborough, John Churchill, 1st Duke of, Biog., IV 354; relations with Lady Castlemaine, IV 74–5*n*; in AP poems, III.i 155*n*; IV 126 and *n*, 166–7*n*, 167, 288*n*; VI 59, 157, 160*n*, 181, 184*n*, 290–1, 293*n*, 358–9; other ref., I 40, 186*n*; III.ii 20*n*, 26*n*, 27*n*, 167; VI 119*n*; VII ccxli

Marlborough, Sarah Churchill, Duchess of, AP corres., III.ii 164; in AP poems, III.ii 74*n*; IV 63 and *n*; not Atossa, III.ii xi *n*, xi–xii, 59*n*, 160–70; other ref., III.ii 26–7*n*, 56*n*, 101*n*, 167; IV 112*n*, 118*n*; VI 359*n*

Marlborough, Charles Spencer, Duke of, Biog., IV 386; in AP poems, IV 335 and *n*

Marlow, Charles, VII xxiv

Marlowe, Christopher, VII lii and *n*

Marmontel, trans. *R. of the Lock* into French, II 105*n*

Maro. See Virgil

Marriot, Mrs, AP corres., II 120; VI 135*n*

Mars, in AP poems, I 398; II 72, 135, 202; V 348

Marseilles, the 1720 plague in, III.i 138 and *n*

Marston, J., II 193*n*

Marten, F., II 411

Martial, in AP poems, II 125, 139; VI 166–7; other ref., I 291*n*; II 91, 141; IV 314*n*; V 357; X 242

Martianus Capella, II 30*n*

Martin, Mr, VI 395*n*

Martin, L. C., II 382*n*

Martyn, J. (editor of *The Grub-street Journal*), VI 325*n*

Marvell, Andrew, I 79*n*; III.i 122*n*, 128*n*, 129*n*, 164*n*

Mary of Modena, I 176*n*, 194*n*

Mary, Queen of Scots, in AP poem, VI 291, 293*n*

Masham, Samuel, Baron, VI 342*n*. See also Dives

Mason, William (poet), II 4*n*, 302, 308; III.ii 47*n*; IV 157*n*, 225*n*; VI 340*n*

Massieu, Guillaume (writer on Homer), VII xxxix and *n*; VIII 343

Massinger, Philip, IV 220*n*

Masson, David, I 208*n*

Masson, Jean (writer), VI 25, 28*n*

Master Key to Popery, III.ii xxx ff., 175–88

Matthews, John, II 416

Matthews, William, II 104*n*; VII cvii *n*

Maty, H., VI 442*n*

Maty, Matthew, III.ii 136*n*

Maudlin (College, Oxford), in AP poem, IV 168*n*, 169

Mauger, Claude (teacher of French), IV 165*n*

Maupas, Charles (teacher of French), IV 164*n*

Mausolus, in AP poem, II 69

Maximus of Tyre (sophist, author of lectures, 2nd c. AD), VII 69–70; IX 300, 361–2, 384; X 173, 215, 306

Maxwell, J. C., IV 339; V 460, 468, 470; VI xx

Maxwell, John (translator of Cumberland), III.i 22*n*, 57*n*, 67*n*, 105*n*, 163*n*

May [Maia], in AP poems, I 428 and *n*; II 13, 26, 30, 34, 35, 38, 39, 43, 49, 52, 71

May, Thomas, trans. Lucan, II 277*n*; his poetic and dramatic works, III.i 149*n*; III.ii 89*n*, 107*n*

Maynard, François, AP trans. of his poetry, VI 168

Maynwaring, Arthur, trans. *Iliad*, VII cxi, cxxxvi–cxxxvii; X 495, 496, 501, 560–72, 575, 579–80

Mayor, J. B., I 101*n*; III.i 110*n*

Mazon, Paul, VII l

Mead, Richard, Biog., IV 372; in AP poems, III.ii 136 and *n*; IV 283; V 379*n*; other ref., III.i 19*n*; III.ii 134*n*; V 449; VI 395–6*n*; IX xiii

Mead, W. E., *Grand Tour*, V 374*n*

Meadows, Sir Philip (diplomatist), VI 167*n*

Meadows, Miss (Court lady), in AP poems, VI 181, 184*n*, 201, 342, 343*n*

Meander. See Maeander

Mears, William (publisher), Biog., V 447; in AP poems, V 111, 152, 301, 321; other ref., II 295*n*; V 431

Medea, in AP poems, V 192 and *n*, 353, 407

Medina, Sir Solomon (army contractor), III.ii 26*n*

Medusa, in AP poem, I 437

Mee, Peter. See My

Melcombe. See Dodington

Melmoth, William, VII cvii *n*

Melville, Herman, VII ccvii *n*, ccxiii and *n*

Memnon, in AP poem, V 87

Memoirs of the Family of Guise, III.ii 172*n*

Mémoires de Trévoux, III.i xviii

Menander, in AP poem, I 81 and *n*; other ref., IX 46; X 81

Mendelssohn, Moses, his and Lessing's *Pope ein Metaphysiker!*, III.i xxvii *n*, xli *n*

Menelaus, in AP poem, VI 107

Menestheus, in AP poem, I 451

Mercury, in AP poem, II 75

Merdamante, in AP poems, V 139, 314

Méré, Georges Brossin, VII lxxii and *n*

Merlin, in AP poems, IV 175, 206*n*, 207, 224–5*n*, 225, 291

Messiah, in AP poem, I 122

Metamorphosis, in AP poem, VI 174

Methuen, Sir Paul, Biog., IV 372; in AP poems, IV 83 and *n*, 333 and *n*

Mexico, in AP poem, I 192 and *n*

Meystayer, Henry (watchmaker), V 88*n*

Michelangelo Buonarroti, I 319*n*

Midas, in AP poems, IV 100, 101; V 335

Middlesex, Charles, Earl of, V 402*n*

Middleton, Conyers, Biog., IV 372; in AP poem, IV 303–4*n*, 304; other ref., V 351*n*

Migne, Jacques Paul, VII 63

Milbourne, Luke, Biog., V 447; critic, V xlv; in AP poems, I 291; V 141, 172, 314; his *Notes on Dryden's Virgil*, I 291*n*; V 151*n*, 230 ff., 322*n*, 447

Miles, Josephine, III.i lxxv *n*, lxxviii *n*

Mill, John Stuart, VII ccv

Miller, James (poet), V xlv *n*, 342*n*, 373*n*, 396*n*, 402*n*, 405*n*

Miller, Philip (botanist), V 371*n*, 382*n*

Mills, A. H., II 306n

Milo, in AP poems, V 135, 309

Miloyevitch, V., III.i 68n

Milton, John, AP admiration for his early poems, I 44; a poet of "Magnificence", III.i lxxiv; AP youthful imitation of, VI 20n; VII xxxv; in AP poems, III.ii 150; IV 108 and n, 159, 175, 203, 209; V 165, 175 and n, 328, 331, 352, 363; VI 328, 332n; Bentley's ed. of PL, IV 108n; V 175n, 237–8n, 363n; sonnet attrib. to AP in imitation of, VI 373, 374n; in AP Preface, VII xlviii, 5; X 412; AP use of, I 44; VII lxvii, lxx, xci, ci, ccxxxvi; X 495; echoed by Dryden in trans. Homer, VII xcii; his similes, VII clxxv, clxxix; as part of epic tradition, VII clxxxiii, clxxxvi, ccvi; his treatment of deities, VII clxxxix; AP on his language, VII 19, 22; influence on Fenton, X 574, on Broome, X 585; other ref., I 127, 132, 136, 149n, 254n, 257n, 261n, 276n, 352; II 117, 160n, 216 f., 230, 231, 301 ff., 402; III.i 39n; VI 193n; VII lxxviii, lxxxix, ccxxxv; IX xiii, 77; X 390–1, 437

WORKS:

Prose, III.i lii, 13n, 62n, 67n, 69n, 81n; VI 193n, 332n; L'Allegro, I 150n; II 67n; V 354n, 466n; VII cxxii n; X 509, 510, 511; Arcades, I 63n; V 140n; At a Vacation Exercise, I 71n, 183n, 184n; Comus, I 79n, 84n, 92n, 119n, 188n; II 37n, 44n, 189n; III.i 43n, 86n; IV 40–1n, 326n; VI 384n; IX 133, 155; X 504, 509, 510–11; Epitaph on the Marchioness of Windsor, II 281n; In Quintum Novembris, II 228; Lycidas, I 46 and n, 73n, 75n, 93n, 117n, 148n, 179n, 254n; III.i 128n; IV 105n, 305n; X 501, 502, 503, 509, 510; Of Education, I 224n; On the Late Massacre at Piemont, X 510; On the Morning of Christ's Nativity, I 113n; X 512; On Time, III.i l

Paradise Lost, I 60n, 63n, 94n, 114n, 115n, 116n, 117n, 148n, 151n, 160n, 161n, 163n, 186n, 190n, 210, 270n, 282n, 283n, 286n, 312n, 324n, 379n, 416n, 419n, 428n, 432n, 437n, 442n, 445n, 455n, 456n, 460n

II 33n, 120, 147n, 149n, 151n, 153n, 154n, 157n, 164n, 168n, 179n, 206n, 211n, 227, 254n ff., 277n, 283n, 330n, 331n, 337n, 363n, 381, 382

III.i conceptualizing the Biblical story, lxiv; a reply to Hobbes?, lxix–lxx; likenesses to E. on Man, liii–liv, lvii–lviii, lxvi, lxx, lxxii, lxxiii; differences from Essay, lxxiii–lxxiv; other ref., v, l, li, lii, lvii, lxiv, lxxvii, 12n, 13n, 14n, 18n, 24n, 29n, 31n, 32n, 35n, 39n, 46n, 49n, 53n, 56n, 79n, 81n, 93n, 102n, 103n, 104n, 106n, 108–9n, 110n, 112n, 114n, 116n, 119n, 129n, 135n, 147n, 148n, 163n, 166n

III.ii 24n, 116n, 118n

IV 108n, 118n, 202n

V 10n, 54n, 56n, 61n, 65n, 66n, 77n, 96n, 105n, 108n, 109n, 130n, 139n, 143n, 152n, 155n, 157n, 178n, 179n, 256, 296–7n, 299n, 339n, 355n, 363n, 383n, 388n 466n ff.

VII xv n, lviii, lix and n, lxii–

lxiii, c, cxxii *n*, cxxvi, cxxix–
cxxxvi, cxliv, cxlv *n*, cxlvii,
clviii, ccix and *n*, ccx and *n*, ccxi
and *n*, ccxiii and *n*, ccxxv, 85, 91,
111, 139–40, 148, 154, 168–9,
176, 275, 287–8, 293, 310–11,
313, 338, 365, 391, 395–6, 400–1,
414
VIII 124, 176–7, 181–2, 193,
199, 206, 246, 256–7, 278–9, 310,
353, 397, 457, 553
IX xiii, 155, 356, 373, 419–20
X 191, 245, 347, 494, 495, 501,
502, 503, 504, 505, 506, 508–12
Paradise Regained, I 60*n*, 210*n*; II
330*n*; III.i 61*n*, 129*n*, 130*n*, 144*n*,
147*n*, 149*n*; X 502; *Il Penseroso*, I
74*n*, 81*n*; II 277*n*; III.ii 147*n*;
X 503, 509; *Samson Agonistes*, I
116*n*; II 228, 267*n*, 367*n*, 406;
III.i 39*n*, 51*n*, 98*n*; VII cxxxi,
343; X 503, 509; Sonnets, I 62*n*;
II 228; IV 171*n*; VI 167*n*
Mimnermus (poet, 7th c. BC), IX
430
Minerva, in AP poems, I 436, 468;
II 258, 266
Minos (pseudo-Platonic dialogue),
III.i 151*n*
Mint (London), in AP poems, IV
14*n*, 15, 96, 107; VI 283
Mirror for Magistrates, III.i 71*n*; IV
19*n*
Miscellaneous Poetical Novels, II 7
Miscellany on Taste, AP poem *To
Burlington* included, III.ii 128 f.,
and characters identified, III.ii
128 f., 135*n*, 137*n*, 138*n*, 139*n*,
145*n*, 146*n*, 176, 182*n*; other ref.,
III.ii 149*n*
Misson, F. M., II 263*n*
Misson, H., II 156*n*, 400
Mist, Nathaniel, Biog., V 448; in

AP poems, V 86 and *n*, 184 and
n, 285 and *n*. See also next
entry
Mist's Journal (*The Weekly Journal*,
ed. Nathaniel Mist), V xxiii,
83*n*, 86*n*, 134*n*, 184*n*, 212*n*, 437,
448 f.; cited, V xii, xxiv *n*, xlviii *n*,
14*n*, 21*n*, 29*n*, 30*n*, 31*n*, 32*n*, 41*n*,
46*n*, 47*n*, 73*n*, 86*n*, 110*n*, 115*n*,
123*n*, 136*n*, 153*n*, 233*n*; VI 294*n*
Mitchell, Joseph, Biog., V 448; in
AP poem, V 162, 163*n*
Mitford, John, X 474
Mitford, Mary Russell, II 373, 374
Mitra, in AP poem, I 446 and *n*
Mizener, Arthur, article on Duke
of Buckingham, III.ii 117*n*
Moeonian, in AP poem, I 312
Moeotis, in AP poems, V 156, 324
Mohun, Charles, Baron, III.ii
122*n*; his wife, IV 84–5*n*
Moivre, Abraham de, in AP poem,
III.i 102 and *n*
Mole (river), in AP poem, I 184
and *n*
Molesworth, William, VII cxxi *n*;
X 495
Molière, I 290*n*; III.i 154*n*; III.ii
97*n*; V 279, 289; VI 178
Moll. See Hervey, Mary (Lepell),
Lady
Molloy, Charles, Biog., V 448;
other ref., V 134*n*
Molly. See Molyneux
Molyneux, Samuel (astronomer),
in AP poems, VI 171, 172, 175*n*,
259–64*n*
Momentilla, in AP poem, II 166
Momus, in AP poem, III.ii 83 and *n*
Monk, J. H., *Life of Bentley*, IV 77*n*;
V 362*n*, 363*n*, 371*n*
Monk, S. H., I 255*n*, 258*n*, 272*n*,
316*n*, 323*n*

Monmouth Street (London), in AP poem, VI 178

Monro, Dr James, Biog., IV 372–3; in AP poems, IV 169 and n; V 271; his epigram, IV 353

Montagu. See Halifax

Montagu, Edward Wortley, Biog., IV 373; in AP poems, as Avidieu, IV 57–9, 57n; as Worldly, III.ii 90 and n, 97n; IV 181

Montagu, Edward Wortley, son, Biog., IV 373; in AP poems, IV 59 and n, 77 and n

Montagu, Elizabeth (bluestocking), III.ii 66n

Montagu, Mary, Duchess of, III.ii 56n, 58n; VI 160n

Montagu, Lady Mary Wortley, Biog., IV 373; relations with AP, I 209; II xiii, 311–13, 312–13n, 325n, 348n, 354–5n; III.ii xxxix–xl, 30n, 51n, 102n, 147n, 178n; IV xv–xix, 95n; V 212n; VI 226n; VII xxvi; her letters quoted, III.ii xl, 31n, 32n, 56n, 57n, 58n, 101n; guardian to her sister, IV 76–7n, 306 and n, 314; supposed author of A Popp upon Pope, IV 120–1n; V 72n; her autograph MSS of AP poems, VI 50n, 149n, 212n; author of Basset-Table and Roxana, VI 416; Burnet's verses to, VI 423; Reply upon Mr Pope ascribed to, VI 444n; in AP poems, IV 57–9, 57n, 74n, 75, 85 and n, 89, 291 and n, 306 and n, 314; V 112 and n, 162n, 301; VI 160n, 173, 176n, 225, 226–7n, 236 and n, 256–7, 258n; as Fufidia, IV 77 and n; as possible Rufa, III.ii 51 and n; as Sappho, III.ii 51 and n, 102 and n; IV xv–xxii passim, 13 and n, 103,

123, 133, 298; VI 357 and n; AP poems addressed to, VI 211–12, 212n, 357, 439; AP corres., II 186n; III.i 58n, 123n; IV 123n; VI 115n, 198n, 212n, 236n; other ref., II 6; V 104–5n

Montaigne, Michel Eyquem de, his conception of ruling passions, III.i xxxvi; his ambivalent view of passions, III.i xxxvii; his anti-anthropocentrism, III.i lxvii, lxix; echoes of Cotton version, III.ii 17n, 20n; AP preferred Charron, III.ii 27 and n; in AP poems, III.ii 27; IV 9, 89, 281; other ref., I 245n; II 200n, 233, 236, 269n, 363n; III.i xxiv, 15n, 17n, 24n, 30n, 31n, 38n, 43n, 53n, 60n, 61n, 66n, 67n, 68n, 70n, 72n, 76n, 77n, 82n, 83n, 96n, 97n, 100n, 101n, 102n, 108n, 110n, 111n, 112n, 129n, 150n; III.ii xx f., xxxv, 16n, 33n; IV 9, 280n, 281

Montalto, in AP poem, V 351. See Hanmer

Monthly Chronicle, III.i xxxvii n

Monthly Review, III.i xxx n

Montrose, James Graham, Marquis of, AP [?] imitation of, VI 23n

Moore, A. (publisher), V 210

Moore, Arthur, Biog., IV 374; in AP poem, IV 97; other ref., V 110n

Moore, C. A., III.i xxvii n, xxviii n

Moore, James. See Smythe

Moore, James (hack-writer), III.ii 96n; IV 356

Moore, John, AP poem to, VI 161–4 and n; other ref., VI 330n

Moore, Mrs John, III.i 86n

Moore, J. R., II 152n, 157n, 159n

Mordaunt. See Peterborough

Mordaunt, Anna Maria (court lady), VI 342, 343n
Mordington, Lord, IV 326 and n
More, H., of Fawley Hall, VI 127n
More, Henry (Platonist), ambivalent view of passions, III.i xxxvii n, xxxviii n; other ref., II 149n; III.i 14n, 26n, 48n; V 387n
More, St Thomas, III.i 66n
Morgan, Sir, in AP poem, III.ii 90 and n
Morgan, Thomas, Biog., V 448–9; in AP poem, V 317
Morice, Mrs Mary (daughter of Bishop Atterbury), VI 343–5
Morley, Mrs, II 191n, 376
Morley, Henry Parker, Lord, II 251n
Morley, John, *Walpole*, IV 394
Morpheus, in AP poem, VI 31
Morphew, John (publisher), II 295n; V 207
Morrah, Dermot, II v, 386 ff.
Morrice, Bezaleel, Biog., V 449; his poems, III.i 55n; V 126n, 128n, 166n; praises *E. on Man*, III.i xv–xvi, 136n; V 43n; attacks AP, V 110n, 208, 211n; in AP poems, V xx n, 111, 165n, 301, 328; other ref., V 448; VI 294–5n
Morris, E. E., his notes cited, III.i 26n, 40n, 43n, 48n, 49n, 68n, 78n, 128n, 129n, 144n, 150n
Morse, J. M., I 274n
Moschus (poet, 2nd c. BC), I 20, 47, 91n; V 140n, 229
Moses, in AP poems, V 159, 325; VI 6, 290
Moses, Thomas, VII 63
Moss, Robert (divine), III.i 133n
Moss, varieties of, III.ii 17n
Mossner, E. C., III.i xxiv

Motte, Andrew, trans. Newton, III.i 57n
Motte, Benjamin (publisher), V xv
Motteux, Peter Anthony, Biog., IV 374; in AP poems, V 146, 147, 317; other ref., I 16n; II 199n, 218n, 233n; IV 29; VII cxi, cxxvii, cxxviii, cxxxvi and n; X 495, 498, 572–4
Mottley, John (dramatic biographer), III.ii 174; V 68n, 112n
Moule, H. F., II 402
Mt St Michel, in AP poem, IV 140, 141
Mountford, W., II 187n
Mummius, Biog. (identity discussed), V 449–50; in AP poems, V 338, 379 f.
Munby, A. N. L., 472
Mundungus, in AP poem, V 287
Münster, Sebastien, VIII 39
Murphy, Arthur, IV 346
Murray, William (later 1st Earl of Mansfield), Biog., IV 374; bequest in AP will, II 239n; co-executor of AP will, III.ii x n, xii, xiii n; in AP poems, IV xxxvii, 151, 175, 237–46 and n; V 357; VI 333 and n; other ref., IV xxiv, xxxv, 301n; IX xiii
Murry, Middleton, III.i 40n
Musaeus (mythical pre-Homeric Greek poet), VII 65, 335; IX 217
Museo Archeologico, Naples, IX xiii
Muses Mercury, VII cxi
Musgrave, Sir Christopher (Tory politician), III.ii 92n
My, Peter, VI 237n
Mycenè, in AP poem, I 425 and n, 429
Myra, in AP poems, I 176 and n; VI 158

N

Nabal, in AP poem, II 18

Naevius, in AP poem, IV 59

Naiads, in AP poems, I 72, 386

Narcissa, in AP poems, III.ii 36 and n, 54 and n; VI 288

Narcissus, in AP poems, V 351; VI 9, 47

Nardac, in AP poem, VI 279

Narses, in AP poem, III.ii 97 and n

Nash, Richard ("Beau"), in AP poems, IV 288n; VI 360, 361n

Nashe, Thomas, I 176n

Naso, in AP poems, IV 40; V 147 and n

Natalis Comes (author of *Mythologia*), VII 311

National Portrait Gallery (London), X xii

Nearchus (painter), VIII 360

Nectar, in AP poem, I 450

Ned, in AP poem, III.ii 37

Needham, Francis, VI xx

Needham, Mother, Biog., IV 374–5; in AP poems, IV 87 and n; V 293, 293–4n; VI 232, 233n

Needler, Henry (poet), III.i 20n

Neill, Desmond, VI xx

Nemea, in AP poem, I 434, 438

Nemesius, III.i 95n

Nepenthe, in AP poem, IV 305

Neptune, in AP poems, I 170, 469, 473; II 135, 203, 272; VI 269

Nereids, in AP poems, I 466 and n, 473

Neritus, in AP poem, I 473

Nero, in AP poems, III.i lxii, 79 and n; 84n; III.ii 144 and n

Neufgermain, Louis de (poet), VI 88, 90n

Newcastle, William Cavendish, Duke of, IV 207n; his wife Margaret, in AP poems, V 78, 280

Newcastle, John Holles, 1st Duke of, III.ii 108n

Newcastle-upon-Tyne, Thomas Pelham-Holles, 1st Duke of, Biog., IV 377; in AP poems, IV 335?; VI 172, 175n; other ref., III.ii 108n; IV 359; V 126n, 187n, 350n, 440, 453

Newcomb, Thomas (publisher), II 402

Newcomb, Rev. Thomas (poet), V 155n, 364n

New Court (London), in AP poem, VI 222

Newdigate, B. H., III.ii 51n

Newfoundland, in AP poem, VI 273

New Foundling Hospital for Wit, II 415n

Newgate, in AP poem, IV 313 and n

Newman, John Henry, II 179n; VII xcv, xcvi

Newmarket, in AP poems, IV 207 and *n*; VI 275

New System of the Nat. Hist. of Quadrupeds, III.i 41*n*

Newton, Sir Isaac, symbol of intellect and its limits, III.i lviii; in AP poems, III.i 60 and *n*; IV 159; V 175–6 and *n*, 331; VI 204, 317, 318*n*; other ref., III.i lv, lxviii, 34*n*, 48*n*, 56*n*, 57*n*, 59*n*, 63*n*, 125*n*; III.ii 17*n*, 33*n*; V 114*n*, 193*n*, 343*n*, 384*n*, 387*n*, 390*n*, 427; VII clxxxv; IX xiii

Newtonianism; tendency of, III.i lxvii; taken account of in *E. on Man* but qualified, III.i lxviii; other ref., III.i xxviii *n*

New York Public Library, X 587–8, 590

Nias, J. B., *John Radcliffe*, IV 381

Nicholas, Duke, in AP poems, VI 218, 219, 220, 222, 223

Nichols, John, *Literary Anecdotes*, I viii, 125*n*; II 104*n*; IV ix, 31*n*, 367–8, 373; V xix *n*, 76*n*, 79*n*, 103*n*, 379*n*, 391*n*, and Biog. App. *passim*; VII xlvi *n*; X 574–5; biographer of Hogarth, III.ii lvii f.; *Literary Illustrations*, V 83*n*, 85*n*, 88*n*, 129*n*, 355*n*, and Biog. App. *passim*; other ref., V 328*n*, 440

Nicoll, Allardyce, IV 15*n*, 220*n*; V 190*n*; VII ccxviii *n*; X 474, 495

Nicolson, Marjorie, III.i lxx *n*, 44*n*, 59*n*; III.ii 17*n*

Niemcewicz, II 105*n*

Nierembergius, III.i 99*n*

Nieuwentyt, Bernard (natural philosopher), III.i 38*n*

Niger, C. Pescennius, V 379, 472

Nightingale, J., II 209*n*

Nigrina, in AP poems, V 139, 314

Nile, in AP poems, I 243; VI 66, 203

Nilsson, Martin, VII ccvii *n*

Nilus, in AP poems, I 185 and *n*, 425; III.ii 149; IV 29

Nimrod, in AP poems, I 138, 139, 155 and *n*; other ref., I 165*n*

Ninus, in AP poem, II 260 and *n*

Niobe, in AP poems, V 310; VI 67

Nisus, in AP poems, I 429 and *n*; II 130, 177

Noah, in AP poem, IV 27

Noble, M. (biographer), V 454

Non-juror. See *Compleat Key*

Norden, John (poet), III.i xlix, 70*n*, 123*n*

Norfolk Poetical Miscellany, III.ii 137*n*, 138*n*

Norman, in AP poem, I 155

Norris, John (Platonist), II 154*n*; III.i 62*n*, 85*n*, 136*n*; V 78*n*, 408

Notes and Queries, IX xiii

Nourse, Timothy (moralist), III.i 68*n*

Novels. See *Miscellaneous Poetical Novels*

Noyes, G. R., X 494

Nugent, Mrs Anne (Craggs), VI 364, 365*n*

Nugent, Robert, Earl Nugent, IV 289*n*, 319*n*; VI 365*n*

Numa, VII ccxxxii *n*

O

Oakley (Gloucestershire), VI 195–6n

Observator, V 118n, 457

Ockley, Simon (translator), III.i 58n

Octavius, in AP poem, VI 66

Odin, in AP poem, II 264

"Odious", in AP poems, III.ii 36 and n, 53

Odysses, in AP poem, I 465

Odyssey. Entries occur under Homer or names of translators. See especially AP entry, Works

Oechalia, in AP poem, I 385

Oedipus, in AP poems, I 410, 413, 424, 444

Oenides, in AP poem, I 434

Oenomäus, in AP poem, I 426 and n

Oete, in AP poem, I 417 and n

Of Good Nature, an attack on *Ep. to Burlington*, III.ii 138n

Ogilby, John, in AP poems, V 78 and n, 94 and n, 280, 294; trans. Virgil's *Eclogues*, I 72n, 73n, 77n, 79n, 82n, 83n, 321n; II 180n; trans. Virgil's *Georgics*, II 253n; trans. *Aeneid*, VII cviii; AP debt to his trans., VII xl, cviii n, cxii, cxxix, cxxxvi, cxl, clii, clvi, ccxxi; X 494, 508; trans. Homer, I 331, 353, 417n; VII xxxv, lxxxiv, cvii–cviii, cxxxvii n,

cxlvii, cxlviii, cxlix and n, cl n, clii, clvi n, clx, 21–2, 166, 207, 223, 310; X 36, 233, 440, 476–7, 578; compared to other trans., VII cxlviii, clx; characteristics of trans., VII cxviii–cxx; facts about his Homer, VII cix; trans. *Iliad*, VII xxxix, cxxvii; X 496, 497, 498, 499, 500, 515–17, 575, 579–81, 584; trans. *Odyssey*, I 466n; VII cxi, cxxv; X 495, 506, 507, 508; plates in his *Iliad*, VIII xiv; other ref., I 4n; V xlv

Ogle, George, II 4

Oglethorpe, J. E., Biog., IV 375; in AP poem, IV 185

O'Hara. See Tyrawley

Oileus, in AP poem, I 453

Okes, Nicholas, II 112

Oldfield, Anne, Biog., IV 375; in AP poems, IV 75, 223 and n; VI 113–15 and n, 410 and n, 438 and n; other ref., III.ii 36n

Oldfield, Richard, Biog., IV 375; in AP poems, IV 54n, 55, 171; other ref., V 402n

Oldham, John (poet and translator), AP knowledge of his work, IV xxvi n; practises poetical "imitation", IV xxvi–xxvii, 34n; other ref., I 47, 79n, 80n, 90n, 91n, 92n, 93n, 260n, 264n, 308n, 312n, 313n, 318n; II 112,

260*n*, 345*n*; III.i 122*n*, 130*n*,
150*n*, 152*n*; V xxxix, 86*n*, 100*n*,
287*n*, 340*n*, 365*n*, 392*n*
Oldisworth, William, as translator of Dacier *Iliad*, VII xiii,
xvii–xviii *n*, xl *n*, cix; VIII xii; X
495, 504. See also Ozell
Oldmixon, John, Biog., IV 375; V
450; attacks AP, II 90*n*; V 25 f.,
207*n*, 208, 209, 211, 232*n*, 233*n*;
praises AP, V 29, 40; in AP
poems, IV 31, 106; V 125–6 and
n, 134, 309 and *n*; other ref., I
252*n*; II 159*n*, 199*n*, 293*n*, 294 ff.,
357*n*; IV 200*n*; V xvi, xlv, xlvii,
13*n*, 60*n*, 134*n*, 153*n*, 178*n*, 186 f.,
276*n*, 347*n*; VI 105*n*
Oldys, William (antiquary), III.ii
44, 59, 112*n*; VI 396*n*
Oliver, William (physician), VI
384*n*
Olympus, in AP poems, I 151, 170;
II 135, 203
Omar, Caliph, V 156*n*
Ombre, in AP poems, II 134, 150,
171, 197; other ref., I 320*n*; II
383–92; III.ii 71*n*; VI 24
One Epistle to Mr A. Pope, II 226*n*
Onslow (adulterer in AP poem),
IV 89 and *n*
Onslow, Arthur, Biog., IV 375–6;
in AP poems, IV 31, 335; his
opinions quoted, IV 345, 349,
379, 381; other ref., III.ii 92*n*
Opera, in AP poems, V 334*n*, 345
ff., 374 f., 395 f.
Ophyr, in AP poem, I 121 and *n*
Oppian, *Halieutica*, III.i 111*n*; IX
389; *Cynegetica*, VII 417; VIII
390
Opsopaeus, X 441
"Opus Magnum", projected by
AP, III.ii xvi ff., xxiii

Orcades, in AP poem, III.i 82
Orcas, in AP poem, IV 223
Orestes, in AP poem, VI 76
Orford. See Walpole
Original Weekly Journal, VI 175*n*
Orion, in AP poem, I 95 and *n*
Orleans, Philip, Duke of, Regent,
III.ii 28*n*
Ormerod, G., *History of Cheshire*, IV
184*n*
Ormonde, James Butler, 2nd Duke
of, III.i 152*n*; V 62*n*
Orpheus, in AP poems, I 78; II
259; VI 7, 15, 32, 34, 275
Orrery. See Boyle, Charles
Orrery, John Boyle, 5th Earl of O.
and Cork, AP corres., III.i 51*n*;
III.ii 60*n*, 61*n*; V 446; VI 397–
8*n*, 405*n*; in AP poems, VI 405
and *n*; other ref., III.ii 173; IV
xxv *n*, 65*n*, 115*n*, 141*n*, 350; VI
354*n*, 399*n*
Orrery, Roger Boyle, 1st Earl of,
III.i 159*n*; IV 207*n*, 350
Orsilochus, in AP poem, I 470
Orsini, in AP poems, III.ii xi *n*,
60*n*, 169
Orwell, George, VII clvi and *n*
Osborn, James M., I xiii; III.ii
xxii *n*, 12*n*; V 473; VII xii; X
594, 606
"Osborne, Francis" [pseud.]. See
Pitt, James
Osborne, Thomas, Biog., V 450; in
AP poems, V 121*n*, 303 f.; other
ref., III.ii 112*n*
Osenburg, F. C., III.i 107*n*
Ostrogoths, in AP poem, V 157, 324
Osyris, in AP poem, I 446
Othello, in AP poem, II 136, 208
Otho, M. Salvius (Roman em-
peror), in AP poems, III.ii 27;
V 379, 472; VI 204

Ottemiller, John, VII xxiii

Otway, Thomas, I 133, 177*n*, 178*n*,
298*n*, 339; II 32*n*, 288*n*; III.i
24*n*, 63*n*; IV 175, 218*n*, 219; VII
lvii

Overton, Henry (engraver), VI
338*n*

Overton, J. H., I 301*n*, 302*n*

Overton, John (print-seller), VI
337, 338*n*

Ovid, in AP poems, I 364; II 40,
74; IV 104, 175; V 357; VI 171,
172, 174 and *n*; other ref., I 281*n*,
309*n*; II 91*n*, 202*n*, 219, 299–303,
380; V 265*n*; VI 20; VII xxxv,
lxvii, ccxxxv
WORKS:
Amores, I 90*n*; X 257, 281; *Ars
Amandi*, I 163*n*; II 33*n*, 162*n*,
207*n*; *Elegies*, I 224; II 356, 357;
Epistles, I 349; II 205*n*, 294*n*,
356, 363*n*, 367*n*; VI 98*n*; X 348;
Fasti, II 329*n*; *Heroides*, I 156*n*;
VII 190; X 62, 70; *Ibis*, X 305;
Metamorphoses, I 67*n*, 74*n*, 93*n*,
120*n*, 122*n*, 132, 149*n*, 151*n*,
153*n*, 160*n*, 163*n*, 165*n*, 166*n*,
167*n*, 168*n*, 170*n*, 172*n*, 184*n*,
185*n*, 189*n*, 193*n*, 244*n*, 248*n*,
268*n*, 279*n*, 320*n*, 331, 352, 353,
416*n*, 423*n*, 438*n*, 439*n* (anon.
trans. *Story of Arethusa*, I 165*n*,
168*n*); II 116 f., 130*n*, 150*n*,
153*n*, 157*n*, 162*n*, 183*n*, 187*n*,
191*n*, 192*n*, 203*n*, 210*n*, 241,
254*n*, 284*n*, 367*n*, 405; III.i 24*n*,
39*n*, 70*n*, 92*n*, 93*n*, 94*n*, 108*n*,
109*n*, 140*n*; V 61*n*, 87*n*, 107*n*,
135*n*, 142*n*, 143*n*, 144*n*, 186*n*,
192*n*, 272*n*, 288*n*, 310*n*, 353*n*,
374*n*; VII clxx, 53, 104, 207, 404,
466; VIII 264, 358; IX 44, 99–
101, 217, 280, 331, 362, 371, 381,

399, 415, 417, 443; X 13, 160,
275, 324, 336, 501, 505; *Pont.*, VI
159*n*; *Tristia*, IV 104*n*

Ovidius Exulans, II 293*n*

Oxenden, Sir George, Biog., IV
376; in AP poems, IV 80*n*, 81,
298 and *n*

Oxford (the town), in AP poem,
II 69

Oxford (university and colleges),
V xxiv *n*, 191, 336, 353*n*, 360 f.,
399; VI 168*n*; VII xlii, cvii *n*

Oxford, Edward Harley, 2nd Earl
of (formerly Lord Harley), annotates AP poems, I viii; IV ix, 84–
5*n*; gives AP portrait to Oxford,
I xiv; complimented by AP,
III.ii xxxii f.; returns AP "translation" of Donne, IV xli, 3*n*;
Bodleian MS notes, III.ii 48*n*,
103*n*; V 33*n*; VI 370*n*; his part in
publication of *Dunciad Variorum*,
V xxviii, 460–4 and *n*; in AP
poems, III.ii 108*n*, 112; VI 294–
5, 368, 370*n*; his copies of AP
poems, VI xiv, xix, 89*n*, 130*n*,
138*n*, 155*n*, 238*n*, 265*n*, 267*n*,
380*n*, 394*n*, 440*n*; AP corres.,
III.i xiii, 33*n*, 107*n*, 136*n*; III.ii
xxxii f., 112*n*, 131*n*; IV xiv, xxv,
66*n*; V xxiii, xxiv *n*, xxv, 212*n*,
456, 460*n*, 461–2*n*; VI 241*n*;
other ref., V xxi, 213*n*, 305*n*,
410*n*, 443, 445, 450; VI 374*n*

Oxford, Robert Harley, 1st Earl of,
urges AP to imitate Donne, IV
xli, 3; his MS volume of poems,
IV xlii, 143*n*, 293*n*; invited to
Scriblerus Club in AP poems, VI
116–19, 196, 197*n*; in other AP
poems, III.ii 26*n*; IV 255, 273;
VI 238–42 and *n*, 392, 394*n*;
other ref., II 93, 285*n*; V 13*n*,

19n, 305n, 306n, 439, 445, 468;
VI 298n; VII ccxxviii, ccxlvi

Oxford Classical Texts, VII xvii

Oxford English Dictionary, III.i 12n,
16n, 17n, 18n, 19n, 24n, 28n, 32n,
38n, 42n, 45n, 53n, 68n, 102n,
103n, 117n, 125n

Oxford Sausage, II 6n

Ozell, John, Biog., V 450–1; in AP
poems, V 91, 91–2n, 198 and n,
290, 397n; VI 37, 37–8n, 59, 60n,
123, 124n, 173; trans. Boileau, I
273n; II 114n, 272n; V xlv n;
other trans., II 379n; V 108n; as
translator of Dacier *Iliad*, V 431,
457; VII xiii, xvii, xl n, cxv n; X
495, 500, 501, 522–36; VIII xii;
Ozell – Oldisworth – Broome
trans. of Dacier *Iliad*, V 431; VII
cix; X 494, 536–9, 574–84, 585

P

Pack, Richardson, III.i 89*n*
Pactolus, in AP poem, I 66
Padua, in AP poem, V 158, 325
Padua-soy, in AP poem, IV 35
Page, Sir Francis, Biog., IV 376; V
    451; in AP poems, IV 12*n*, 13,
    135, 322; V 343 and *n*; other ref.,
    IV 367; V 401*n*
Page, Sir Gregory, Biog., IV 376;
    as possible Sir Job, IV 289*n*
Paget, Thomas Catesby, Lord, *E.
    on Man* attributed to, III.i xv
Pa-god, in AP poems, IV 45, 309
Paintin, H., II 100*n*
Pakington, Sir Herbert, Biog., IV
    376; in AP poems, IV 75*n*
Palaemon, in AP poem, I 417
Palestrina, Giovanni, I 320*n*
Palingenius, Marcellus, III.i 13*n*,
    23*n*, 59*n*, 94*n*, 104*n*
Palinurus, in AP poem, V 404*n*, 405
Palladio, Andrea, Palliadian, in
    AP poems, III.ii 140, 155; IV
    263; other ref., II 227*n*; III.ii
    xxv, 128, 134*n*, 139*n*, 177*n*
Pallas, in AP poems, I 469, 472,
    473; II 135, 202; V 61, 269; VI
    106, 336–7
Pall Mall Miscellany, VI 342*n*
Palmer. See Cleveland
Palmer, Sir Thomas, Biog., IV
    376–7; in AP poem, IV 81 and *n*
Pam, in AP poem, II 172

Pams, in AP poem, VI 367
Pamela, in AP poem, VI 63
Pan, in AP poems, I 75, 86, 151,
    166; V 159, 325
Pancirollas, Guido, II 341*n*
Pandion, in AP poem, I 453
Panegyric on a Court, V 398*n*
Pantomimes, V 176 and *n* ff.
Panza, Sancho, in AP poem, III.ii
    153 and *n*; other ref., IV 166*n*
Papillia, in AP poem, III.ii 40*n*, 53
    and *n*
Pappus of Alexandria (fl. *c* 300 AD),
    III.i 111*n*
Paraclete, in AP poem, II 348
Parian, in AP poems, I 400; II 255
    and *n*; III.ii 117; IV 239
Paridel, in AP poems, V xxxii,
    376*n*, 376–7
Paris, in AP poems, II 31; IV 117;
    V 127, 306; Parliament of, III.ii
    93*n*
Parker. See Macclesfield
Parker, F. H. M., I 152*n*
Parker, G., II 176*n*
Parker, Samuel, II 200*n*
Parmenides of Elea (philosopher,
    5th c. BC), IX 262
Parnassus [–ian], in AP poems, I
    250, 277, 296, 417, 441; III.i
    129; IV 96, 102; V 97, 161, 296,
    326 ; VI 79
Parnell, Thomas, Biog., IV 377;

his poems, II 98*n*, 374; IV xxv; V 67*n*, 109*n*, 138*n*; VII xxvi; AP ed. of his poems, VI 240–2*n*, 437*n*; VII xxvi; in AP poems, IV 255; VI 196, 197*n*, 239, 240*n*, and as member of Scriblerus Club, 115*n*, 116, 117, 118, 120, 197*n*; as AP collaborator, VI 115–18*n*, 120*n*, 196–7, 414*n*; his *E. on Homer*, VII xiv, xv, l, lxxviii, lxxx–lxxxii, lxxiv, lxxxv *n*, 13; text of *Essay*, VII 26–80; headpiece for, in AP *Iliad*, VII xii; assists AP in *Iliad*, VII xviii, xxxix; AP corres., VII xxxvii *n*, xxxviii and *n*, lxxxi; on Homer authorship, VII lxxvi; AP acknowledgements to, VII 23; VIII 578; other ref., II xii, xiii, 155*n*; VI 346*n*; VII xxv, xxvi, xliv *n*

Parr, R. (engraver), II viii

Parthenia, in AP poem, VI 126

Partridge, John (almanac-maker), in AP poems, II 111, 137, 211 and *n*; other ref., II 286*n*; IV 206*n*

Pascal, Blaise, AP associates his religious opinions with, III.i xxii; his ambivalent view of man, III.i xxxviii; other ref., III.i 17*n*, 35*n*, 44*n*, 53*n*, 54*n*, 55*n*, 56*n*, 71*n*, 82*n*, 87*n*, 99*n*, 158*n*

Pasquin (weekly paper), V 39, 163*n*, 168*n*, 170, 327*n*, 329

Passeran. See Radicati

"Paston, George" [pseud.], *Life of Pope*, III.ii 51*n*

Pastor, Ludwig von, I 319*n*, 320*n*, 322*n*

Pastora, in AP poem, III.ii 49

Pater, Walter, VII lvii

Paterculus (Gaius Velleius Pater-

culus, author of *Historia Romana*, 1st c. AD), VII 42, 46

Patriots, in AP poems, III.ii 88 and *n*, 105 and *n*; IV 281, 299 and *n*, 301, 302*n*, 324

Patritio, in AP poem, III.ii 26 and *n*

Patroclus, in AP poems, I 457, 458, 459, 460; II 271 and *n*

Pattison, Mark, his notes cited, III.i 11*n*, 14*n*, 18*n*, 20*n*, 22*n*, 23*n*, 24*n*, 25*n*, 32*n*, 33*n*, 40*n*, 45*n*, 46*n*, 53*n*, 54*n*, 57*n*, 59*n*, 64*n*, 66*n*, 68*n*, 70*n*, 71*n*, 73*n*, 77*n*, 80*n*, 88*n*, 93*n*, 94*n*, 95*n*, 99*n*, 100*n*, 101*n*, 102*n*, 103*n*, 104*n*, 108*n*, 110*n*, 113*n*, 116*n*, 122*n*, 128*n*, 130*n*, 131*n*, 132*n*, 134*n*, 135*n*, 145*n*, 147*n*, 148*n*, 151*n*, 152*n*, 153*n*; IV 6*n*, 8*n*, 68*n*, 105*n*, 120*n*, 216*n*, 220*n*, 299*n*, 319*n*; other ref., III.i xxiv *n*

Pattison, William (poet), II 293*n*, 415; VI 441*n*

Paul, in AP poem, III.ii 37

Paul, H. G., *John Dennis*, V 127*n*

Paulet. See Bolton

Paulus Silentiarius, II 160*n*

Pauly, Alphonse, II 227*n*

Pausanias, *Description of Greece*, VII 45, 52, 107, 178–80, 218, 259, 271, 371; VIII 195, 301, 355, 496; IX 209, 216, 276, 283, 388; X 194, 226, 230, 259

Paxton, Nicholas, Biog., IV 377; in AP poems, IV 313 and *n*, 321; V 311*n*

Peacham, Henry, I 313*n*; III.ii 140*n*

Peacock, T. L., II 386

Peake, A. S., *Commentary on the Bible*, III.i 109*n*

Peche, William, VII xxxix

Pedasus, in AP poem, I 459
Peg, in AP poem, IV 77
Pegasus [–aean], in AP poems, I 257; IV 279; V 165, 328; VI 79
Peleus, in AP poem, IV 169
Pelham. See Newcastle
Pelham, Henry, Biog., IV 377; in AP poem, IV 316 and n
Pelion, in AP poem, VI 31
Pembroke, Henry Herbert, 9th Earl of, V 377n, 384n, 452; VI 343n
Pembroke, Margaret (Sawyer), Countess of, III.ii lviii, 48n, 49
Pembroke, Mary (Howe) Herbert, Countess of, III.ii 48n
Pembroke, Mary (Fitzwilliams), Countess of. See Fitzwilliams
Pembroke, Thomas Herbert, 8th Earl of, III.ii lviii, 48n, 134, 135n; VII 55
Pendarves. See Delany
Penkethman, William, Biog., IV 377; in AP poem, IV 220n, 221
Pennell, in AP poem, VI 276
Pennington, Montagu, Memoirs of Mrs Carter, IV 376
Pentheus, in AP poem, I 429
Pentlow (gamester), in AP poem, VI 25, 28n
Pepys, Samuel, I 276n, 299n; II 7; IV 260n
Perceval. See Egmont
Percy, Thomas, Bishop, I 41n, 202n, 348n, 353n, 355n, 356n, 359n
Perigord truffles in AP poem, V 397
Perizonius (Voorbroek), Jacob, X 22
Perkins, Francis, II 99, 101n, 374 f.
Perks, S., Water Line of the City of London after the Great Fire, IV 63n
Perolla, in AP poem, V 288

Perrault, Charles, Parallèle des Anciens et des Modernes, I 253n; VII 16, 229, 245; IX 108, 113, 228, 457; X 66, 90, 148, 205, 233; Les Murs de Troye, VII 349; in AP poem, VI 37, 38n; other ref., III.i 155n; VII xxxix, lxxii, lxxvi, xcvii; X 431, 446
Perry, Charles (traveller), V 449
Perseus, in AP poems, I 395, 423, 437; II 258
Persian[–s], in AP poems, I 283, 446; II 30, 260; IV 109, 183; VI 173, 284
Persius Flaccus, Aulus (author of satires, 1st c. AD), I 77n, 112n, 241n, 276n; III.i 152n; V 178n, 291n, 356n; VII 62, 223; VIII 381
Peru[–vian], in AP poems, I 192 and n; IV 241
Pescennius, in AP poem, VI 203
Peter, in AP poems, IV 5; VI 348. See also St Peter
Peter the Great, III.ii 21n
Peterborough, Charles Mordaunt, 3rd Earl of, Biog., IV 374; mediates between AP and Lady Mary, IV xvii–xviii; scandalized by Burnet's History, IV 30n; his garden, IV 278n; his attributions of poems to AP, VI 436–7n, 440n; in AP poems, IV 17 and n; VI 247n; other ref., III.ii 28n, 51n, 63n, 140n; V 35; VIII 461
Peteus, in AP poem, I 452
Petra, Gabriel de, VII 244
Petrarch, Francesco, I 321n; II 156n, 220, 226n, 251n, 252, 260n, 300; IV 320n; VII ccxxxix
Petre, M. D., The Ninth Lord Petre, II 91n, 92, 375n

Petre, Mary, II 98
Petre, Robert, Lord, I 299n; II 81 ff., 115, 375–6
Petre, Thomas, Lord, II 82
Petre (family), II 81 ff., 371 ff.
Petronius, *Satyricon*, I 241n, 256n, 271n; III.i 146n; IX 24; in AP poem, I 315 and n
Phaeacia, in AP poems, I 465, 468, 472
Phaedrus (1st c. AD), *Fables*, III.i 24n
Phaenician, in AP poem, I 470
Phaëton, in AP poem, VI 12
Phaon, in AP poem, I 393 ff.
Pharian, in AP poem, I 446 and n
Phemius (supposed author of a supposed work about the Greek return from Troy), VII 33
Pherecydes of Athens (genealogist), VII 77; VIII 549
Phidias (sculptor), in AP poems, V 159, 325; other ref., VII 79, 119
Philemon, in AP poem, V 80, 281
Philip II of Spain, in AP poem, III.ii 19 and n; other ref., I 189n
Philip V of Spain, III.i 146n; III.ii 28n
Philippa, Queen, I 177n, 178n
Philips, Ambrose, Biog., IV 377–8; V 451; his pastorals, I 17, 18, 20, 42, 78n, 93n, 275n; II 164n, 170n, 181n, 211n, 272n, 308n, 332n; his list of qualifications for writing epistles, III.ii xxxviii; AP *Guardian* 40 ironically praising, V 222–9 and n; his *Thule*, V 89, 289; parodies of, VI 441, 442n, 461; in AP poems, IV 102 and n, 109 and n, 231; V ix–x, 71n, 72, 188 and n, 276n, 277, 336 and n; VI 112 and n, 123, 124n, 129, 131n, 173, 176n, 284, 286n, 307, 309n; in AP

poems as Macer, VI 137–8, 138–9n; other ref., II 188n, 366n; V xi, xvi, 112n, 166n, 433, 435; VI 141n
Philips, John, *Cyder*, I 162n, 171n, 173n, 180n, 181n, 190n; II 260n; III.i 32n; III.ii 90n; other poems, I 163n, 186n; II 109n
Philips, Katherine (poetess), II 307, 321n, 325n, 341n; III.i 45n, 60n; IV 105n
Phillimore, Sir Robert Joseph, Bart., *Memoirs of Lyttelton*, IV xxxv n
Phillips, E., II 171n, 183n
Phillips, Teresia Constantia ("Con"), Biog., IV 378; in AP poem, IV 75
Philomedé, in AP poems, III.ii xlvii and n, 40 ff., 55 ff.
Philomel, in AP poems, I 63, 401 and n; II 67
Philomela, in AP poems, I 94; III.i 97
Philosophical Transactions, V 401n
Philosophical Translations (of the Royal Society), III.i 42n
Philostratus, Flavius P. (author of *Heroica*), VIII 112, 118, 134, 235, 275
Philostratus, P. Lennius (author of *Imagines*), VIII 497
Phlegeton, in AP poem, VI 32
Phlegias, in AP poem, I 445 and n
Phocais (work attributed to Homer), VII 54
Phocian, in AP poems, I 414; II 269 and n
Phoebe, in AP poems, I 416; V 378
Phoebus, in AP poems, I 65 and n, 72, 81, 163 and n, 190, 254, 394, 403, 411 and n, 419, 423, 430, 433, 435, 437, 438, 441, 442, 443,

444, 461; II 44, 128, 161; III.ii
73; V 127, 306, 335, 347, 350;
VI 171, 188, 212
Phoenix, in AP poem, VI 22
Phorcys, in AP poem, I 466, 473
Phoroneus, in AP poem, I 424 and n
Phosphor, in AP poem, I 63 and n
Phrygian, in AP poems, I 400 and
n, 437 and n, 445 and n, 458, 461;
VI 230
Phryne, in AP poems, III.ii 101
and n; VI 49–51n
Picavet, C.-G., III.i 137n
Pickenburg. See Bucquenbourg
Pico della Mirandola, Giovanni,
VI 297–8
Pierian, in AP poem, I 264 and n
Pigott, Nathaniel (barrister), VI
255, 256n
Pilkington, Mrs Laetitia (poetess),
V 115n
Pindar, in AP poems, II 272 and n,
273; IV 112 and n; V 62n, 165
and n, 328; other ref., I 326n; II
223; V340n; VII 59; VIII 285,
564–5; IX 34, 305; X 306
Pindus, in AP poems, I 112 and n;
IV 324
Pinky. See Penkethman
Pinto, V. de S., I 299n
Piobetta, J. B., III.i 100n
Piozzi, Mrs Hester Lynch (for-
merly Mrs Thrale), II 99 f.; VI
150n
Piper, David, VII xxiii
Pisa, in AP poem, V 140, 314
Pisander (of Rhodes, author of an
epic on Hercules), VII 6; X 14
Pisistratid Recension, VII lxxxi, 58
Pisistratus (tyrant of Athens, 6th c.
BC), VII lxxvi, 44, 58–9; IX 425
Pitholeon, in AP poem, IV 99–100,
99n

Pitt, Christopher (poet and translator), III.i 152n; V 85n, 102n,
137n; VI 438n
Pitt, James, Biog., IV 378; V 451;
as "Mother Osborne" in AP
poems, IV 302 and n; V 93n, 311
and n; as "Old James", V 146
and n
Pitt, Thomas, Governor of Madras,
III.ii 121n, 122n, 123n
Pitt, William (later 1st Earl of
Chatham), III.ii 121n; IV xxxiii,
xxxiv, 344
Pix, Mary, Biog., V 452; other ref.,
V 162n
Placebo, in AP poem, II 21, 25
Plain Dealer, in AP poems, VI 37,
59; other ref., III.i 69n, 74n, 75n,
94n, 105n, 145n, 146n; V 430,
444; VI 244n, 439n
Plantin, Christopher (printer), in
AP poem, VI 82, 84n
Plato, in AP poems, III.i 57 and n;
V 365; VI 96, 114, 151, 204;
other ref., III.i 58n; V 89–90n;
VII 64; VIII 285, 343; IX 361
WORKS:
Alcibiades, VII 427; Apology,
VIII 283; Axiochus, X 81;
Charmides, X 152; Cratylus, VIII
178; Euthyphro, VIII 342; Hip-
parchus, VII 59; Ion, X 285–6;
Laws, III.i 21n, 24n; VIII 404;
IX 310; X 151; Menexenus, X 54;
Minos, X 203; Phaedo, X 232;
Phaedrus, III.i vii; VII 53; IX
155; Politicus, III.i 108n; Repub-
lic, VII 72, 222, 225, 287, 293,
316, 466; VIII 324, 476, 535,
564; IX 300, 413; X 111, 160,
219, 346–7, 476; Sophistes, III.i
50n; Symposium, VII 150; Ti-
maeus, II 154n, 365n; VII 319;

VIII 204; *Theaetetus*, VII 396; IX 262

Platonism and neo-Platonism, pervasive in *E. on Man*, III.i xxii, xxviii, xxix, xxx, xxxii, xxxiii *n*, xxxv, xlvi, liv; anti-Platonism, III.i lviii; other ref., III.i xliii, xlviii, li, 58*n*; VIII 204. See also Plotinus

Platonists, Cambridge, III.i 124*n*. See also Ralph Cudworth, Henry Moore, John Smith, Benjamin Whichcote

Plautus, in AP poems, I 80; V 91, 290; other ref., III.ii 37*n*; VIII 40; IX 324; X 103, 270

Pleiades, the, in AP poem, I 70 and *n*

Pliny the Elder, *Hist. nat.*, II 260*n*, 264*n*; III.i 33*n*, 36*n*, 40*n*, 42*n*, 102*n*, 110*n*, 111*n*; V 19*n*; VII 43, 54, 183, 337; VIII 40, 169, 245, 289–90, 306, 359, 363, 390; IX 31, 209, 218, 242–4, 309, 315, 338, 344–5, 415, 425, 452; X 37, 84, 151, 156, 192, 222, 314; in AP poems, V 365, 396*n*

Pliny the Younger, *Letters*, I 240*n*; X 361

Plotinus, III.i xxxii *n*, xxxiii *n*, 48*n*, 58*n*, 139*n*, 142*n*

Pluche, N. A. (natural philosopher), III.i 103*n*

Plume, Sir, in AP poems, II 133, 135, 194, 206

Plutarch, AP indebtedness to *Lives*, II 232–3, 235–6, 236*n*; in AP poems, VI 114; other ref., II 258*n*, 265*n*, 266*n*; VII xl, lxxvi, xc, c; X 48
WORKS:
Bruta ratione uti, IX 164; *Coniugalia praecepta*, IX 376; *De aud.*

poet., VII 51, 64, 85, 87, 90, 92, 95, 101, 187, 217, 241, 286, 399, 435, 463; VIII 504, 542; IX 225, 283, 291; X 11–12, 18, 120, 183, 186; *De cupiditate divitiarum*, IX 123; *De curiositate*, VII 336; IX 386; *De exilio*, IX 204; *De garrulitate*, IX 330; X 206, 224, 292; *De invidia et odio*, VII 140; *De Iside et Osiride*, X 197, 359, 362; *De laude ipsius*, VII 103, 371; IX 273, 444; *De liberis educ.*, X 310; *De musica*, VII 33, 444–5; X 305; *De prof. in virt.*, VII 84; *De pythiae oraculis*, VII 226; *De vita et poesi Homeri*, VII 52, 176, 382; IX 280; X 173; *Instit. Lacon.*, VII 279

Lives, II 267*n*, 268*n*, 269*n*, 270*n*; X 203, 243; *Agesilaus*, VIII 504; *Alexander*, VII 30, 36, 40, 45, 60, 265, 445; VIII 235; *Antony*, VIII 59; *Aratus*, VIII 477; *Caesar*, IX 452; *Cato*, III.i 163*n*; VI 114, 115*n*; *Cicero*, X 362; *Coriolanus*, X 153–4; *Lycurgus*, VII 43–4, 56; *Numa*, III.i 58*n*; *Pelopidas*, VIII 184; *Pompey*, VIII 467; *Solon*, III.i 112*n*; IX 33; X 44, 47; *Sylla*, VII 178; *Themistocles*, IX 246; *Theseus*, VII 158; IX 237, 315, 425

Morals, III.i 55*n*, 61*n*, 76*n*, 77*n*, 80*n*, 83*n*, 99*n*, 102*n*, 103*n*, 110*n*, 117*n*, 118*n*; *Of the Face in the Moon*, VIII 493; *Of Knowing a Flatterer from a Friend*, VII 346–7; *Opin. of Philos.*, VIII 175; *Orat. de fort. Alex.*, VII 154, 193, 203; *Praec. gerendae reipub.*, IX 371; *Quaest. conviv.* (or *Symposiacs*), VII 35, 150, 221, 287, 446, 447; IX 100–1, 133, 144, 191, 210,

223, 247; X 102, 104; *Reg. et imp. apothegmata*, VII 57, 454; *Sept. sap. conviv.*, VII 35; VIII 112; IX 284–5; X 260

Pluto, in AP poem, V 185, 335

Po, in AP poems, I 67, 170 and *n*

Poet finish'd in Prose, III.i xx *n*

Poitiers, in AP poem, IV 287

Poland, in AP poems, III.ii 103; IV 38; The Succession, IV 38*n*

Pole, William, II 383 ff.

Politian, Angelus, *Praefatio in Homerum*, VII 43, 78, 136; *Ambra*, VII 31; IX xiv

Poll, in AP poem, II 134, 197

Pollio, Biog., V 452; in AP poems, I 112; V 376*n*, 377, 380 f.; VI 204

Pollux, Julius (scholar, rhetorician, 2nd c. AD), IX 311

Polybius (historian, 3rd/2nd c. BC), VII 180–1, 237; IX 308, 337, 339, 437

Polybus, in AP poem, I 413 and *n*

Polynices, in AP poem, I 428

Polypheme, in AP poems, V 334; VI 216

Polyphemus, in AP poem, I 365–6

Pomfret, Henrietta Louisa (Jeffreys) Fermor, Countess of, II 274*n*; VI 384*n*, 389*n*

Pomfret, John (poet), II 148*n*, 184*n*, 201*n*, 294, 321*n*, 343*n*; III.i 37*n*, 53*n*, 136*n*; IV 99*n*, 228*n*

Pomona, in AP poems, I 151, 377, 381

Poole, Benjamin (lawyer), VI 411*n*

POPE, ALEXANDER

Chronological tables, I xviii–xxi; II xii–xv; III.i lxxxi–lxxxiv; III.ii lix–lxii; IV xlv–xlvii; V xlix–lii; VII xxv–xxviii; in his own poems, IV 97, 255, 279; VI

40, 108, 116, 117, 118, 135, 140, 173, 180, 196, 211, 232, 242, 255, 294, 302, 369, 392, 397; portraits, VII xii; VIII xii, xiii; IX xii; X xii, xiii

I: Notes on his own works. Dispersed under works below where notes occur

II: His poetical art, v f., 302; epigrammatic concentration, 235 ff.; experiments in "forms", vi; poetic diction, vi, 358; "imitation", vi, 10; vocabulary, 241 f., 296*n*; views on seventeenth-century French romances, 36*n*; views on typography, x; his learning, 231–5 (see also Homer trans. below); defends allegory, 220 ff., 251 f., 410

III.i: See *Essay on Man* below

III.ii: His distinction between satire and libel, xxxix f., xliv; interest in philosophical theories, xx ff., 106*n*, 153*n* (see also *E. on Man* below); theory of ruling passions, xxi, xxxv, xxxvii, 30, 67, 106; his concept of virtue, xl–xlii; political views, xli f.; his Overlooked Revisions of his text, lii ff., 5, 40, 76, 129 f.; interest in pictorial arts, 48*n*, 49*n*, 58*n*

IV: View of satire, xxi, 11, 19 and *n*, 95, 109, 116 and *n*, 217, 307, 313*n*, 314–15, 325–7; political sympathies and activities, xxxvi–xli, 10*n*; in his own poems, expressing moral ends of poetry, 14*n*, 15–17, 120 and *n*, 309, 318–19, 324, expressing character of the Poet, 18*n*, 19, 65 and *n*, 114, 120, 273, 317–18, and his "lively Eye", 104, 270*n*, 271, 283 and *n*; *Nil admirari*, 27,

236n, 237; contrasts his earlier and later poetry, 106, 120; plans a dictionary of standard English usage, 177n, 372, 379
V: Views of his contemporaries on his life and writings, 11 f., 23 ff., 207 ff., 231 ff., notes to Dunciad A and B passim
VI: Autograph manuscripts, xiii, xiv, xvii f., 4n, 38n, 40n, 52n, 61n, 74n, 111n, 124n, 127n, 144n, 159n, 174n, 183n, 194n, 195n, 197n, 198n, 200n, 201n, 214n, 228n, 231n, 235n, 236n, 240n, 243n, 246n, 249n, 256n, 258n, 298n, 316n, 319n, 332n, 337n, 339n, 342n, 355n, 359n, 360n, 363n, 390n, 397n, 404n, 405n; his dogs, 52n, 366–72; AP in his own poems, 196, 333, 380; his will, 213n, 376n

WORKS:
The following references include prose works. Attributed works are in brackets. The titles are strictly alphabetized, but cross references are given for names and parts of poem titles.
Achilles. See Prologue to
Acis and Galatea. See Lines from
Addison. See Prologue to Mr Addison's Tragedy; To Mr Addison, Occasioned by his Dialogues on Medals
Adriani Morientis ad Animam, VI 91–5
Alcander, I 8n, 263n; IV xxix; VII xxxv. See also Lines from
Alley. See English Poets, Imitations of, Spenser
Andover. See On Mr James Moore's pretty Verses
[Answer to an Epigram], VI 450, 451n

Answer to Mrs Howe, VI 201–2
[An Answer to What is Love], VI 448
Arbuthnot. See Epistle to Dr; Mr P— to Dr A—T
Argus, VI 51–2; VII cxii
Argyle. See In behalf of Mr Southerne; To His Grace the Duke of
Arrival of Ulysses in Ithaca, I 158n, 167n, 331, 463–74; VII xxxvi, cxi
Artimesia. See English Poets, Imitations of, Dorset
Art of Sinking. See Lines from; Peri Bathous
Atterbury. See Epitaph. For Dr Francis; Translations of
Atticus, VI 98n, 137n, 141n, 142–3, 144–5n, 235n. For longer version, see Fragment of a Satire
Augustus. See Horace, Imitations of, Ep. II i
Autumn. See Pastorals
Balance of Europe, VI 82
[Ballad. Nelly], VI 447
[Basset-Table], VI 416
Bathurst. See Epistles to Several Persons, Ep. III; Lines to Lord
Beggar's Opera. See Songs from
Belinda. See To Belinda
Bethel. See Horace, Imitations of, Sat. II ii
Blount. See Epistle to Miss Blount, on her leaving the Town; Epistle to Miss Blount, with the Works of Voiture; Inscription; To Mrs. M. B. on her Birth-day
Boethius. See From Boetius
Boileau. See Epigram. Occasion'd by Ozell's Translation of Boileau's Lutrin; Verbatim from
Bolingbroke. See Horace, Imitations of, Ep. I i; Lines to
Bononcini. See Epigram on the Feuds

Bounce to Fop, VI 366–71

Brutus; unwritten epic, III.i xii; VI 193*n*. See *Diana's Answer to*; *Fragment of Brutus an Epic*; *The Prayer of*; *Two Chorus's to the Tragedy of*

Buckingham. See *Epitaph. On Edmund Duke of*; *Occasion'd by some Verses of his Grace the Duke of*

Buckingham, John Sheffield, 1st Duke of, AP ed. of his *Works*. See references under Buckingham.

Buckinghamshire. See *The Character of Katharine, late Duchess of*

Budgell. See *To Eustace*

Burlington. See *Epistles to Several Persons, Ep. IV*; *On the Countess of*; *On a Picture of Queen Caroline*; *To the Earl of*

Canticle, VI 308, 310*n*

Capon's Tale, VI xiv, 256–7, 258*n*

Captives. See *Epilogue to*

Caroline. See *On a Picture of Queen*; *On Queen Caroline's Death-bed*

Caryll. See *Epitaph on John Lord*

Cato. See *Epigram. On Cato*; *On a Lady who P—st at the Tragedy of*; *Prologue to Mr Addison's Tragedy of*

Catullus. See *Fourth Ode of*

[*Catullus. Ad Peninsulam Sirmionem*], VI 417

[*Celia*], VI 462

Chalfont. See *Sonnet written upon occasion of the Plague*

Challenge (1735 title). See *The Court Ballad*

A Character [Marlborough], VI 358–9

[*Character of Katharine, late Duchess of Buckinghamshire*], III.ii 59*n*, 61*n*, 166

Characters. See *Macer, Umbra, Atticus*

Characters of Men. See *Epistles to Several Persons, Ep. I*

Characters of Women. See *Epistles to Several Persons, Ep. II*

Chaucer, AP trans. of, discussed, II 4–12; dated, II 5; AP method in modernizing, II 8–12; AP imitation of, VI 41–2, 405; other ref., I 329, 352–3, 361; *January and May*, (text) II 13–24; ref. to, I 18*n*, 41, 352; II xi, 4*n* ff; VI 24, 109*n*

Wife of Bath Her Prologue, (text) II 55–78; ref., I 358; II xi, 4*n* ff., 189*n*; VI 24

See also *English Poets, Imitations of*; *Temple of Fame*

Chorus of Youths and Virgins. See *Two Chorus's to the Tragedy of Brutus*

Cibber. See *Epigram on Cibber's declaration*; *Epigrams occasioned by Cibber's verses*

Cleland. See *To Mr C*

Cleopatra. See *On the Statue of*

Cloe: a character, III.ii 42; VI 377

Cobham. See *Epistles to Several Persons, Ep. I*

Coningsby. See *Epitaphs from the Latin*

Corbet. See *Epitaph. On Mrs*

Correspondence (where recipient is identified, entry occurs under that name), VII cxcii *n*, cxcvi *n*, cciii *n*; VIII 390, 461; IX xii, xiv

[*Cosmelia*], VI 438, 439*n*

Couplet from Horace. See *Horace, Couplet from*

Couplet on his Grotto, VI 392, 394*n*

[*Couplet. On Sappho*], VI 409

Couplets and Versicles, 1708–10, VI 74; 1711–20, VI 228; 1721–30, VI 306; 1731–40, VI 390

Couplets on Wit, VI 234–5

Court Ballad, III.ii 174; VI xiii,
xviii, 180–4, 465n
Cowley. See English Poets, Imitations
of; Fourth Ode of Catullus; Verses in
imitation of
Cowper. See Verses to Mrs Judith
Craggs. See Epistle to James;
Epitaph on
Critical Specimen. See Lines from
Cromwell. See An Epistle to Henry;
Letter to
Crux-Easton Epigrams, VI 353–4
Cuckold. See Two or Three
Curll. See Full and True Account of;
Lines on
[Dawley Farm], VI xiv, 452–5
Dennis. See Prologue for the benefit of
A Dialogue, VI 211
[Dialogue on a Birth-Day in October],
VI 461
Dialogues on Medals. See To Mr
Addison
[Diana's Answer to Brutus], VI 421
Digby. See Epitaph on the monument of
Dignity, Use and Abuse of Glass-
Bottles, II 188n; V 432, 445; VI
131n
Discourse on Pastoral Poetry, I xii,
xvi, 7n, 23–33, 37, 38, 43, 48, 51,
53, 100; AP notes to, I 23n–31n
Discovery, VI 259–64, 446n
Donne, Imitations of, ref., IV xli–
xliii; Satire II, (text) IV 129–45;
ref., III.i 82n; III.ii 51n, 91n,
102n; V 375n; VI 17n, 361; VII
ccxxviii and n; Satire IV (The
Impertinent), (text) IV 23–49; ref.,
III.i xv n; III.ii 24n; IV 24; V
71n, 117n, 126n, 130n, 142n,
144n, 147n, 344n; VI 105n, 279n,
354
Dorset. See English Poets, Imitations
of; Epitaph. On Charles Earl of
H

Drew. See Epitaphs on John Hewet
and Sarah Drew
Dryden. See Epitaph designed for Mr
Dryden's Monument
Dryope. See The Fable of
Duke upon Duke, III.ii 172n; VI
217–24
Dulness. See Lines on
Dunciad (1728), its origin, V ix ff.,
201–2n; publication, V xvii ff.;
effect on the Dunces, V xxii ff.;
Keys to the poem, V xxiii f.; as
mock-epic, V xxxvii f.; AP debt
to predecessors, V xxxviii ff.
Dunciad Variorum (1729), authorship, V xxiv ff.; publication, V
xxvii f., 460 ff.; annotation, V
xxiv ff., xl; (text, Dunciad A) V
57–245; ref., I v, vi, viii, 4n, 114n,
121n, 179n, 188n, 249n, 263n,
269n, 285n, 318n, 322n, 360n; II
xiv, xv, 151n, 161n, 186n, 187n,
209n, 239, 284n, 393, 401, 411,
414; III.i xii, xv n, xxvii, lxviii n,
lxxviii, 13n, 16n, 33n, 39n, 43n,
68n, 72n, 79n, 87n, 164n; III.ii
17n, 87n, 91n, 135n; VI 17n, 55n,
116n, 180n, 205n, 207n, 234n,
274n, 279n, 281n, 292n–5n,
299n, 300n, 303n–5n, 309n,
310n, 330n, 331n, 344n, 345n,
363n, 371n, 380n, 385n, 386n,
393n, 394n, 397n, 401n, 402n;
VII xviii, xix, xxvii, xxviii, xliv,
ccxxxv, ccxl and n, ccxlvi,
ccxlvii; X 501, 502, 503, 505, 512
New Dunciad (1742), its origin, V
xxx f.; Warburton's share in it,
V xxx f.; its obscurity, V xxxi f.;
other ref., V xxix ff., 248 f., 410 f.,
418n
Dunciad in Four Books (1743), its
new hero, V xxxiii ff.; altera-

tions in the text, V xxxvi f.;
Warburton's contributions, V
xxxvii, 249, 254 ff.; (text,
Dunciad B), V 247-426; other
ref., V xxxii ff., 248 ff., 412 ff.;
X 501, 504, 505, 510, 511
Durastanti. See *Signora Durastanti*
Durfy. See *Prologue Design'd for*;
Verses Occasion'd by an &c.
Dying Christian to his Soul, VI 94-5
Elegy [earlier *Verses*] *to the Memory
of an Unfortunate Lady*, (text) II
361-8; ref., II xi, 313*n*, 351-9;
III.i 26*n*; IV 111*n*; VI 69*n*, 192*n*,
311*n*; VII xxvi, ccxxxviii–
ccxxxix, ccxlvi, ccxlviii; X 502,
503, 505, 510, 511
Eloisa to Abelard, (text) II 317-49;
ref., I 156*n*, 177*n*, 279*n*, 343, 346,
432*n*; II x, xi, 293-315, 364*n*,
368*n*, 411-16; III.i lxviii *n*,
lxxviii, 26*n*; V 28; VI 69*n*, 192*n*,
279*n*, 281*n*, 311*n*, 394*n*; VII
xxvi; X 501, 503, 505, 510, 511,
512, 600
English Poets, Imitations of, VI 8*n*,
13*n*, 19*n*
Chaucer, II 10; VI 41-2
Cowley. *The Garden*, I 70*n*; III.ii
146*n*; VI 47-8
E. of Dorset. *Artimesia*, III.ii 51*n*;
VI 48-9, 265*n*; *Phryne*, VI 49-51,
164*n*
Spenser. *The Alley*, III.ii 29*n*; VI
43-5
Swift, VI 111*n*
Waller. *On a Fan*, VI 45-7
*Epigram. Engraved on the collar of a
dog which I gave to his Royal High-
ness*, VI 372; VII ccxlii and *n*
Epigram from the French, VI 347-8
*Epigram, in a Maid of Honour's
Prayer-Book*, VI 264, 265*n*

[*Epigram* "Lo! Surrey's Lord"], VI
462
*Epigram. Occasion'd by Ozell's Trans-
lation of Boileau's Lutrin*, VI 37-8
Epigram on Authors and Booksellers,
VI 75
Epigram on the Balance of Europe, VI
82
Epigram. On Bishop Hough, VI 399,
400*n*
[*Epigram. On Cato*], VI 304*n*, 410
[*Epigram on Celia*], VI 443-4
*Epigram on Cibber's Declaration that he
will have the Last Word with Mr
Pope*, VI 397-8
[*Epigram on the Feuds between Handel
and Bononcini*], VI 447
Epigram. On Laureates, VI 402
Epigram. On lopping trees in his garden,
VI 385-6
*Epigram. On One who made long Epi-
taphs*, VI 363-4
Epigram. On Poets, VI 75
*Epigram. On seeing the Ladies at Crux-
Easton*, VI 353-4
[*Epigram. On some snow melting in a
lady's breast*], VI 413
*Epigram. On the Toasts of the Kit-Kat
Club*, VI 177
[*Epigram Papal. On the Female
Canticle*], VI 446
Epigram "Peter complains", VI
348-9
Epigram. The Translator, V 450
Epigram "When other Ladies",
III.ii 69*n*; VI 316-17
*Epigram. Wrote by Mr P in a Volume
of Evelyn on Coins*, III.ii 182*n*; VI
340-1
Epigram "You beat your Pate", VI
348
Epigrams from The Dunciad, VI 235*n*,
298-305, 325*n*

Epigrams from The Grub-Street Journal, VI 324–33

[*Epigrams from The Grub-Street Journal*. 1730–1], VI 450

Epigrams occasioned by Cibber's verses in praise of Nash, VI 85n, 360–1

Epigrams, Occasion'd by An Invitation to Court, VI 185–8

Epigrams on Shakespear's Monument, VI 395–7

[*Epilogue to The Captives*], VI 438

Epilogue to Jane Shore, VI 105n, 113–15

Epilogue to the Satires, Dialogue i, (text) IV 295–309; *Dialogue ii*, (text) IV 311–27; ref., I 117n; II xv, 281n; III.i xii, 154n; III.ii 24n, 29n, 51n, 87n, 88n, 99n, 100n, 102n, 138n, 174; IV xxxvi, xxxix; V 148n, 312n, 404n, 428, 440 f.; V 148n, 312n, 404n, 428, 440 f.; VI 235n, 275n, 365n, 375, 379n, 380n, 392n, 394n, 400n; VII xxviii, ccxxxii and n, ccxxxiii and n, ccxxxv and n, ccxxxix, ccxlvii, ccxlix; X 511

Episode of Sarpedon, I 160n, 186n, 282n, 292n, 331, 352, 353, 356n, 358, 447–62; II 199n; VII xxxv and n, cxi, cxxvii, cxxxvi

Epistle to Addison. See To Mr Addison

Epistle to Augustus. See Horace, Imitations of, Ep. II i

Epistle to Bathurst. See Epistles to Several Persons, Ep. III

Epistle to Burlington. See Epistles to Several Persons, Ep. IV

Epistle to Cobham. See Epistles to Several Persons, Ep. I

Epistle to Dr Arbuthnot, (text) IV 91–127; ref. I vi, 117n, 287n, 469n; II xiv, 37n, 81n, 104n, 160n, 215n, 240n, 241, 364n, 401; III.ii 29n, 138n, 151n, 172, 178n; IV xxi–xxiv, xxxix; V 18n, 64n, 71n, 72n, 126n, 129n, 149n, 258n, 292n, 340n, 350n, 366n, 372n, 392n, 416n, 432, 445; VI 144n, 145n, 166n, 285n, 330n, 333n, 339n, 357n, 361, 371n, 380n; VII xxvii, xxxviii, clvii and n, ccxxxii and n, ccxlvii; X 502, 510

Epistle to Henry Cromwell, Esq, VI 24–9, 265n, 292n, 446n

Epistle to James Craggs, Esq; Secretary of State, VI 209–10, 211n

Epistle to Jervas. See Epistle to Mr Jervas

Epistle to a Lady. See Epistles to Several Persons, Ep. II

Epistle to Miss Blount, on her leaving the Town, after the Coronation, VI 124–6, 191n; *Lines suppressed at the end of*, VI 232–3

Epistle to Miss Blount, with the Works of Voiture, I 311n; II 190n, 365n; VI 62–5, 191n

Epistle to Mr Jervas, with Dryden's Translation of Fresnoy's Art of Painting, (text) VI 156–8; ref., I 265n; II 238n, 375; III.ii 58n; VI 72n, 81n, 82n, 109n, 159–60n, 205n, 207n, 281n, 455n; X 512

Epistle to Robert Earl of Oxford, and Earl Mortimer, II xiii, 368n; VI 238–42; VII xxvi, ccxlvi and n

Epistles to Several Persons (Moral Essays), relation to AP ethical programme, III.i xi–xii; preparation of definitive edition with Warburton, III.ii ix f.; "death-bed" issue destroyed by Bolingbroke, III.ii x ff.; title "Moral Essays" fabricated by Warburton, III.ii xiv f.; rela-

tionship to *E. on Man*, III.ii xvi
ff.; process of composition, III.ii
xx ff.; AP theory of the ruling
passion, III.ii xxi, xxxv, xxxvii,
30, 67, 106; satire "in the Horatian way", III.ii xxxvii ff.; satire
and libel, III.ii xxxix f., xliv;
social basis, III.ii xli f.; factual
satire and type-names, III.ii
xliii ff.; textual problems, III.ii
xlix ff.; Overlooked Revisions,
III.ii lii f., 5, 40, 76, 129 f.; spelling, punctuation, etc., III.ii liv
f.; apparently false rhymes, III.ii
19*n*, 28*n*, 35*n*, 56*n*, 58*n*, 67*n*, 147*n*;
minor poems partly incorporated
in, III.ii 38*n*, 42, 51*n*, 54*n*, 67*n*,
70*n*, 146*n*; other ref., I v, vi; II
xiv, 12, 57*n*, 158*n*, 189*n*, 192*n*,
193*n*, 200*n*, 209*n*, 241, 363*n*, 383;
III.i xiv, lxxviii, 41*n*, 80*n*, 130*n*,
132*n*, 154*n*; V 98*n*, 153*n*, 343*n*,
384*n*, 402*n*, 452

Identification of satiric characters, III.ii: Adonis, 91; Ar-
cadia's Countess, 48; Atossa, xii
ff., 59, 159–70; Babo, 139*n*;
Bubo, 138; Calista, 52; Catius,
25; Clodio, 30*n*; Cloe, 63; the
Cottas, 108; Courtine, 24*n*;
Curio, 108*n*, 135*n*; Euclio, 37;
Fannia, 49; Flavia, 51*n*; Fulvia,
96; Harpax, 97; Hellno, 35, 57;
Hippia, 96; Lesbia, 102*n*; Manly,
24; Narcissa, 36, 54; Orsini, 169;
Papillia, 53; Pastora, 49; Patri-
tio, 26; Philomedé, 57; Phryne,
101; Rufa, 50; Sabinus, 146;
Sappho, 51, 102; Scoto, 28;
Shylock, 23, 97, 137*n*; Silia, 52;
Simplicius, 52; Sir Balaam, 121;
Sir Morgan, 90; Sir Visto, 137;
Timon, 146; Umbra, 24; Uxorio,
91; Vatia, xxvi *n*; Villario, 145;
Virro, 137; Worldly, 90

Epistle I (*To Cobham. Of the Characters of Men*), (text) III.ii 15–38;
connection with *E. on Man*, III.ii
xx ff., xxxiv f.; type-characters
and contemporary originals,
III. ii xlvi; before publication,
III.ii xx f., xxxiv; publication,
III.ii 4; Warburton's interference
with text, III.ii 6 ff.; other ref.,
III.ii 24*n*; VI 344*n*, 357; VII
xxvii, ccxxxv and *n*

Epistle II (*To a Lady. Of the Characters of Women*), (text) III.ii 46–
80; process of composition, III.ii
xxxv ff.; publication, III.ii 40;
the scandalous characters, III.ii
40 ff.; textual problems, III.ii 40
ff. For Atossa, see above, identification of satiric characters.
Other ref., III.i lxxi; VI 72*n*,
247*n*, 265*n*, 287–8*n*, 308*n*, 317*n*,
361, 377*n*, 404*n*; VII xxvii, ccxli
and *n*

Epistle III (*To Bathurst. Of the Use
of Riches*), III.ii (text) 81–125;
before publication, xxi f., xxxii
ff., 35*n*; connection with *E. on
Man*, xxiii f.; AP meticulous
work over composition, xxxiv;
publication, 76; real and ficti-
tious names, xlv f.; Warburton's
interference with text, 76 ff.;
autograph MSS, xxxii f, 4*n*, 89*n*,
96*n*, 97*n*, 107*n*, 133; other ref., I
vi; VI 349; VII xxvii, clvii and *n*,
ccxxviii and *n*, ccxxix and *n*,
ccxxxv

Epistle IV (*To Burlington. Of
Taste*), (text) III.ii 131–56; mis-
interpretation of, III.i xv, xvi,
xxix *n*; links with *E. on Man*,

III.ii xxi ff.; embryonic "Gardening Poem", III.ii, xxiv f.; project of prefixing to Burlington's Palladio sketches, III.ii xxv; publication, III.ii 128; Timon mistaken for Chandos, III.ii xxvi ff., xliv, 146 ff., 170–4; AP unpublished retort *A Master Key to Popery*, III.ii 175–88; textual problems, III.ii 128 ff.; MSS, III.ii xxiv *n*, xxxi *n*, 129*n*, 144*n*, 171*n*; Richardson's variant readings, III.ii xxxi *n*, 4*n*; other ref., I 177*n*; VI 48*n*, 281*n*, 334, 338*n*, 339*n*, 365*n*, 393*n*; VII xxvii, ccxxix and *n*, ccxlvii

[*Epitaph* "As she was once"], VI 447

Epitaph designed for Mr Dryden's Monument, VI 209*n*, 237, 238*n*

Epitaph. For Dr Francis Atterbury, III.ii 38*n*; VI 343–5

Epitaph. For One who would not be buried in Westminster Abbey, VI 376

[*Epitaph. From the Latin in St Botolph's, Aldersgate*], VI 449

Epitaph intended for Mr Rowe, VI 208–9

Epitaph. Intended for Sir Isaac Newton, VI 317, 318*n*, 344*n*

Epitaph. Of By-Words, VI 346–7

Epitaph. On Charles Earl of Dorset, VI 334–6

Epitaph. On Edmund Duke of Buckingham, II 268*n*; VI 362–3

Epitaph. On G——, VI 295–7, 346*n*

Epitaph. On General Henry Withers, VI 320–1

Epitaph. On Himself, VI 386, 387*n*

Epitaph on the Honble Simon Harcourt, VI 242, 243–4*n*

Epitaph on James Craggs, Esq; in Westminster-Abbey, VI 281–3

Epitaph. On John Knight, VI 364–5

Epitaph on John Lord Caryll, III.i 56*n*; VI 81, 160*n*, 170*n*

Epitaph on Lady Kneller, VI 249

Epitaph on the monument of the Honble Robert Digby, and of his sister Mary, III.i 138*n*; VI 313–14, 315–16*n*, 329*n*

Epitaph. On Mr Elijah Fenton, VI 318, 319*n*

Epitaph. On Mr Gay, VI 349–52

Epitaph. On Mr Rowe, VI 170*n*, 209*n*, 400, 401*n*

Epitaph. On Mrs Corbet, VI 322–4

Epitaph on P. P. Clerk of the Parish, VI 233, 234*n*

Epitaph on Sir Godfrey Kneller, VI 312–13

Epitaph. On Sir William Trumbull, VI 81*n*, 169, 170*n*, 335*n*, 401*n*

[*Epitaph* "See here, nice Death"], VI 460

[*Epitaph* "When purer Skies"], VI 447

Epitaphs from the Latin on the Count of Mirandula, VI 297–8; *Lord Coningsby's Epitaph*, III.ii 124*n*; VI 297; *Applied to F. C.*, VI 297

Epitaphs on John Hewet and Sarah Drew, III.i 99*n*; VI 197–201

Erinna, III.ii 70*n*

Essay on Criticism, (text) I 233–326; AP notes to, I 197, 240*n*, 241*n*, 250*n*, 252*n*, 254*n*, 256*n*, 261*n*, 265*n*, 266*n*, 272*n*, 275*n*, 276*n*, 278*n*, 283*n*, 289*n*, 294*n*, 301*n*, 306*n*, 309*n*, 310*n*, 312*n*, 314*n*, 316*n*, 317*n*, 320*n*, 323*n*; other ref., I xiv, xv, xvi, 3*n*, 5*n*, 6*n*, 7*n*, 9*n*, 19, 72*n*, 81*n*, 93*n*, 100, 107, 131*n*, 164*n*, 173*n*, 336, 340–2, 395*n*, 418*n*, 458*n*, 482–3, 484–6; II xii, 85, 92*n*, 215*n*, 245, 271*n*, 287*n*,

289n, 343n, 349n, 363n; III.i xix, lxxi, 70n, 89n, 117n, 124n, 155n; III.ii 65n, 70n; V 8n, 12n, 17–18n, 25 ff., 68n, 84n, 117n, 157n, 164n, 172n, 359n, 366n, 439; VI 40, 68n, 106n, 235n, 275n, 279n, 281n, 292n, 393n, 455n; VII xxv, xlvi–xlvii, cxliv; X xii, 504

Essay on Man, (text) III.i 1–166
History of the poem, place in scheme, III.i xi f; composition dated, III.i xii ff.; anonymous publication, III.i xv; authorship guessed, III.i xv n; highly praised, III.i xv f; esteemed abroad as a "system", III.i xli; translated, III.i xli n; AP thinks of continuing, IV xli, 327 and n
Problem of orthodoxy, III.i: not at first seriously questioned, xvii f.; vouched for by Silhouette and Jesuits, xviii; later questioned by Jesuits, xviii, by Crousaz, xix ff., by Louis Racine, xxii; defended by Warburton, xxi f
AP letter to Racine, III.i xxii
Problem of intention, III.i: address to the Saviour, xxiii; inscription on the Morgan MS, xxiv; testimony of Lyttelton, Chesterfield, J. Richardson the younger, xxiv f; duality of the age and the poet, xxv–xxvi
Philosophical content, III.i: influence of Leibniz, xxvi, xli n, of Shaftesbury, xxvii f., of King, xxviii f., of Bolingbroke, xxix ff.; traditional theodicy, xxxii ff.; traditional ethics, xxxv ff., ruling passions, xxxvi f.; ambivalent view of passions, xxxvii ff., of man, xxxix f.; traditional social and political theory, xxxix; mis-

interpreted as a "system", xli; limitations as a philosophical argument, xlii; common criticisms of its thought: unoriginal, xliii, fails to solve problem of evil, xliv, cheerless, xlv, incompatible with ethics, xlvi
Content as a poem, III.i: favourite structural patterns of the Renaissance, xlvii ff., reflected in the *Essay*: order, liv–lvii, violation, lvii–lx, restoration, lx–lxiii
Relation to Augustan concerns, III.i: the Fall-theme conceptualized, lxiii–lxv; transcendent order asserted, lxv–lxvii; new facts and values normalized, lxvii–lxx; permanently relevant in theme, lxx–lxxii
Distinctive qualities, III.i: magnitude of subject, lxxii–lxxiv; limitations in the handling, lxxiii–lxxiv; a public and classical poem, lxxiv–lxxvii; compared with Donne, lxxiv, with Wordsworth, lxxv–lxxvii, with *Religio Laici*, lxxviii–lxxx; a poem of abstractions, lxxvii ff.
MSS, III.i xiv, xxiv, 11n, 41n, 69n, 83n
AP notes to, III.i 11n, 14n, 17n, 23n, 25n, 29n, 31n, 36n, 37n, 41n, 44n, 46n, 47n, 49n, 53n, 62n, 66n, 71n, 74n, 76n, 78n, 81n, 83n, 85n, 90n, 92n, 95n, 98n, 99n, 102n, 103n, 105n, 107n, 110n, 111n, 113n, 114n, 116n, 120n, 121n, 128n, 130n, 132n, 134n, 135n, 137n, 143n, 147n, 149n, 152n, 157n, 160n
Other ref., I v, vi, vii, 172n, 264n, 293n, 317n; II xiv, xv, 211n, 265n, 284n, 287n, 288n, 324n,

327n, 411; III.ii xvi n, xvii, xxi, xxiii, 17n, 27n, 28n, 67n, 84n, 106n, 107n, 133, 164; V 18n, 43n, 258, 316n f., 386n, 388n f., 392n, 429, 435, 443; VI 74n, 82n, 109n, 149n, 305n, 352, 357, 358–9, 371n, 393n, 394n, 455n; VII xxvii, xxviii, lxxi, ccxi and n, ccxii and n, ccxiv–ccxvi, ccxviii n, ccxxvi, ccxxxv and n, ccxxxvi and n, ccxli and n, ccxlvi; X 502, 510, 511, 512

[*Esther. An Oratorio*]. See *Haman and Mordecai*

Evelyn. See *Epigram. Wrote by Mr P*

[*Extempore Distich*], VI 442

Fable of Dryope, I 163n, 331, 338–9, 383–90, 294n, 401n, 404n, 439n; X 504

Fable of Vertumnus and Pomona, I 375–82; VI 91

Fan. See *Lines from*

Farewell to London. In the year 1715, VI 128–32; VIII xii

Fatis agimur. See *Lines "Fatis agimur"*

First Book of Statius His Thebais, (text) I 405–46; Thebais in AP poem, I 409; AP notes to, I 413n, 417n, 422n, 426n; other ref., I xvi, 64n, 184n, 296n, 329, 331, 340, 341, 346–52, 353, 359, 387n, 400n; II 208n, 210n, 258n, 411; III.i 43n, 129n; VI 60, 70n, 109n; X 503

Fortescue. See *Horace, Imitations of, Sat. II i*

Four Poems from A Key to the Lock, VI 132–6

[*Fourth Epistle of the First Book of Horace's*], VI 459

[*Fourth Ode of Catullus. Paraphras'd in the manner of Cowley*], VI 417

Fragment of Brutus an Epic, VI 404–5

Fragment of a Satire (longer version of *Atticus*), VI 283–6

[*Friendship*], VI 462

From Boetius, de cons. Philos., VI 73–4; X 502

[*From Claudian: On a Globe of Crystal containing Water in it*], VI 418

Full and True Account of Mr Edmund Curll, V 74n, 105n, 112n, 118n, 119n, 429, 433, 450; VI 236n

Further Account, V 429, 433, 451

Garden. See *English Poets, Imitations of*, Cowley

[*Garden of Eden*], VI 459

Gardens of Alcinous, I 331; VI 103–4; VII xxxvi, cxi

Gay. See *Epitaph. On G—*; *Epitaph. on Mr*; *To Mr*

George II. See *Lines to King*

God's Revenge against Punning, VI 136n

Grotto. See *Couplet on his*; *Verses on a*

Grub-Street Journal. See *Epigrams from*

Guardian, No. 40, (text) V 222–9; ref., I 18, 20, 42, 46, 48n, 78n, 93n, 101n, 275n; V 24n, 68n, 200, 451; VI 113n; No. 61, III.i 24n, 29n, 108n, 109n, 163n; No. 78, I 251n; No. 173, III.ii 141n, 149n; VI 104n; VII xxxvi, cxi, ccxxiv n

Gulliver's Travels. See *Verses on*

[*Haman and Mordecai* (later *Esther. An Oratorio*)], V 348n, 442; VI 423–35; X 503

Handel. See *Epigram on the Feuds*

Happy Life of a Country Parson, VI 110–11

Harcourt. See *Epitaph on the Honble Simon*

Harvey. See *On Miss*

Hatton. See *Lines on Mr*

Hervey. See *To Ld Hervey & Lady Mary Wortley*

Hewet. See *Epitaphs on John*

Homer, AP trans., VII: AP learning, and knowledge of Greek, xxxv–xxxvi and *n*, xlii, lxxxi and *n*, lxxxiii–lxxxv and *n*, lxxxviii, lxxxix, cxiii *n*; motives for translating, xlii, xlvi, l; AP on imagination and judgement, xlvi–xlvii; AP awareness of "pastness" of poetry, xlix; characteristic of age, l and *n*, li–lii, lxxviii, lxxxix–xci, xcvii, contrasted with Romantic, ciii–civ; pictorialism, liii–lvi; generalizing process, lvi–lix and *n*; reflects range of Western literary culture, lviii–lxii; interplay of the directly observed and the formulaic, lx–lxii, lxviii; elements AP could not render, lxii; use of heroic couplets, lxii–lxiv and *n*, lxx, cxii, cxxvi, cxxviii, cxxix, cxxxvi, cxxxviii–cxxxix, cliv; the Homeric hexameter, lxiii; trans. of Homer's "fire", lxiv; of rhythm, lxv–lxvii; of epithets, lxvii–lxviii, xciii; its virtues, lxvii–lxviii, lxx, ciii, cliii–cliv, cix, clxi, clxii, clxiii, cxcii–cxciii, and errors, lxxxv, lxxxviii and *n*, cxiv; AP life related to, VII lxx–lxxi, ccxxi–ccxxii; VIII xii; IX xii; opinion of Homer, VII lxxvi, lxxxix, xciii *n*, cvi, clvii, ccxxii–ccxxiii, and response, clxiv, to Homeric firmness of design, clxv, economy, clxvi–clxviii and *n*, extensive complexity, clxix, coherent complexity, clxx, characterization, clxx–clxxii and *n*, inner assessment of force and action, clxxii–clxxiii, as work of art, clxxiv, and AP concept of the whole and responsibility to the original, clxxvi–clxxix; Thersites episode, lxxxvii and *n*, lxxxix *n*; method of making English poetry out of Greek, xci–xcii; the Homeric similes, xcvi–c, clxxiv–clxxvi, clxxxvii, and AP response to, clxv–clxvi, clxxi–clxxii; characterization (in trans.), civ; touchstone for choice of words, cvii; rendering of Homeric implications, ci–ciii; AP ideas of translation, civ–cv, and commitment to, clxxxiv, clxxxv; audience for, cvii; tenseness and organization of verse, clviii; mitigates French modernist charges, cxxxv *n*; as interpreter of Homer, clxxxvii–clxxxviii; treatment of Zeus as deity, clxxxviii–cxci; commitment to human order, cxci–cxcii, and conception of the good society, ccxxxiii; difference from Homer in terms of moral relations, ccv; AP Axylus, ccxxvi–ccxxvii, ccxxix; use of Homeric allusion, ccxxxiv, epic vocabulary, ccxxxv–ccxxxvi, character and event, ccxxxvi–ccxxxvii, ccxxxix, ccxl, in poems written after Homer trans., ccxxxix–ccxlv; use of epic formulas, attitudes, situations, ccxlv–ccxlviii; the epic hero related to satire, ccxlviii–ccxlix

Other ref., I v, 103, 318*n*, 352–60, 465–74; V 40, 41, 76*n*, 112*n*, 146*n*, 233, 279*n*, 432, 444, 449, 451; VI 132*n*

Predecessors, VII: general parallels, xv *n*, cxii; ed. read by AP, lxxvii *n*; debt to Mme Dacier, lxxix; use of and contrast with Parnell, lxxxii; rivalry with other translators, cviii; list of English trans., cix–cxi; debt to Milton and Dryden, cxxix–cxxxiii and *n*, cxxxv–cxxxvi; AP trans. compared to Dryden passage, cxxxvii, and to *Iliad* original, cxxxvii *n*; reaction against Dryden's *Iliad*, cxli–cxlii, compared to Congreve, cxl–cxli; AP works within a tradition, clxii; debt to Tooke, cxliv–cxlv, cxlviii, cxlix–cl, clii, clv; debt to Chapman, cxvii, and criticism of, cxviii *n*; AP early reading of Ogilby, cxviii, and trans. compared with, cxxi; debt to Hobbes, cxxii, cxxiii; AP rejects burlesque tradition, cxxv–cxxvi; other use and comparisons, xciv and *n*, xcv, xcvii and *n*, cviii and *n*, cix, cxii–cxiv, cxv, cxxxviii, clvi and *n*, clix, ccxv, ccxxv

AP notes, VII xviii and *n*, xix, xxxix and *n*, xl *n*, xli *n*, lxxii, lxxx *n*, xc–xci, c–ci (see also ref. for Zimmermann, H.-J.)

MSS and revisions, VII xviii–xx, xli and *n*, clxxvi; of collaborators' work, cxxii *n*, in *Odyssey*, cxciv–cxcv, the MS leaf, cxcvi–cci and *n*; AP and collaborators share Augustan values, ccx

Iliad and *Odyssey* compared or contrasted: VII: AP on imagination and judgement (Preface to *Iliad* and Postscript to *Odyssey*), xlvii–xlix; styles, lx; Achilles and Odysseus, lxi and *n*; use of pre-

decessors in each, cxii–cxiii; comparative worth, cxciv; number of similes, clxxiv–clxxv; the Homeric works, clxxxvi–clxxxvii, ccv–ccviii; the Augustan trans., ccxxxi, ccxxxiv; the illustrations, IX xii, xiii; parallels, X 501

Iliad, AP trans., VII clxiv–cxciii; cited *passim* in VII, Introduction; related to *Dunciad*, V 81*n*, 100*n*, 103*n*, 107*n*, 355*n* Proof pp. illus., VII xii–xiv; text used, xvi; first proposals for trans., xxv; publication, VI 132*n*, 135*n*, 136, 137*n*, 160, 188*n*, 189, 194, 217; VII xxvi–xxvii, cxliii; boyhood trans., xxxv and *n*; announcement of forthcoming trans., xxxvi and *n*; AP comments on his trans., xxxvii *n*, xxxix; his editorial method, xli; financial profits, xlii and *n*, xliv and *n*; X xiii; Catalogue of Ships, VII xli *n*, ccxli; attacked by Mme Dacier, xliii–xliv; AP on Achilles' shield, l; Essay on Battles, l, ccv *n*; the aural complexity, lxiv–lxv; norms of discourse in, lxviii–lxx; impossible to "Christianize", lxxii; AP view of in epic tradition, lxxvi; Parnell's help in, lxxxi; accuracy of AP Greek in notes, lxxxiv; attacked by Dennis, lxxxvi; influence of predecessors, cxxvi–cxxvii; variation on Homeric theme, cxxix; AP similes compared to *PL*, cxxxiv–cxxxv

AP Preface, I 222, 314*n*, 335*n*, 359; II 270*n*, 271*n*, 398; VII ccxxxiii *n*, ccxxxiv, ccxxxvi; X xiv; text, VII 1–25; MS text, X 409–44, mentioned, 445–6

Texts and editions of AP trans., VII ccl and *n*, ccli *n*
Engraving of Shield of Achilles illus., VIII xii; MS leaf with AP sketch of Shield illus., VIII xiii; the book in Kneller's portraits, VIII xiii–xiv; IX xii; Lintot ed. illus. reproduced, VIII xiv; anon. designs for, IX xiii–xiv; title page of quarto illus., IX xiv
Mentioned in AP Postscript, X 453; proofs of folio, 469; AP proof corrections in quarto, 469–73; AP holograph leaf, 474; tabulation of AP indebtedness to earlier translators, 492–506, 512–86; parallels to *Odyssey* trans., 509–10; early printings, 587–93; ref. to in Spence's *Essay*, 595–6; Spence on, 603; AP agreement with Lintot for trans., 606
References to in the notes to the *Odyssey*, IX 25–6, 28–9, 31, 35, 38, 43–4, 54, 58, 60, 66, 69, 79, 82–5, 87–8, 91, 94, 98, 101, 109–10, 114–15, 118–19, 125, 127–8, 131, 137, 141, 152, 154, 157, 191–2, 197, 205, 210, 221, 223, 232, 239–40, 259, 265–6, 268, 270, 275–6, 283, 290–1, 297, 304, 327, 333, 371, 394–5, 410, 412, 414–16, 418, 428, 451, 457; X 19, 27, 32, 35, 38, 53, 58–9, 63, 75, 84, 101–2, 105–6, 113, 115, 148–9, 158, 168–9, 176, 186–7, 191, 198, 201, 205, 211, 219, 233, 261, 266–7, 275, 278, 282, 286, 298–9, 302, 305, 308–9, 324, 334, 338–9, 346, 349, 351–3, 360–1, 366, 374, 378, 382–6, 389, 391–3, 395–6
Other ref., I 74*n*, 134, 154*n*, 162*n*, 181*n*, 186*n*, 222, 244*n*, 314*n*, 331, 354, 359, 386*n*, 397*n*, 422*n*, 430*n*, 467*n*; II xiii, 104*n*, 127*n*, 146*n*, 147*n*, 153*n*, 154*n*, 158*n*, 162*n*–8*n*, 170*n*, 171*n*, 173*n*–7*n*, 180*n*, 182*n*, 187*n*, 188*n*, 190*n*–2*n*, 195*n*, 196*n*, 199*n*, 200*n*, 202*n*, 203*n*, 206*n*–8*n*, 212*n*, 277*n*, 287*n*, 322*n*, 362*n*, 366–8*n*, 392, 398; III.i 14*n*, 17*n*, 28*n*, 35*n*, 67*n*, 75*n*, 80*n*, 95*n*, 103*n*, 118*n*, 129*n*, 135*n*, 165*n*; III.ii 85*n*, 150*n*, 173; IV 169*n*, 239*n*; V 28 ff., 81*n*, 103*n*, 107*n*, 111*n*, 122–3*n*, 191*n*, 193*n*, 207, 355*n*, 368*n*, 445, 470; VI 68*n*, 70*n*, 71*n*, 74*n*, 109*n*, 117*n*, 135*n*, 136, 137*n*, 160, 188*n*, 189*n*, 191*n*, 194, 217*n*, 227*n*, 231*n*, 235*n*, 240*n*, 435*n*; VII lviii *n*, lxxi, lxxvii, lxxxv
Odyssey, AP trans. discussed, VII cxciii–ccxxi; cited *passim* in VII Introduction
Text used, VII xvi; publication, VI 248; VII xxvii; proof corrections, xxxviii *n*; AP announcement of subscription for, xliii; AP collaborators, xliii, xliv, ccviii–ccix (see also Broome; Fenton); division of returns from, xliv–xlv, and payment for, xlvi and *n*; Postscript, xliv, lviii *n*, lx, ccxx–ccxxi and *n*; procedures in translating, l; Augustan feasts in, liii and *n*; sententiae in, lvi and *n*; norms of discourse, lxviii; AP trans., ccii–cciii, fits style to hierarchic levels, cciii and *n*, cciv; the Augustan Odysseus, ccxi–ccxviii; relations of culture and power in, ccxxxiii; first p. *Odyssey IV* with revisions illus., IX xii; head and tail pieces illus., IX xiii; MS pp. with revisions illus., IX xii; X xii–xiii

Compared with *Aeneid*, VII 15; on Chapman's trans., VII 21; ref. to in the notes to the *Iliad*, VII 84, 125, 271, 323, 353; VIII 39, 157, 194, 196, 248, 264, 265, 316, 327, 344, 374, 493, 578; AP trans. editorially quoted, VII 85; VIII 265, 374, 493

Postscript, I 268*n*, 359; MS text, X 445–6; tabulation of AP indebtedness to earlier translators, X 492–5, 506–12; collaboration with Broome, X 575; indenture for printing, X 589; Spence's *Essay* on, and AP annotations, X 594–605

Other ref., I 117*n*, 331, 350, 359, 386*n*, 473*n*; II xiv, 147*n*, 154*n*, 161*n*, 175*n*, 178*n*, 190*n*, 195*n*, 196*n*, 200*n*, 207*n*, 277*n*, 332*n*, 366*n*, 367*n*, 381*n*; III.i 32*n*, 35*n*, 55*n*, 158*n*; IV 67*n*; V 31, 32*n*, 76*n*, 98*n*, 112*n*, 133*n*, 191*n*, 431; VI 68*n*, 109*n*, 227*n*, 248; VII lxxvi–lxxvii, clviii; X 509. See also in AP Works, *Argus*; *Arrival of Ulysses in Ithaca*; *Episode of Sarpedon*; *Gardens of Alcinous*

Horace, Couplet from, VI 391, 394*n*

Horace. [*The Fourth Epistle of the First Book of Horace's Epistles*], VI 459

Horace, Imitations of, IV: origin, xiii; relation to *Moral Essays*, xiii–xiv, 4*n*, 7*n*, 8*n*; early attempts at "imitation", xxix; other ref., I v, vi, xvi; II 241; III.ii xl f.; VI 292*n*, 393*n*, 401*n*

Epistle I i (to Bolingbroke), (text) IV 275–93; ref., II xv; III.ii 52*n*, 140*n*; VI 265*n*, 279*n*, 375, 455*n*; VII xxviii, ccxxxvi and *n*

Epistle I vi (to Murray), (text) IV 233–46; ref., I 284*n*; II xv; III.i 50*n*, 146*n*, 149*n*; III.ii 173; V 376*n*, 392*n*; VI 371*n*, 375; VII xxviii, ccxxxii and *n*

Epistle I vii (in the manner of Swift), (text) IV 265–73; ref., II 104*n*; VI 376; X 598

Epistle II i (to Augustus), (text) IV 189–231; ref., I 324*n*; II xv, 8*n*, 9*n*, 147*n*, 230; III.ii 34*n*, 36*n*, 102*n*, 138*n*, 156*n*; V 283*n*, 317*n*, 322*n*, 361*n*, 446, 465; VI 279*n*, 286*n*, 365*n*, 401*n*; VII xxviii, ccxxxii and *n*, ccxxxv, ccxxxix–ccxl and *n*, ccxlix; X 506, 510

Epistle II ii, (text) IV 161–87; ref., I 276*n*, 281*n*, 303*n*; II xv, 268*n*; III.i 71*n*, 74*n*; III.ii 90*n*; V 129*n*, 175*n*, 371*n*, 400*n*, 402*n*; VII xxviii, xxxv, ccx *n*, ccxx *n*; X 502

Ode IV i (to Venus), (text) IV 147–53; ref., VI 372

Ode IV ix, (text) IV 155–9; ref., VI 373; VII ccxxxiii *n*

Satire II i (to Fortescue), (text) IV 1–21; ref., I 318*n*; II xiv; III.i xv *n*, lxviii *n*; III.ii 51*n*, 66*n*, 97*n*, 102*n*, 121*n*, 131*n*, 145*n*, 176; V 189*n*, 407*n*; VI 196*n*, 349, 454*n*; VII xxvii, clvii and *n*, ccxxix–ccxxx, ccxxxii and *n*, ccxxxv and *n*, ccxlii and *n*, ccxlvii, ccxlix

Satire II ii (to Bethel), (text) IV 51–69; ref., I 187*n*, 188*n*; II xiv; III.i 92*n*, 109*n*; III.ii 89*n*, 90*n*, 102*n*, 156*n*, 164; V 402*n*; VI 359; VII xxvii, ccxxviii and *n*; X 511

Satire II vi, (text) IV 247–63; ref., VI 375

Sober Advice from Horace (*Serm. I i*), (text) IV 71–89; ref., II xiv;

III.ii 34n, 36n, 83n; IV xxiv–xxv;
V 402n; VI 361, 392n; VII xxvii,
xlii n
  See also *Epilogue to the Satires*
Horace, Lines from, VI 390, 392n;
  Horace III iv, Lines from, VI 233
Horace, Satyr 4. Lib. 1. Paraphrased,
  VI 338–40
Hough. See *Epigram. On Bishop*
Howe. See *Answer to Mrs*
Hymn of St Francis Xavier, VI 77, 78n
Hymn Written in Windsor Forest, VI
  xiii, 194
Imitation of Martial. See *Martial,
  Imitation of*
Imitation of Tibullus. See *Tibullus,
  Imitation of*
Imitations of Donne. See *Donne, Imita-
  tions of*
Imitations of English Poets. See *Eng-
  lish Poets, Imitations of*
Imitations of Horace. See *Horace,
  Imitations of*
Impertinent. See *Donne, Imitations of,
  Sat. IV*
Impromptu, To Lady Winchelsea, VI
  120–2
*In behalf of Mr Southerne. To the Duke
  of Argyle*, VI 214–15
[*In her own Isle the Goddess lay*], VI
  417
Inscriptio, VI 307, 309n
Inscription. Martha Blount; *A:P:*, VI
  231
Inscription "Nymph of the Grot",
  VI 248–9
*Inscription on a Grotto of Shells at
  Crux-Easton*, VI 353
Inscription upon a Punch-Bowl, VI
  224–5
Jane Gray. See *Prologue to Lady*
Jane Shore. See *Epilogue to*
January and May. See Chaucer

Jervas. See *Epistle to Mr*
Key to the Lock, II xiii, 89n, 102n,
  104, 119n, 378; VI 131n, 132n;
  Four Poems from, VI 132–6
[*King's Box to Aurelia*], VI 417
Kit-Kat Club. See *Epigram. On the
  Toasts of the*
Kneller. See *Epitaph on Lady*; *Epi-
  taph on Sir Godfrey*; *To Sir Godfrey*
Knight. See *Epitaph. On John*
Lady Jane Gray. See *Prologue to*
[*Lady M. Wortley's Resolve Imitated*],
  VI 439
[*Letter from the world to come*], VI 458
Letter to Cromwell, VI 39–40, 446n
Letter to a Noble Lord, III.ii xxxii; IV
  xv, xvi n, xx, 4n, 117n, 118n
Lines, added to Wycherley's poems, VI
  53–60
Lines "Fatis Agimur", VI 75
Lines from Acis and Galatea, VI 215–
  17, 433n, 435n; X 503
*Lines from Alcander and the Early
  Poems*, VI 20–3
Lines from The Art of Sinking, VI 288
[*Lines from The Art of Sinking*], VI
  413
Lines from The Critical Specimen, VI
  79, 80n, 357n
Lines from The Fan, VI 411
Lines from Horace. See *Horace, Lines
  from*
Lines from The Shepherd's Week, VI
  412
Lines in Conclusion of a Satire, VI 307,
  309n
Lines "My Pylades", VI 76
Lines on Bounce, VI 405
Lines on Coffee, VI 229
Lines on Curll, VI 236
Lines on Dulness, VI 53
Lines on his Birthday, IV 13n; VI
  247n

Lines on Ministers, VI 391, 393*n*

Lines on Mr Hatton's Clocks, VI 237

Lines on Swift's Ancestors, VI 251–2

Lines on Writing a Tragedy, VI 230

Lines to Bolingbroke, VI 307, 308*n*

Lines to a Friend. Written at his Mother's bedside, VI 333–4

Lines to King George II, VI 392, 394*n*

Lines to Lord Bathurst, VI 195–6

Lines suppressed. See *Epistle to Miss Blount, on her leaving the Town*

[*Lines* "Why shine thine Eyes"], VI 460

Lintot. See *Verses to be prefix'd*

London. See *A Farewell to*

[*The Looking-Glass*], VI 419–20

[*A Love Song In the Modern Taste*], VI 457

[*Lydia, Imitated from the Lyric of Cornelius Gallus*], VI 417

Macer, VI 137–8, 139*n*, 141*n*

Malherbe. See *Stanza's. From the french of*

Marlborough. See *A Character*; *Upon the Duke of*; *Verses upon the late D—ss of*

Martial, Imitation of, Book 10, Epig. 23, VI 166–7

Master Key to Popery, III. ii xxx ff., 29*n*, 175 ff.; IV xix, 4*n*

Memoirs of Martinus Scriblerus, II 146*n*; III.i 69*n*; V 343*n*, 445; VI 115*n*, 197*n*, 207*n*

[*Memoriae Sacrum D. M. T., E. B., & L. P.*], VI 457

Messiah, (text) I 109–22; introduction, I 99–107; AP notes to, I 113*n*–22*n*; other ref., I 9*n*, 28*n*, 63*n*, 77*n*, 88*n*, 143, 192*n*, 264*n*, 337*n*; II 145*n*; V 66*n*, 177*n*; VI 71*n*, 91; VII xxv; X 501, 510, 511, 512

Miscellaneous Thoughts, III.i 89*n*, 159*n*

Miscellanies. See *Poems from*

Miscellanies, 1732. See *Poems from*

Miscellanies (Pope–Swift), IV xvi, 108*n*; V xv and *n*, 108*n*, 110*n*; VI (1727) xiii, 258*n*; (1732) xiii, 291*n*, 345–6*n*; (1742) 346*n*, 400*n*; VII xxvii, cxii

Miscellany, Lintot's (ed. AP). See Lintot, Barnaby Bernard

[*Molly Mog*], VI 371*n*, 443

[*The Monster of Ragusa*], VI 418

Montagu. See *Lady M. Wortley's Resolve Imitated*; *On Lady Mary Wortley Montagu's portrait*; *To Ld Hervey & Lady Mary Wortley*; *To Lady Mary Wortley*

Moore. See *On Mr James Moore's . . .*; *To Mr John*

Moral Essays. See *Epistles to Several Persons*

Mortimer. See *Epistle to Robert Earl of Oxford, and Earl*

[*Mr P— to Dr A—t*], VI 444–6

Murray. See *Horace, Imitations of, Ep. I vi*

Narrative of Dr Robert Norris, I 243*n*, 306*n*; II 286*n*; V 72*n*, 82*n*, 437

Nash. See *Epigrams occasioned by Cibber's verses in praise of*

[*News from Court*], VI 421

Newton. See *Epitaph. Intended for*

[*Nightingale*], VI 441

Norris. See *Narrative of Dr Robert*

Nostradamus. See *A Prophecy of*

Occasion'd by some Verses of his Grace the Duke of Buckingham, VI 188–9

[*Ode for Musick on the Longitude*], VI 415, 451*n*

Ode for Musick on St Cecilia's Day, (text) VI 29–36; ref., II 245,

363n; VI 40n, 68n, 106n, 189n;
X 500-1, 505, 509, 510
[An Ode for the New Year], VI 458
[Ode on Science], VI 460
Ode on Solitude, I 171n; VI 3-5
Of the Characters of Women. See
Epistles to Several Persons, Ep. II
Of her Picture, VI 9
Of her Sickness, VI 10
Of her Sighing, VI 11
Of her walking in a Garden after a
Shower, VI 10-11
Of a Lady Singing to her Lute, VI 7-8
Of the Lady who could not sleep in a
stormy Night, VI 9
Of Taste. See Epistles to Several Per-
sons, Ep. IV
Of the Use of Riches. See Epistles to
Several Persons, Ep. III
[The Old Gentry], VI 420
On the Benefactions in the late Frost,
1740, VI 389
[On the bridge at Blenheim], VI 461
On a certain Lady at Court, VI 250-1
On the Countess of Burlington cutting
Paper, VI 336-8
On Dr Alured Clarke, VI 391, 393-4n
On Lady Mary Wortley Montagu's
Portrait, VI 211-12
On a Lady who P—st at the Tragedy of
Cato, VI 99
On lying in the Earl of Rochester's Bed
at Atterbury, VI 380-2
[On Miss Harvey, being a Day old],
VI 441, 442n
[On Mr James Moore's pretty Verses
on the Birth-day of the Lord
Andover], VI 451-2
[On Mrs Tofts], VI 413
[On an Old Gate Brought from Chelsea
to Chiswick], VI 459
[On a Picture of Mrs Catherine L—],
VI 420

On a Picture of Queen Caroline drawn
by Lady Burlington, VI 390, 393n
On Queen Caroline's Death-bed, VI
390, 392n
On receiving from the Right Hon. the
Lady Frances Shirley a Standish and
two Pens, VI xiv, 378-80
[On the River Danube], VI 420
On Silence, VI 17-19, 463-4
On the Statue of Cleopatra, made into a
Fountain by Leo the Tenth, I 73n,
319n; II 268n; VI 66-9, 72n; X
506
One Thousand Seven Hundred and
Forty, (text) IV 329-37; ref.,
III.ii 24n, 102n; IV xli; V 147n,
376n; VI 386n
Orrery. See Tom Southerne's Birth-
day Dinner at
Ovid, AP trans., I xvi, 329, 331,
332-46, 352; AP use of Addi-
son's trans., II 191n; of Dryden's,
I 153n, 160n, 166n, 167n, 168n,
169n, 184n, 268n; II 162n, 254n;
V 144n, 288n; of C. Hopkins's, I
279n; of Sandys's, I 44, 151n,
160n, 166n, 167n, 347, 439n; II
167n, 183n, 191n, 192n, 203n,
208n; III.i 95n. See Fable of
Dryope; Polyphemus and Acis;
Sapho to Phaon; Story of Arethusa;
Vertumnus and Pomona
Oxford. See Epistle to Robert Earl
of; To the Right Honourable the
Earl of
Ozell's Translation. See Epigram.
Occasion'd by
[Palaemon, a Pastoral], I 402n; VI
417
Paraphrase on Thomas a Kempis, VI
5-7
Parnell, Thomas, Poems (ed. AP).
See Parnell, Part of the Ninth Ode

of Horace. See *Horace, Imitations of*, under *Ode*

[*Parson's Daughter*], VI 421

Pastorals, (text) I: *Autumn*, 80–7; *Spring*, 59–70; *Summer*, 71–9; *Winter*, 88–95; AP notes to, I 59n–66n, 68n–76n, 78n–80n, 83n–6n, 88n–91n, 93n–5n; other ref., I xii, xvi, xvii, 9n, 13, 14, 17, 37 ff., 100, 105, 126–8, 130, 148n, 151n, 156n, 158n, 160n–2n, 176n, 194n, 207, 279n, 322n, 324n, 331, 352, 353, 436n, 477–82; II xii, 14, 181n, 252n, 259n; VI 8n, 14n, 24, 69n, 217n, 455n; VII xxv, cxxvii; X 503, 509

Peri Bathous, or The Art of Sinking in Poetry, I 251n; II 127n, 209n; III.i 13n; V xv f., xxi n, xxxiii; cited 71n, 72n, 146n, 148n, 166n, 201, 202, 277n, 358n, 378n, 391n, 431, 434 f., 437 ff., 441, 444, 450 f., 456 f.; VI 20n, 115n, 288–9, 292n, 452n; VII xliv, cxcv, cxcvi. See also *Lines from The Art of Sinking*

Phryne. See *English Poets, Imitations of*, Dorset

Pigott. See *Presentation Verses to Nathaniel*

Plays, VI 85

Poems from Miscellanies, The Third Volume (1732), VI 345

Poems on Several Occasions (ed. AP), I 9n; VI xiii, 8, 68n; VII cxii

Polyphemus and Acis, I 331, 332, 336, 338, 346, 363–73

Pope. See *Epigram. Wrote by Mr P*; *Miscellanies*, Pope–Swift; *Mr P— to Dr A—t*; *To Mr Pope*; *To Mr Pope on his Translation of Homer*

Prayer of Brutus, VI 192–3

Preface of 1717, (text) I 1–10; ref., I xii, xvi, 130n, 293n

Presentation Verses to Nathaniel Pigott, VI 255–6

Presenting a Lark, VI 13–14

[*Prologue to Achilles*], VI 457

Prologue Design'd for Mr Durfy's last Play, VI 76n, 101–2

Prologue for the benefit of Mr Dennis, VI 355–7

[*Prologue to Lady Jane Gray*], VI 415

Prologue to Mr Addison's Tragedy of Cato, VI 68n, 96–8, 145n, 180n, 311n; VII xxv

Prologue to Sophonisba, VI 98n, 310–11

Prologue to The Three Hours after Marriage, V 167n; VI 178–80

[*Prophecy of Nostradamus*], VI 411

Psalm I. See *A Roman Catholic Version*

Psalm XCI, I 120n; VI 69–71; X 501, 503

Pylades. See *Lines "My Pylades"*

[*Question by Anonymous*], VI 450, 451n

[*Quidnuncki's*], VI 438

[*Ramble*], VI 415

Rape of the Lock, (text) II 144–212; II: AP debt to Caryll, 81–3; dated, 83–7; threatened by Sir Plume, 88; indecencies censured, 90n; substitution of mottoes, 91n; difficulty with the dedication, 93 f.; presentation copies, 96 ff., 140n; expansion, 102 f.; popularity, 104 f.; changes between the two versions, 123 f.; dedicatory letter to Arabella Fermor, 142 f.; Belinda as mock-heroic Homeric, 396

Rape of the Locke, (text) II 125–37; ref., II 83 ff., 243, 362n

Other ref., I 9n, 63n, 94n, 131,
320n, 450n, 471n; II xi, 57n, 70n,
79 ff., 240, 243, 244, 253n, 282n,
286n, 288n, 298, 308n, 315, 362n,
365n, 371 ff., 408; III.ii 36n, 52n,
72n–4n, 105n; V xxxvii, xli, 18n,
80n, 293n, 450; VI 71n, 91, 107,
108–9, 132n, 189n, 191n, 227n,
229n, 237n, 281n, 435n; VII xxv,
xxxvi n, xlvi, lviii, cxxvii, cxxviii,
cxxix, clvii and n, ccxxxv,
ccxxxvii, ccxlii and n, ccxliii,
ccxliv and n, ccxlv, ccxlvi; X 500,
501, 502, 503, 504, 505, 506, 509,
510, 511
Receipt to make a Cuckold. See Two or
Three, on
Receipt to make Soup. For the use of
Dean Swift, VI 253–5
Receit to make an Epick Poem, II 103
River, VI 14–15
Rochester. See On lying in the Earl of
Rochester's bed
Roman Catholic Version of the First
Psalm, VI xiii, 164–5, 166n, 292n
Rondeau, VI 61
Rowe. See Epitaph intended for Mr;
Epitaph. On Mr
[Roxana], VI 416
St Cecilia's Day. See Ode for Musick on
Sandys's Ghost, (text), VI 170–6;
ref., I 287n; IV 112n; VI xiv,
205n, 330n; X 502, 504
Sapho to Phaon, (text) I 391–404;
ref., I xii, xvi, 169n, 331, 348,
386n, 428n; II 272n, 293n, 338n,
343n; V 71n, 432; VI 29, 279n;
X 502, 504
Sarpedon. See Episode of Sarpedon
Satires of Donne Versifyed. See Donne,
Imitations of
Scriblerian. See Verses in the Scrib-
lerian Manner; Verses in the Scrib-

lerian Manner. To the R^t Honble the
Earl of Oxford
Serm. I ii. See Horace, Imitations of;
Sober Advice from Horace
Shakespeare, AP ed. of, see Shake-
speare entry. See also Epigrams
on Shakespear's monument
Shepherd's Week. See Lines from
Shirley. See On receiving from the
Right Hon. the Lady Frances
[Signora Durastanti's Cantata], VI
440
Silence. See On Silence; Upon
Silence
Six Maidens, VI xiii, 341–3
Sober Advice from Horace. See Horace,
Imitations of
[Song "Say Phoebe, why is Gentle
Love"], VI 461
[Song " 'Twas in this shade"], VI
416
[Song "When thy Beauty appears"],
VI 436–7
[Songs from The Beggar's Opera], VI
448
Sonnet written upon occasion of the
Plague, and found on a glass-
window at Chalfont, VI 373–5
Sophonisba. See Prologue to
Southerne. See In behalf of Mr;
Tom Southerne's Birth-day Dinner
Spenser. See English Poets, Imitations
of
Spring. See Pastorals
Stanza's. From the french of Malherbe,
III.ii 68n; VI 71–2
Statius His Thebais. See The First
Book of
[The Story of Arethusa], I 165n, 168n;
VI 409
Successio. See To the Author of a Poem,
intitled,
Summer. See Pastorals

Swift. See *Horace, Imitations of, Ep. I vii*; *Lines on Swift's Ancestors*; *Miscellanies*; *Receipt to make Soup*; *Verses on Gulliver's Travels*

Sylvia, a fragment, III.ii 54*n*, 67*n*; VI 286–7

Temple of Fame, (text) II 249–89; treatment of *Hous of Fame*, II 215, 220–7, 403–10; *Temple of Fame* dated, II 242 ff., 285*n*; presentation copies, II 245*n*; AP reply to Dennis's *Remarks*, II 392 ff.; other ref., I 172*n*, 257*n*, 293*n*, 296*n*, 418*n*; II xi, 4*n*, 5*n*, 84*n*, 147*n*, 157*n*, 213–47, 326*n*, 331*n*, 333*n*, 367*n*, 379*n*, III.i 149*n*, 164*n*; IV 175*n*, 194*n*, 207*n*, 326*n*; V xvii, 68*n*, 145–6*n*, 152*n*; VI 35*n*, 36*n*, 68*n*, 91, 127, 128*n*, 176*n*, 233*n*; VII xxvi; X 512

Thebais. See *First Book of Statius*

Thomas a Kempis. See *Paraphrase On*

Thoughts on Various Subjects, I 264*n*; III.ii 34*n*, 59*n*, 64*n*, 111*n*; V 365*n*; VI 15*n*

Three Epitaphs on John Hewet and Sarah Drew, VI 197

Three Gentle Shepherds, II 37*n*; VI 112–13

Three Hours after Marriage (with Gay and Arbuthnot), II xiii; IV 37*n*, 223*n*, 344, 377, 380, 393; V 45, 46*n*, 138*n*, 164*n*, 167*n*, 277*n*, 431, 433, 437 f., 445 f.; VII xxvi. See also *Prologue to*

Tibullus, Imitation of, VI 236. See also *To Phoebus*

[*To Aurelia*], VI 417

To the Author of a Poem, intitled, Successio, V 84*n*; VI 15–17, 56*n*

To Belinda on the Rape of the Lock, VI 107–10, 160*n*; X 501, 502

[*To Brunetta*], VI 417

To the Earl of Burlington asking who writ the Libels against him, VI 355

To Eustace Budgell, Esq. on his Translation of the Characters of Theophrastus, VI 123

Tofts. See *On Mrs*

[*To His Grace the Duke of Argyle*], VI 422

To a Lady. See *Epistles to Several Persons, Ep. II*

[*To Lady Mary Wortley Montagu*], VI 423

To a Lady with the Temple of Fame, VI 127, 128*n*

*To L*d *Hervey & Lady Mary Wortley*, VI 357

To the Memory of an Unfortunate Lady. See *Elegy*

To Mr Addison, Occasioned by his Dialogues on Medals, (text) VI 202–7; ref., I 262*n*; III.ii 135*n*; V 159*n*, 378*n*; VI xv, 144 *n*, 159*n*, 282*n*, 465*n*; VII xxvi

To Mr C, VI xvii, 321, 322*n*

To Mr Gay, I 62*n*; VI 225–7; X 510

To Mr John Moore, Author of the celebrated Worm-Powder, VI 141*n*, 161–4

[*To Mr Pope*], VI 455

[*To Mr Pope on his Translation of Homer*], VI 420

To Mrs M. B. on her Birth-day, III.ii 69*n*; VI xviii, 244–6, 247*n*

*Tom Southerne's Birth-day Dinner at L*d *Orrery's*, VI 398–9

[*To Phoebus, Tibullus eleg. IV. lib. iv*], VI 420

To the Right Honourable the Earl of Oxford. Upon a piece of news in Mist, VI 294–5

To Sir Godfrey Kneller, On his painting for me the Statues of Apollo, Venus,

and Hercules, II 237n, 240n; VI
  212–13
To a Young Lady, with the Works of
  Voiture. See Epistle to Miss Blount,
  with the Works of Voiture
[Translations of Atterbury's Lines on
  Himself], VI 456
Trumbull. See Epitaph. On Sir
  William
Two Chorus's to the Tragedy of Brutus
  (including Chorus of Youths and
  Virgins), III.i 34n, 106n; VI 151–
  4, 155n
Two or Three; or A Receipt to make a
  Cuckold, V 450; VI 104–5, 106–
  7n, 115n
Ulysses. See The Arrival of Ulysses in
  Ithaca
Umbra, VI 137n, 140, 141n
Unfortunate Lady. See Elegy to the
  Memory of an
The Universal Prayer, VI 145–8,
  149–50n
[Upon Aurelia's Shooting at a Deer],
  VI 416
[Upon Cleora's Marriage and Retire-
  ment], VI 418
[Upon the Duke of Marlborough's
  House at Woodstock], VI 412
Upon a Girl of Seven Years old, VI
  xviii, 106–7
[Upon the Lady S—d after she was
  dead], VI 418
[Upon the Phenicians, Inventors of
  Letters], VI 418
Upon Silence in Imitation of a Modern
  Poem on Nothing, VI 463
Venus. See Horace, Imitations of,
  Ode IV i
Verbatim from Boileau, VI xiv, 388
Verses in Imitation of Cowley. By a
  Youth of thirteen, VI xiii; Presenting
  a Lark, VI 13; The River, VI 14

Verses in imitation of Waller. By a
  Youth of thirteen: Of the Lady who
  could not sleep in a stormy Night, VI
  9; Of her Picture, VI 9; Of her
  Sickness, VI 10; Of her Sighing, VI
  11; Of her walking in a Garden
  after a Shower, VI 10
Verses in the Scriblerian Manner
  (Scriblerian Imitations), VI 115–20
Verses in the Scriblerian Manner. To
  the Rt Honble the Earl of Oxford, VI
  196–7
Verses Occasion'd by an &c. at the End
  of Mr D'Urfy's Name in the Title
  to one of his Plays, VI 85–90
Verses on a Grotto by the river Thames
  at Twickenham, VI xviii, 382–5;
  VII ccxxiv and n, ccxxvi
Verses on Gulliver's Travels, VI 266
Verses sent to Mrs T. B. with his
  Works, VI 189–92
Verses to be placed under the Picture of
  England's Arch-Poet, VI 290–3
Verses to be prefix'd before Bernard
  Lintot's New Miscellany, VI 82–3,
  84–5n
Verses to the Memory of an Unfortunate
  Lady. See Elegy to
Verses to Mrs Judith Cowper, VI 306,
  308n
Verses upon the late D—ss of M—, VI
  402–4
Vertumnus and Pomona. See The
  Fable of
Waller. See English Poets, Imitations
  of; Verses in Imitation of
Weeping, VI 12–13, 274n
Wife of Bath Her Prologue. See
  Chaucer
Winchelsea. See Impromptu, To
  Lady
Windsor Forest, (text) I 145–94; AP
  notes to, I 148n, 150n, 153n–6n,

158*n*–63*n*, 165*n*, 168*n*, 169*n*, 171*n*, 173*n*–5*n*, 179*n*, 181*n*, 187*n*, 188*n*, 191*n*; other ref., I xvi, 9*n*, 62*n*, 67*n*, 71*n*, 77*n*, 78*n*, 80*n*, 105, 280*n*, 340, 373*n*, 379*n*, 387*n*, 401*n*, 440*n*, 450*n*, 466*n*, 468*n*; II 164*n*, 245, 277*n*, 392; III.i 27*n*, 70*n*; V xvii, 27 f., 63*n*; VI 36*n*, 95, 106*n*, 189*n*, 274*n*, 394*n*, 435; VII xxv, ccxvii, ccxxxvii, ccxlviii; X 501, 503, 504, 505, 506, 509, 511

Winter. See *Pastorals*

Winter Piece, VI 231

Withers. See *Epitaph. On General Henry*

[*Woman convinc'd*], VI 458

Works, VII xxvi; VIII xii; X 587

Written over a Study; out of Maynard, VI 168, 169*n*

Wrote by Mr P. See Epigram. Wrote by Mr P in a Volume of Evelyn on Coins

Wycherley. See *Lines added to Wycherley's Poems*

Xavier. See *Hymn of St Francis*

[*Yarhell's-Kitchen*], VI 410

Pope, Alexander (father of AP), Biog., IV 378; in AP poems, IV 125–6 and *n*, 273 and *n*; other ref., VI 249*n*, 340*n*; VII xxvi

Pope, Editha (mother of AP), Biog., IV 378–9; in AP poems, IV 125–7; other ref., III.i xiv; III.ii xxix *n*; IV xxiii; VII xii, xxvi, xxvii, cxcvii *n*

Pope, J. C., III.i vi

Pope, Walter, II 288*n*; V xl

Popp upon Pope, IV xvi, 120

Popping, Sarah (publisher), V 208

Popple, William, Biog., V 452; in AP poem, V 327

Porphyry (scholar, philosopher, student of religions, 3rd c. AD), VII lxxvi, cii, 64, 72, 173, 340, 426; VIII 290; X 7, 341

Porson, Richard, II 416; IV 323*n* V xxi *n*; VII lxxxviii *n*

Portia, in AP poems, II 47; VI 153

Portland, Dorothy Bentinck, Duchess of, III.ii 169

Portland, Willem Bentinck, 1st Duke of, I 301*n*

Portland Papers, IV 121*n*, 148, 348, 365, 392

Portsmouth, Louise de Perancoët de Kéroualle, Duchess of, I 298*n*

Post, L. A., VII ccv *n*

Post Boy, in AP poem, IV 38*n*, 39; other ref., II 103, 104, 244, 295*n* f.; V 81*n*, 118*n*, 452, 454; VI 163*n*, 174*n*, 446*n*; VII xlii *n*

Post Man, VI 174*n*, 183*n*; VII xxxvi *n*

Potter, John, Archbishop of Canterbury, V 313*n*, 340*n*, 404*n*, 459

Pottle, F. A., III.i vi

Poulett. See Hinton

Poussin, Nicolas, VIII 359

Powell, L. F., VII lxxxviii *n*

Poyntz, Anna Maria. See Mordaunt

Poyntz, Stephen (diplomatist), VI 343*n*

Praz, Mario, VII li *n*

Present State of the Republic of Letters, III.i xvii, xxvii *n*

"Preston" [pseud., anon.], *Aesop at the Bear Garden*, II 220*n*, 284*n*; V 146*n*, 207

Priam, in AP poem, V 289

Priapus, in AP poems, I 387 and *n*; II 36

Price, C. U., II 372

Price, Mary, VII xxiv

Price, Rebecca, III.i xli *n*
Pride, as subject of AP poems, III.ii xliii
Pride and Discontent Silenc'd (anon. poem), III.i 30*n*
Primer [Prymer; or, Lay Folks' Prayer Book], II 119, 148*n*
Prince, Daniel (printer), V xix
Princeton University, VII xv, xxiii
Prior, Sir James, *Life of Malone*, IV 270*n*, 319*n*, 362; V 373*n*
Prior, Matthew, Biog., IV 379; portrait of, I xiv; praises AP in *Alma*, V 28; in AP poems, IV 259; V 110 and *n*, 112, 112–13*n*, 301; VI 26, 29*n*; other ref., II 6; III.ii 112*n*; IV 10*n*, 280*n*; V 41*n*; VI 92*n*, 410*n*, 444*n*; X 56, 510
WORKS:
Carmen Saeculare, II 262*n*, 266*n*, 279*n*; *Charity*, III.i 157*n*, 158*n*; *Essay upon Opinion*, III.i 83*n*; III.ii 16*n*, 17*n*; *Henry and Emma*, II 197*n*, 296*n*, 329*n*, 413–14; V 468; *The Ladle*, III.i 128*n*; *On Exodus*, III.i 60*n*; *Solomon*, III.i 11*n*, 16*n*, 26*n*, 29*n*, 31*n*, 47*n*, 54*n*, 55*n*, 57*n*, 60*n*, 69*n*, 73*n*, 94*n*, 95*n*, 100*n*, 101*n*, 128*n*, 152*n*, 160*n*; other poems, I 283*n*; II 92*n*, 293*n*, 322*n*, 324*n*; III.i 87*n*; III.ii 66*n*; IV 208–9*n*; V 466, 471, 473
Priscian, in AP poem, V 165, 328
Proclus (neo-Platonist), VII 40, 44, 47, 50; VIII 204, 392
Procopius (historian, 6th c. BC), IX 348; X 92
Procris, in AP poem, VI 45, 46
Proculus, in AP poems, II 137, 210
Progress of Dulness, V xvii, xxi f., xxiv *n*, 41*n*, 430

Promethean, in AP poem, VI 289
Prompter (periodical), III.i xvii *n*; III.ii 156*n*; V 327*n*, 335*n*, 445, 452
Propertius, Sextus (poet, 1st c. BC), II 293*n*; V 363*n*; X 163
Proserpine, in AP poems, V 87, 185, 335; VI 33
Prosymna, in AP poem, I 432 and *n*
Protestant Packet (periodical), V 450
Proteus, in AP poems, IV 290*n*, 291; V 111, 272, 301
Prothero, R. E., II 301*n*
Proudfoot, L., VII cviii *n*, cix *n*, cxii–cxiii *n*
Provençal poets, AP opinion of, II 251 f.
Prynne, William (pamphleteer), V 71, 276
Ptolemy (Egyptian dynasty), VII 33, 60
Ptolemy (geographer), VII 179–80; IX 30
Publisher (short-lived periodical), III.i 13*n*, 23*n*, 59*n*
Pulteney, Anna Maria (Gumley), VI 419*n*
Pulteney, Daniel; Biog., IV 379; in AP poem, IV 336 and *n*; other ref., IV xxxi; V 357*n*
Pulteney, William, later 1st Earl of Bath, Biog., IV 380; his politics, IV xxxi–xxxv, 299*n*; as AP collaborator, VI 263*n*; mock epitaph on, VI 283*n*; his *Proper Reply*, IV 119*n*, 339; in AP poems, IV 317 and *n*, 332 and *n*, 333; V 352*n*, 357 and *n*, 393*n*; other ref., III.ii 187*n*; VI 28*n*, 177*n*, 254–5*n*, 263–4*n*, 419*n*
Pylades, in AP poem, VI 76
Pyle, in AP poem, I 470

Q

Quadrille, in AP poems, III.ii 92 and *n*; IV 7 and *n*

Quaintance, Richard, VII xxiii

Quare, Daniel, II 146*n*

Quarles, Francis, in AP poems, IV 227; V 78, 79*n*, 99*n*, 280 and *n*; other ref., III.i 13*n*, 17*n*, 54*n*; V xxxix, xlv, 321*n*

Quarterly Review, VII liii *n*

Queen Mary College, London, VII xv

Queensberry, Catherine Douglas, Duchess of, in AP poem, III.ii 66 and *n*; other ref., VI 296*n*, 351*n*, 443*n*, 444*n*

Queensberry, Charles Douglas, 3rd Duke of, Biog., IV 358; in AP poem, IV 114; other ref., IV 362

Queensberry, James Douglas, 2nd Duke of, VI 296*n*, 351*n*

Querno, Camillo (poetaster), in AP poems, V 97 and *n*, 297 and *n*; in AP *Guardian* paper on pastorals, V 413–14

Quidnunc, in AP poem, V 64, 290

Quillet, Claude, III.i 72*n*, 79*n*

Quin, James, Biog., IV 380; in AP poem, IV 223 and *n*

Quinault, Philippe, II 216*n*

Quintilian, AP reading in, I 201*n*; II 382; III.i 165*n*; in AP poem, I 315 and *n*; AP use of, VII xl; *Instit. orat.*, I 213–15, 231, 241*n*, 248*n*, 250*n*, 256*n*, 260*n*, 261*n*, 266*n*, 269*n*, 272*n*, 274*n*, 275*n*, 278*n*, 309*n*; II 160*n*, 349*n*; III.i 79*n*; VII 77, 83–4, 143, 205–6, 467; IX 206, 384

Quiny, J., II 188*n*

R

Rabelais, François, in AP poems, V 62 and *n*, 270; VI 307, 309*n*; other ref., II 221*n*; IV 31*n*

Racine, Jean, in AP poems, IV 219, 226*n*, 227; *Iphigenia*, a translation, V 91; *Phèdre*, II 192*n*; other ref., I 285*n*; VII li

Racine, Louis, doubts orthodoxy of *E. on Man*, III.i xxii; AP corres., III.i xxii, xxiii

Racket, Mrs Magdalen, V xxii *n*

Radcliffe, Alexander, II 293*n*

Radcliffe, Ann, II 330*n*

Radcliffe, John, Biog., IV 380–1; in AP poem, IV 211

Radicati, A., Count of Passerano, Biog., IV 381; in AP poem, IV 307 and *n*

Radnor, Charles Bodvile Robartes, Earl of, III.ii 108*n*

Radnor, John Robartes, Earl of, VI 386*n*

Rag Fair, V 63*n*

Raleigh, Sir Walter, in AP poems, IV 176–7*n*, 177; other ref., II 346*n*; III.i 11*n*, 114*n*, 132*n*; VII 187; IX 233

Ralph, James, Biog., V 452–3; in AP poems, V xlii, xliv, xlvi, 165 and *n*, 285, 285–6*n*, 328 and *n*; *Sawney*, II 90*n*, 413; V xliv, 28

and *n*, 60*n*, 63*n*, 110*n*, 172*n*, 204*n*, 210; other ref., V xxiii, xxvi, lvi, 311*n*, 430, 469

Ramsay, Allan (poet), IV 197*n*

Ramsay, A. M. (le chevalier de), III.i xxii, 137*n*

Ramus, Peter, I 214–17

Rand, B., *Berkeley and Perceval*, IV 346

Rand, E. K., I 132*n*, 139*n*

Randolph, M. C., I 305*n*

Ransome, John Crowe, VII ccxiii–ccxiv and *n*

Raphael (painter), in AP poems, I 319*n*, 320 and *n*; VI 157, 159*n*; other ref., VI 313*n*; VII lvii; VIII 359, 365–6

Rapin, René, early reading by AP, I 201*n*; AP use of, VII xl
WORKS:
Comparaison d'Homère et de Virgile, VII xc, 16, 83–4, 173; VIII 544, 548; IX 26–7, 36–8, 154, 182, 186, 214–15, 239, 254–5, 261, 300, 333, 418; X 46–7, 87, 166, 194, 285, 306–7, 317, 338, 342, 430–1; *Dissertatio de carmine pastorali*, I 15, 16, 17, 19, 23*n*, 24*n*, 25*n*, 27*n*, 28*n*, 29*n*, 30*n*, 32*n*, 43; *Horti*, III.ii xxiv *n*; *Reflexions sur l'art poétique d'Aristote*, I 26*n*, 30*n*, 210, 211, 239*n*, 248*n*, 249*n*, 255*n*, 256*n*, 258*n*, 259*n*, 269*n*, 273*n*,

315n; X 61; *Whole Critical Works*, I 230n, 285n

Rawlinson, Richard, II 325n, 328n

Rawlinson, Thomas, in AP poem, VI 83, 85n

Ray, John (natural philosopher), III.i 41n, 111n; III.ii 177n; V 387

Raymond, Robert, 1st Baron, V 395n, 453, 459

Raymond, Robert, 2nd Baron, Biog., V 453; in AP poem, V 395

Read, Sir William (quack doctor), VI 136 and n

Read's Weekly Journal, V 116n, 174n, 212n, 454; VI 351n

Rebecca, in AP poems, II 18, 29 and n

Redgrave, S., II viii

Redriff, in AP poem, VI 276

Rees, Ennis, VII lii n

Reeve, Sir Thomas (judge), IV 288n

Regis, P. S. (metaphysician), III.i 22n

Reichard, H. M., II 204n

Religious Ceremonies and Customs . . . of the World, III.i 27n, 28n

Rémond de Saint Mard, Toussaint, IV xvi, 79n; V 112n, 467

Rendcomb House (Glos.), III.ii 172n

Reynard the Fox, in AP poem, IV 287

Reynolds, Henry, I 226–7, 231

Reynolds, Sir James, Lord Chief Baron, IV 393

Reynolds, Sir Joshua, IV 270n

Rhine, in AP poems, I 186, 410; III.i 151; VI 203

Rhodope, in AP poem, VI 34

Rich. See Warwick

Rich, Christopher, I 200

Rich, Elizabeth (Griffith), Lady, VI 182, 184n

Rich, John, Biog., IV 381; V 453; his theatrical devices, V 176n, 177n; in AP poems, IV 306; V 179, 332; other ref., V 178n; VI 395n

Richard, second son of William I, I 157n, 158n

Richard Cœur de Lyon, in AP poem, VI 218

Richard III, in AP poem, IV 19 and n

Richardson, George (cataloguer), III.ii 135n

Richardson, Jonathan (the elder), *Essay on Theory of Painting*, II 185n; portraits, IV 364; portraits of AP, VIII xii; X xii; AP corres., III.i xvi; III.ii 4n; IV xiii, 5n, 16n; VI 374n; other ref., V xliii, 79n

Richardson, Jonathan (the younger), *Richardsonia*, I 223; III.ii 4n, 37n; testimony about AP deism, III.i xxiv–xxv; other ref., I xvi, 13n, 125n, 197, 201, 340; III.ii xxxi n, 35n; V xliii, 60n

Richardson, Samuel, II 11, 305n

Richelieu, Armand Jean du Plessis, duc de, Cardinal, IV 319; V 358

Richings Park (Bucks.), III.ii 142n

Richmond, Frances Theresa Stuart, Duchess of, III.ii 98n

Richmond, in AP poems, VI 44, 264; other ref., VI 317n

Riddell-Blount, E., VI xix

Rider, Dudley, II 104n

Ridpath, George, Biog., V 453; in AP poems, V 118 and n, 184 and n, 285 and n, 302 and n; other ref., V 458

Rieu, E. V., trans. Homer, VII ci *n*, cxvii *n*, cxxii, cxxxv *n*, cxl *n*, cl *n*; trans. *Iliad*, VII clxii; X 579

Rilke, R. M., II 295*n*

Ring, in Hyde Park, in AP poems, II 149; VI 63; other ref., II 193*n*, 399, 400; III.ii 70

Ripa, Cesare, II 227

Ripley, Thomas, Biog., IV 381–2; in AP poems, III.ii 137; IV 211; V 336 and *n*

Ritter, F., II 411

Robartes. See Radnor

Robartes, Russell (Lord Radnor's brother), III.ii 109*n*

Robert, Duke of Normandy [Robert Shorthose], I 157*n*; X 430

Roberts, J. (publisher), V 207–8, 210–12

Robertson, J. M., III.i xlvi

Robethon, John, I 208

Robey, Richard, I xii

Robin, P. A., III.i 72*n*

Robinson, Anastasia (singer), VI 155*n*, 440*n*

Robinson, J. R., *The Princely Chandos*, III.ii 148*n*, 151*n*

Robinson, Nicholas, *New Theory of Physick*, IV 117–18*n*

Robinson, W. H., VI xix, 7

Roboam, in AP poem, VI 290

Robson, R., V 472

Rochester, John Wilmot, 2nd Earl of, AP opinion of, III.ii 31*n*; *A Letter from Artemisa*, I 242*n*, 325*n*; II 42*n*; III.i 147*n*; IV 245, 339; *Satire against Mankind*, II 320*n*; III.i 109*n*; III.ii 20*n*; V 77*n*; other poems, I 291*n*, 315*n*; II 128*n*; IV 201*n*; V 288*n*; VII cxliii; in AP poems, III.ii 31 and *n*; IV 245; VI 380–2; trans. of

Seneca, V 288*n*; AP imitation of, VI 17–19; other ref., I 163*n*, 298*n*; III.i lxvii; IV xxvi; VI 336*n*

Rodrigo, in AP poem, V 87

Rogers, R. W., author of *Major Satires of Pope*, III.i xvi *n*, xxvi *n*; III.ii xxii *n*, 52*n*, 92*n*; V 43*n*, 463

Rogers, S., *Table Talk*, IV 15*n*

Rogerson, Brewster, II 311*n*

Rolle, Margaret, later Baroness Walpole, III.ii 51*n*

Rolli, Paolo Antonio, Biog., V 453; in AP poems, 124 and *n*, 305 and *n*; other ref., V 126*n*, 335*n*, 402*n*

Roman Catholic. See Legislation

Roman[–s], in AP poems, I 323, 411; II 47, 73, 363; IV 197, 203, 297, 317, 335; V 85, 363, 373; VI 66, 96, 204

Romant of the Rose, II 36*n*

Rome, in AP poems, I 185, 254, 268, 311, 319, 324, 411; II 136, 137, 210, 211, 256; III.ii 89, 102, 139; V 78, 91, 97, 158, 280, 285, 290, 297, 324; VI 66, 67, 97, 101, 134, 156, 157, 202, 204; AP conception of, VII ccxxix

Ronsard, Pierre de, V 340*n*

Rooke, Sir George (admiral), V 405*n*

Roome, Edward, Biog., V 453–4; writer of Pasquin papers, V 39, 327*n*; in AP poems, V 137 and *n*, 162, 162–3*n*, 327 and *n*; VI 301, 304*n*; other ref., V xlvi, 24*n*, 134*n*, 209, 212, 281*n*, 435

Root, R. K., *Poetical Career of Alexander Pope*, I 103*n*; II 108*n*, 295*n*; III.ii 147*n*

Roper, Abel, Biog., V 454; in AP poems, V 118 and *n*, 302 and *n*

Rosalinda, in AP poem, I 75

Rosamonda, in AP poems, II 211; III.ii 57

Rosamonda's Lake, II 400

Roscoe, William, ed. of AP, II 224; III.i xxix *n*, xxx *n*, 161*n*; VI 128*n*, 348*n*, 447*n*, 460*n*

Roscommon, Wentworth Dillon, 4th Earl of, in AP poems, I 324 and *n*; IV 212*n*, 213; other ref., I 61*n*, 158*n*, 208, 246*n*, 253*n*, 260*n*, 261*n*, 263*n*, 264*n*, 273*n*, 277*n*, 281*n*, 297*n*, 307*n*, 311*n*, 312*n*, 314*n*, 318*n*; III.i 71*n*, 113*n*, 155*n*; V 27*n*, 135*n*, 136*n*; VII cxliii

Rose, H. J., VII lxxvi *n*

Rosebery, Archibald Primrose, 5th Earl of, *Chatham*, IV 344

Rosenbach, A. S. W., VI xix

Rosenbloom, Charles J., VII xiii; X 474

Ross, Man of, III.ii xxi f., 113 ff.

Rossetti, Dante Gabriel, X 505

Røstvig, Maren-Sofie, I 171*n*

Roubillac, L. F., his bust of AP, VI xii

Rousham House (Oxon.), III.ii 141*n*

Rousseau, J. B. (poet), V 373*n*

Rousseau, Jean Jacques, II 297; III.i xlv *n*

Rowe, Mrs Anne, VI 400

Rowe, Nicholas, Biog., IV 382; his trans. of Lucan, II 178*n*, 357*n*; III.i 32*n*; in AP poems, IV 201 and *n*; VI 25, 29*n*, 37, 38*n*, 128–9, 131*n*, 140 and *n*, 173, 175*n*, 450; AP Epilogue to his *Jane Shore*, VI 113–15 and *n*; AP Prologue to his *Lady Jane Gray*, VI 415*n*; AP epitaphs on, V 236; VI 170*n*, 208–9, 238*n*, 400–1; as AP col-laborator, VI 100*n*; AP ack-nowledgements to, VII 23; X 443; other ref., II 187*n*, 357; III.i 35*n*, 122*n*; III.ii 52*n*; IV xxviii *n*, 370; V xlvii, 45*n*, 81*n*, 105*n*, 207*n*, 433

Rowe, Ruth M., III.i vi

Rowe, Thomas, II 327*n* f.

Royal Exchange, in AP poems, II 129, 170

Royal Magazine, VI 461*n*

Royal Masonic Cyclopaedia, V 399*n*

Royal Society, V 398

Rubens, Peter Paul, VIII 368, 369

Rubicon, in AP poem, III.i 151

Rudder, Samuel, *New History of Gloucestershire*, III.ii 172*n*

Rufa, in AP poems, III.ii 50–1 and *n*; IV 77

Ruffhead, Owen (author of *Life of Pope*), II 356, 393*n*, 414; III.i xxx *n*, 64*n*, 140*n*; III.ii xix *n*, xxxiv, xxxvi, 49*n*, 59*n*, 63*n*; V xxxii *n*; VI 4*n*, 20*n*, 109*n*, 126*n*, 127*n*, 193*n*, 232*n*, 361*n*, 394*n*, 404*n*, 405*n*, 458*n*; VII xxxv *n*

Rufinus, Tyrannius (4th/5th c. AD), VII 64

Rufus. See William II

Ruling passion. See AP entry, under III.ii

Rundle, Thomas, Biog., IV 382; in AP poem, IV 316

Ruskin, John, III.i lxxv

Russel, R. (ed. *Grub-street Journal*), VI 325*n*

Russell ["a Lord R."], in AP poem, IV 244*n*, 245

Russell. See Bedford

Rutland, John Manners, 3rd Duke of, V 371*n*

Ryder, Dudley, VII cvii and *n*

S

Sabaean, in AP poem, I 121 and *n*

Sabin, in AP poem, III.ii 34

Sabinus, in AP poem, III.ii 146 and *n*

Sacheverell, Henry, I 301*n*, 303*n*

Sackville. See Dorset

Sackville, Lord John (son of 1st Duke of Dorset), V 402*n*

St André, Nathaniel (surgeon), in AP poem, VI 260–4*n*

St Anne's Church (London), IV 62*n*

St Augustine, his theodicy, III.i xxxiv, xxxvii, 35*n*; *Confessions*, III.i 47*n*, 48*n*, 56*n*, 61*n*, 125*n*; VII 64; IX 239; *De civ. dei*, III.i 50*n*, 66*n*, 84*n*, 122*n*, 131*n*, 147*n*; *De immort. animae*, III.i 48*n*; *Liber meditationum*, X 149; other ref., I 101

St Botolph's, Aldersgate, in AP poem, VI 449

St Chrysostom, X 55

St-Evremond, Seigneur de, Charles de Marquetel de St-Denis, I 240*n*, 315*n*; II 151*n*, 187*n*, 197*n*, 221*n*, 222*n*, 236*n*, 237, 240, 265*n*, 337*n*, 362*n*; III.i 55*n*, 65*n*, 67*n*; V 397*n*; VII xl, lxxiii, 332; VIII 166; X 115

St Francis Xavier, AP version of his hymn, VI 77

St James's Chronicle, VI 296*n*, 440*n*, 462*n*

St James's Coffee-house, in AP poems, IV 285; VI 172, 175*n*

St James's Evening Post, VI 243*n*, 262*n*, 323*n*, 450, 455*n*

St James's Journal, V 33*n*, 136*n*, 448; VI 136*n*

St James's Magazine, VI 461*n*

St James's Palace (London), in AP poems, III.ii 92, 124; IV 287; V 371, 404; other ref., II 400

St James's Park (London), II 399, 400

St James's Park: A Satyr (anon.), II 373

St James's Post, V 458

St James's Register, VI 458*n*

St Jerome, in AP poem, II 74; other ref., VI 207*n*; VII 64, 259

St John. See Bolingbroke

St John, in AP poem, II 62

St John's Church (Westminster), IV 62*n*

St John's College (Cambridge), in AP poem, V 362 and *n*

St Luke's Church, IV 62*n*

St Margaret's Church (Westminster), IV 63*n*

St Martin-in-the-Fields, IV 62*n*

St Mary-le-Bow Church, in AP poems, II 133, 193; V 183, 333

St Paul, in AP poems, II 58, 59, 60; IV 281 and *n*; VI 110; III.i: parable of body and members,

lvi–lvii, lviii, 123*n*; faith, hope, and charity, lx; other ref., xxiv

St Paul's Cathedral, in AP poems, I 310 and *n*; IV 285

St Peter, in AP poems, IV 297; V 159, 325

St Stephen's Chapel (Westminster), in AP poem, III.ii 124 and *n*

Saintsbury, George, VII cxciv *n*

Salel, Hugues, VII lxxxviii *n*, cx; X 441, 539

Salem, in AP poem, I 120 and *n*

Salisbury, James Cecil, 6th Earl of, V 401

Salisbury, John of, III.i 113*n*

Sallust, V 262*n*; VIII 64; IX 13; X 33

Salomon, in AP poem, VI 290

Samaritan, in AP poem, II 57

Sammes, Aylett, II 264*n*

Samos [–ian], in AP poems, I 425; VI 275

Samson, in AP poem, II 75

Samuel, in AP poem, VI 6

Samuel, Deborah Hobson, VII xxiii

Sandwich, John Montagu, 4th Earl of, V 379*n*, 402*n*, 449 f.

Sandys, George, translator of Ovid, I 44, 122*n*, 151*n*, 160*n*, 166*n*, 167*n*, 331, 332–4, 336–8, 343, 347, 349, 365–73*n*, 377–81*n*, 385–90*n*, 439*n*; II 155*n*, 191*n*, 192*n*, 208*n*, 367*n*; III.i 93*n*; poetic paraphrases of Bible, II 160*n*, 321*n*; III.i 13*n*, 55*n*; AP poem on, VI 170–4, 175*n*; other ref. to him as translator and as author of *Relation of a Journey*, V 379*n*; VII lxxvii *n*, lxxviii *n*, cv *n*; VIII 463; IX 378, 433; X 20

Sandys, Samuel, 1st Baron of

Ombersley, Biog., IV 383; in AP poem, IV 332 and *n*

Sanger, Egbert (bookseller), in AP poem, VI 37, 38*n*

Sannazaro, Jacopo, I 95*n*; II 337*n*; VIII 352

Sanson, Nicolas (map-maker), VII 177

Santayana, George, III.i lxxi–lxxii

Saperton's . . . Dale (Gloucestershire), in AP poem, IV 183 and *n*

Sappho, Greek poetess, references to her life, I 393*n*, 394*n*, 402*n*; AP spelling of, I 339*n*; AP knowledge of, VI 92*n*, 95*n*; in AP poems, II 273; III.ii 51 and *n*, 52, 102 and *n*; IV 13, 103, 123, 133, 298; VI 120, 306, 357 (see Lady Mary Wortley Montagu for her identification as Sappho); other ref., VIII 406; X 286, 348. See AP Works for *Sapho to Phaon*

Sarah, in AP poem, II 29 and *n*

Sarazin, J. F., V 97*n*

Sargeaunt, John, I 245*n*

Saron, in AP poem, I 115 and *n*

Sarpedon, in AP poem, I 449, 450, 453, 454, 457, 460, 461, 462

Satan, in AP poems, II 20; III.ii 122, 124; IV 140, 141

Saturnian, in AP poems, V 63, 186, 271, 335, 341; VI 307

Satyrion, in AP poem, II 32 and *n*

Saul, in AP poem, V 363

Saumaise, Claude de, I 348*n*

Savage, Richard, AP corres., IV 351; his *Collection of Verse and Prose*, V xvi *n*, xxii *n*, 202*n*; his connection with the *Dunciad*, V xxv f., xxvi *n*, 8*n*, 14*n*, 199; *An Author to be Let*, V 15*n*, 110*n*, 113*n*, 163*n*, 375*n*, 437; VI 329*n*; other

ref., II 413; III.ii xxi; V 102n,
430, 435; VI 299n, 311n, 332n
Savile ["The Name of S."], in AP
poem, VI 337, 338n
Savile. See Halifax
Savile, Sir Henry (scholar), VI 110,
111n; VII 82
Sawbridge, Thomas, Biog., IV 384;
in AP poem, IV 78n, 79
Sawney and Colley, V 289n, 302n
Sawyer, Robert G., VI 141n, 206n
Saxon, in AP poem, I 157
Scaliger, J. C., *Poetices libri septem*, I
313n; VII xxxviii, xl, lxxii, lxxxi,
16, 102, 119–20, 132, 135, 152–3,
191, 202, 244–7, 272, 295, 359,
400; VIII 2, 16, 107, 143, 174–5,
358, 361; IX 212, 214, 217, 223,
234, 236, 245, 251, 260, 279–80,
292, 302, 320, 348, 352, 386, 394,
397, 402, 444, 446, 455; X 9, 13,
410, 431
Scarborough, Richard Lumley,
2nd Earl of, Biog., IV 371; in AP
poems, III.ii 24n; IV 316 and n,
336 and n; VI 173, 176n
Scarron, Paul, II 107
Scarsdale, Nicholas Leke, 4th Earl
of, Biog., IV 370; in AP poems,
IV 8n, 9
Schade, A., II 4n
Scheemakers, Peter (sculptor), VI
395n
Schiller, J. C. F. von, VII ccxxxiii
and n
Schmitz, L., I 182n
Schmitz, R. M., I xiii, 125n, 130n;
VII xxxvii n
Scholem, G., II 157n
Scholes, Percy, V 346n
Scholia and Scholiasts, VII xcii, 59,
125, 189, 197, 210, 223, 226, 283,
313, 426; VIII 10, 106, 140, 181,

194, 252, 356, 381, 530; IX 115,
226; X 126–7, 167, 202, 266, 338
Schutz, Augustus, Biog., IV 384; in
AP poems, IV 286n, 287; VI 181,
184n
Scipio, P. Cornelius Africanus, in
AP poems, I 172 and n; II 267;
III.ii 33 and n; other ref., I 141;
VII ccxxx
Scot, Thomas, II 217n, 228
Scotists, in AP poem, I 289 and n
Scotland [Scots], in AP poems,
III.i 82; IV 31, 140, 141, 197
Scoto, in AP poem, III.ii 28
Scots Magazine, VI 461n
Scotsman, in AP poem, IV 269
Scott, Francis. See Delorain
Scott, John A., VII ccvii n
Scott, Russell, VII xxiii
Scott, Sir Walter, III.ii 96n; VI
251–2n, 412n
Scotus, Duns, I 289n
Scriblerus Club, II xii; V xiv, xv,
xxxix; VI 115–18n, 234n, 242n,
414n; VII xxv
Scrope, Sir Carr, I 339 ff., 342 ff.,
393n, 394n, 395n, 396n, 397n,
399n, 400n, 401n, 403n
Scudamore, Frances, Lady, III.ii
113n
Scudéri, Mlle Madelène de, II 217
Scylla, in AP poems, I 365, 429
and n; II 130, 177
Scyron, in AP poem, I 429 and n
Scythian, in AP poem, II 264
Searle, John, Biog., IV 384; *Plan of
Pope's Garden*, IV 164n; V 384n;
VI 384n; VII ccxxiv; in AP
poem, IV 96 and n
Seaton, Mary E., II 154n
Sebon, Raymond (theologian),
III.i lii, 17n, 31n
Secker, Thomas, Biog., IV 384; *E.*

on Man attributed to, III.i xv *n*; in AP poem, IV 316 and *n*; other ref., IV 284*n*, 382

Sedley, Sir Charles (poet), trans. Virgil, II 144*n*; in AP poem, IV 204*n*, 205; other ref., I 93*n*, 298*n*, 299*n*; II 321*n*; III.i 65*n*, 89*n*; VII cxliii; X 501

Segrais, Jean de, trans. Virgil, VIII 410

Seine, in AP poem, V 373

Sejanus, in AP poem, IV 301

Selby-Bigge, L. A., III.i 105*n*

Selden, John, II 260*n*

Selkirk, Alexander, III.i 58*n*

Selkirk, Charles Douglas, 2nd Earl of, Biog., IV 358; V 438; in AP poems, III.ii 23*n*, 101*n*; IV 305 and *n*, 316 and *n*, 322 and *n*; V 148*n*; other ref., IV xix; VII ccxlix

Semele, in AP poems, V 186 and *n*, 335

Senault, J. F. (moralist), III.i 47*n*, 68*n*, 69*n*, 77*n*

Seneca, Lucius Annaeus, *De beneficiis*, I 292*n*; III.i 36*n*, 37*n*, 148*n*, 158*n*; *De constantia*, X 318; *De providentia*, VI 98*n*; IX 199; *Ep.*, III.i 22*n*, 26*n*, 60*n*, 61*n*, 86*n*, 130*n*, 132*n*, 136*n*, 143*n*, 145*n*, 157*n*, 159*n*, 162*n*; IX 431; *Herc. furens*, III.i 71*n*; V 157*n*; *Hippolytus*, V 157*n*, 466*n*; *Medea*, V 192*n*; *Nat. quaest.*, III.i 33*n*; other ref., II 18; III.i xiv, xxviii, 38*n*; III.ii xxvii *n*; V 288*n*; VII 41, 43, 180

Seneca the elder (Marcus), I 215

Senesino, P. W. (operatic singer), V 346*n*

Senior, F. Dorothy, I 200*n*; VI 360*n*

Sense, in AP poems, III.ii 18, 140

Septimuleius, in AP poem, VI 26

Serenissa, in AP poem, VI 9, 10, 11, 13

Serenus Sammonicus (Roman author, 2nd c. AD), VII 251

Serle, John. See Searle

Serpentine, II 400; III.ii 70*n*

Servius (author of commentary on Virgil, 4th c. AD), I 254*n*; IX 337; X 231

Sesostris, in AP poem, II 262

Session of the Poets, IV 216*n*

Settle, Elkanah, Biog., IV 385; *Empress of Morocco*, II 328*n*, 362*n*; V 454; in AP poems, IV 231; V 54, 56, 61*n*, 69, 69–70*n*, 85, 92, 153 ff., 153*n*, 205, 276 and *n*, 280 and *n*, 319, 322 ff., 322*n*; other ref., I 291*n*, 339; V xiv, xxxviii, xlv, xlvi *n*, 76*n*, 151*n*, 183*n*, 391*n*; VI 16*n*

Several Letters between Two Ladies, II 201*n*

Severn, in AP poem, III.ii 114

Seville (Spain), in AP poem, VI 136

Seward, William (littérateur), III.ii 95*n*

Sewell, George (hack writer), in AP poem, VI 283, 286*n*; other ref., II 330*n*; VI 174*n*

Seymour. See Hartford

Seymour, Richard, II 383 ff.

Shades, in AP poem, IV 69

Shadwell, Thomas, Biog., V 454; in AP poems, IV 201; V 91*n*, 141 and *n*, 151*n*, 287 and *n*, 321; his works, II 217*n*; III.i 56*n*, 76*n*, 79*n*, 112*n*; other ref., I 291*n*; IV 226*n*; V xxxviii, xlv

Shaftesbury, Anthony Ashley Cooper, 3rd Earl of, his doc-

trines, II 81*n*; III.i xl; influence
on *E. on Man*, III.i xxvii f., xxxi;
Characteristics, I 218; II 189*n*,
200*n*, 278*n*; III.i lxxxviii, 13*n*,
16*n*, 36*n*, 85*n*, 93*n*; IV xxviii *n*,
14*n*, 229*n*; V 389–90*n*, 409*n*
Shakespeare, William, in AP
poems, I 289*n*; IV 108, 175, 199
and *n*, 201, 203, 219; V 82*n*, 83,
127, 279 and *n*, 290, 307, 351*n*,
352, 352–3*n*, 398 and *n*; VI 283,
302, 304–5*n*, 395–7, 400, 401*n*;
AP ed. of, II xiv, 208*n*; III.ii
18*n*; V xi f., 30 f., 40*n*, 76*n*, 112*n*,
191*n*, 444, 448; VII xxvii; his
view of egoistic individualism,
III.i lxx *n*; his conceptual world
and AP's, III.i lxxii; a poet of
"Magnificence", III.i lxxiv; AP
opinion of, III.ii 18*n*; 18th c.
attribution of *Double Falshood* to,
V 180–1*n*; his monument, V
267–8*n*, 428; VI 395–6*n*; verbal
parallels with AP Homer, VII
xv *n*; AP compares with Homer,
VII xlviii, 5; X 412; his similes,
VII clxxv; sense of character,
VII ccxiii; AP bust of, IX xiii;
other ref., I 215; II 117, 188*n*,
230–1, 301; III.i lxx; IV 204–5*n*,
218*n*; V 167*n*; VII lxxiii, c
WORKS:
Antony and Cleopatra, II 159*n*,
329*n*; V 470; *As You Like It*, III.i
86*n*; X 503, 504; *Comedy of
Errors*, III.i 48*n*; *Cymbeline*, II
299*n*; III.i 154*n*; V 180*n*;
Hamlet, I 274*n*, 297*n*; II 299*n*,
335*n*, 362*n*, 367*n*; III.i l, liii, 63*n*;
V 165*n*, 180*n*; *1 Henry IV*, V
100*n*; X 511; *2 Henry IV*, III.i
23*n*; V 409*n*; VIII 241; *Henry V*,
II 160*n*; III.i 19*n*, 112*n*, 122*n*;

VII lv, lix; *1 Henry VI*, II 284*n*;
III.i 164*n*; X 505; *3 Henry VI*,
III.i 145*n*; *Henry VIII*, III.i 31*n*;
III.ii 177*n*; *Julius Caesar*, III.i
152*n*; *King Lear*, in AP poem, IV
45; other ref., III.i liii, lxvii,
lxx *n*, 48*n*, 113*n*; VII cxxxix, cxl,
clii *n*, clxxxvi; X 503; *Love's
Labour's Lost*, III.i 132*n*; *Macbeth*,
III.i liii, 88*n*, 148*n*; V 258*n*;
Measure for Measure, III.i 59*n*,
76*n*, 89*n*; *Merchant of Venice*, III.i
40*n*, 158*n*; *Merry Wives*, III.i
46*n*, 65*n*; *Midsummer Night's
Dream*, II 299*n*; V 466; *Othello*,
II 111*n*, 363*n*; III.i liii, lxx *n*; VII
clxxxvi; *Richard II*, X 505;
Richard III, II 205*n*; *Romeo and
Juliet*, II 335*n*; IV 261*n*; *Sonnets*,
III.i 86*n*, 122*n*; *Taming of the
Shrew*, V 91*n*; *Tempest*, I 316*n*; II
45*n*, 153*n*, 168*n*, 382; III.i liii;
III.ii 18*n*; V 268*n*; VII lix *n*;
Timon, III.i 29*n*; *Troilus and
Cressida*, II 344*n*; III.i xxxi, xlix,
lvii, 122*n*; IV 340; VII cxxvi;
Twelfth Night, VIII 307; *Venus
and Adonis*, II 310; *Winter's Tale*,
V 180*n*

Sharon, in AP poem, IV 47
Sharp, A. M., II 87*n*, 99, 197*n*,
374*n*, 375
Shaw, T. E., VII ccvii *n*
Sheers, Sir H., I 38
Sheffield, John. See Buckingham
Shelley, P. B., II 222
Shenstone, William, II 353*n*; III.ii
98*n*
Sheppard, or Shepherd, Edward
(architect), III.ii 138*n*, 183*n*
Sheppard, Jack (criminal), VI xvi,
243*n*
Sherbo, A., V 467

Sherborn, C. D., VI 344*n*

Sherburn, George (author of *Early Career of Alexander Pope*), I xiii, 14, 37*n*, 41*n*, 65*n*, 105*n*, 106*n*, 126*n*, 202*n*, 203*n*, 207*n*, 330*n*, 347*n*, 348*n*, 352*n*, 355*n*, 358*n*; II xii, xiii, 5*n*, 14, 81*n*, 84*n*, 86, 90*n*, 102*n*, 104*n*, 285*n*, 301*n*, 305*n*, 311*n*, 325*n*; III.i vi, xxix *n*, xxx *n*, 170; III.ii xiii *n*, xxii *n*, xxvii f., xxix *n*, liii, 49*n*, 61*n*, 74*n*, 141*n*, 147*n*, 171; IV xv *n*, xvi *n*, xvii *n*, xix *n*, xxiii *n*, xxxviii *n*, xlv, 10*n*, 64*n*, 65*n*, 116*n*, 121*n*, 125*n*, 255*n*, 323*n*, 343*n*, 345*n*, 347*n*, 356*n*, 357*n*, 360*n*, 361*n*, 363*n*, 369*n*, 371*n*, 377*n*, 378*n*, 379*n*, 385*n*, 388*n*; V xiv, xxxii *n*, 442, 460 f., 464, 467, 469, and cited *passim*; VI xx, 29*n*, 111*n*, 149*n*, 193*n*, 256*n*, 291*n*, 416*n*, 420*n*, 421*n*; VII xiii, xxv, xxvi, xxxv *n*, xxxviii *n*, xlii *n*, xliii *n*, xliv *n*, xlv *n*, xlvi and *n*, lxxxvii *n*, cvii *n*; IX xii; X 589

Sherburne, John, II 293*n*, 302

Sheridan, Thomas, AP corres., V xxiv *n*; VI 299*n*

Sheringham, R., II 263*n*

Sherlock, Thomas, Biog., V 454; in AP poems, 313*n*, 330 and *n*

Sherrard, Lord, in AP poems, VI 186, 188*n*

Sherwin, Dr William, IV xx

Ship Tavern (London), VI 197*n*

Shippen, Robert, I xiv

Shippen, William, Biog., IV 385; in AP poems, IV 9, 332 and *n*; V 147, 147–8*n*; other ref., III.ii 30*n*; IV xxxi, xxxv, 350

Shirley. See Ferrers

Shirley, Lady Frances, VI xiv, 378, 379*n*

Shirley, James (dramatist), V 91*n*

Shock, in AP poem, II 127, 134, 145, 154, 166, 197

Shorey, Paul, III.i xxxv *n*, 57*n*, 58*n*

Shovell, Sir Clowdisley, Admiral, V 405*n*

Shower, John, III.i 33*n*

Shrapnel, Susan Andrews, VII xxiv

Shrewsbury, Anna Maria (Brudenell) Talbot, Countess of, in AP poems, III.ii 119 and *n*

Shrewsbury, Charles Talbot, 12th Earl and Duke of, Biog., IV 388–9; his connection with AP *Donne Satires*, IV xli, 3; in AP poems, IV 105, 317 and *n*; other ref., III.ii 148*n*, 187 and *n*; VI 149*n*

Shylock, in AP poems, III.ii 23, 97, 101, 137*n*; IV 15

Sibyl, in AP poems, III.ii 93, V 320

Sican. See Sykins

Sichel, Walter, III.i 76*n*

Sicilian, in AP poems, I 60 and *n*, 396 and *n*, 426

Sidgwick, R., IV xxxiv *n*, 306*n*

Sidney, Sir Philip, in AP poems, III.i 138 and *n*; IV 202*n*, 203; other ref., I 82*n*; II 156*n*, 212*n*; III.i 108*n*; VII lxxviii, ccxx and *n*

Silenus, in AP poems, I 378; V 390 ff., 390*n*

Silhouette, Etienne de, trans. *E. on Man* into Fr., III.i xix, xx *n*; defends orthodoxy of *E. on Man*, III.i xviii

Silia, in AP poem, III.ii 52

Silius Italicus, *Punica*, II 173*n*; VII 6; IX 372–3; other ref., 266*n*; II 203*n*

Simison, Barbara, VII xxiii

Simo, in AP poem, III.ii 58

K

Simois, in AP poem, I 462

Simonides (poet, 6th/5th c. BC), III.i 67*n*; VII 44, 49, 53, 335; VIII 136; X 59

Simplicius of Cicilia (author of commentary on Epictetus, 6th c. BC), III.i xxviii, xxix, lxxi *n*; III.ii 52; IX 32

Simpson, Percy, I xiv, 199*n*

Singer, Elizabeth, II 178*n*, 254*n*, 327*n*, 331*n*; VI 109*n*

Singer, S. W. (editor of Spence), III.ii xxii *n*; X 594. See also Spence

Sirach, in AP poem, II 46

Sirius, in AP poems, I 73, 141

Siserah, in AP poem, VI 290, 291

Sisyphus the Coan (supposititious author from whom Homer is alleged to have plagiarized), VII 33

Skeat, W. W., II 12, 403

Skelton, John, in AP poem, IV 196*n*, 197

Skerret, Maria, III.ii 101*n*

Sloane, Sir Hans, Biog., IV 385; in AP poems, III.ii 136 and *n*; IV 28*n*, 29; AP corres., III.ii 136*n*; other ref., III.ii 139*n*

Small, S. G. P., I xii

Smalley, Donald, VII ccxix

Smalridge, George, Bishop of Bristol, III.i 71*n*; V 126*n*

Smedley, Jonathan, Biog., V 454–5; *Gulliveriana*, V xlviii, 14*n*, 39*n*, 46, 136*n*, 208, 212, 233*n*; *Metam. of Scriblerus*, V 113*n*, 138*n*, 210*n*; in AP poems, V 135–6 and *n*, 139 ff., 309 ff.; other ref., V 116*n*, 460

Smith, A. H., VII xiv

Smith, D. Nichol, *Letters of Burnet to Duckett*, IV 111*n*, 351; V 168*n*, 207*n*, 363*n*, 432*n*, 439*n*; of *Swift to Ford*, V 62*n*; VI 465*n*; other ref., V 434; VI xx

Smith, Edmund, II 340*n*, 342*n*

Smith, G. G., VII ccxx *n*

Smith, J. E., IV 62*n*

Smith, John (trans. Chaucer), II 6

Smith, John (Platonist), III.i 118*n*, 124*n*

Smith, Logan Pearsall, III.ii 49*n*

Smith, Richard (printer), IV 307*n*

Smith, W. C., VI 433*n*

Smith, William, II 210*n*

Smithfield, in AP poems, V 59, 60*n*, 184, 267, 269*n*, 334

Smollett, Tobias George, *Roderick Random*, IV 326*n*

Smythe, James Moore, Biog., IV 385–6; V 455; in *Master Key to Popery*, III.ii 178 and *n*, 184; his *Rival Modes*, III.ii 69–70*n*; V 33–5, 456; VI 247*n*; *One Epistle to Mr Pope*, IV xvii; his plagiarisms, V 33, 52, 101–2*n*; VI 294*n*; in AP poems, IV 97 and *n*, 102 and *n*, 105*n*, 123 and *n*, 126; V 99–101 and *n*, 102*n*, 103*n*, 298, 435, 447; AP epigrams on, VI 300, 303*n*, 325–7, 328–30*n*, 451–2; other ref., IV 121*n*; V xii *n*, 16*n*, 72*n*, 83–4*n*, 110*n*, 116*n*, 163*n*, 209, 211 and *n*, 212; VI 141*n*, 454*n*

Smythe, William, V 110*n*

Snider, Denton, VII ccvi *n*

Soames, Sir William (with Dryden, trans. of Boileau's *L'art poétique*), I 246*n*, 247*n*, 250*n*, 252*n*, 257*n*, 260*n*, 264*n*, 267*n*, 280*n*, 282*n*, 292*n*, 296*n*, 305*n*, 310*n*, 311*n*, 326*n*; III.i 165*n*

Sobieski, John, King of Poland, III.ii 103*n*

Socinus, Laelius, in AP poems, I 300 and *n*, 301*n*, 302*n*

Socrates, in Dryden's Prologue to *Oedipus*, I 314*n*; in Esprit, III.i 34*n*; in AP letter, III.i 51*n*; in Xenophon, III.i 53*n*; in AP poems, II 269 and *n*; III.i 148, 149*n*

Sohoe, in AP poem, IV 231

Sol, in AP poems, I 292; II 127, 145; VI 10

Solinus, Gaius Julius (geographer, 2nd c. AD), V 365; VIII 306

Solomon, in AP poems, II 21, 45 and *n*, 47 and *n*, 48, 57, 74

Solon (statesman and poet, *c* 6th c. BC), III.i 112*n*; V 264*n*; VII 58, 173; IX 33, 283; X 44, 47, 102, 243

Solyma, in AP poem, I 112 and *n*

Somers, John, Baron, Biog., IV 386; in AP poems, IV 105, 106*n*, 317 and *n*; other ref., I 59*n*; VI 117*n*

Somerset, Robert Carr, 1st Earl of, VII ccxviii–ccix, ccix *n*

Sophianus (Nicólaos Sophianós), VII 177

Sophocles, *Ajax*, VII 84, 109, 357, 384; IX 54, 110; *Electra*, VII 441; VIII 507; X 198; Fragments, IX 39, 300, 389; *Lotrices*, IX 213; *Oedipus* plays, VII 470; VIII 285; IX 221, 325, 398; X 17; *Trachiniae*, VIII 252; other ref., I 250*n*, 314*n*; III.i lxix; VIII 285; X 108

Sophonisba, in AP poem, VI 310

Sorbière, Samuel, III.i 88*n*

Souhaitte, S. de, X 441

South, Robert, I 219; V 358

Southcote, Thomas, I 203, 317*n*; IV xx, 300*n*, 391

Southerne, Thomas, Biog., IV 386; his plays, II 193*n*; III.i 153*n*,

156*n*; in AP poems, IV 201 and *n*; VI 214–15, 398–9; other ref., I 38; IV 355

South Sea Company (and Bubble), III.ii 101 and *n*, 104*n*, 166*n*; IV 64*n*, 65, 79*n*, 348, 356; VII xliii

Southwell, Robert (poet), III.i 132*n*

Sozzini, Fausto, I 300*n*

Spadillo, in AP poem, II 172

Spain, in AP poems, III.ii 89; IV 19, 39, 298; V 157, 324; VI 25, 135, 136, 178; The War of Jenkins' Ear, IV 39*n*, 298 and *n*

Spanish [–iard], in AP poems, VI 49, 218

Spalding Club Miscellany, IV 76*n*

Spartan, in AP poems, I 425; II 31, 269; IV 33

Spearman, C. E., III.i 64*n*

Spectator, in AP poem, VI 123; Addison in, I 7*n*, 17, 131, 191*n*, 207–8, 223 and *n*, 273*n*, 289–90*n*, 402*n*; II 121*n*, 167*n*, 296*n*; III.i 14*n*, 20*n*, 22*n*, 28*n*, 44*n*, 48*n*, 49*n*, 54*n*, 83*n*, 86*n*, 101*n*, 106*n*, 110*n*, 115*n*, 133*n*, 141*n*, 145*n*; III.ii 121*n*, 123*n*, 141*n*; IV xxviii, 110*n*, 223*n*, 365; V 98*n*, 128*n*, 143*n*, 178*n*, 347*n*, 373*n*, 387*n*, 398*n*, 467, 469; VI 112*n*, 139*n*, 144*n*; VII xxv, lxxx and *n*, 9; X 62; AP *Messiah* in, I 99, 103, 112*n*; advertisement of AP poems in, I 128; II 92*n*; *E. on Criticism*, published in, I 197*n*; AP *Temple of Fame* recorded in, II 243; AP indebtedness to, II 287*n*, 288*n*; issues attributed to AP, III.ii 19*n*; AP use of Sir Andrew Freeport in, III.ii 99*n*; Steele's contributions, III.i 145*n*, 152*n*, 158*n*; VII xxv; AP *Waller* in, VI 46*n*;

AP letters in, VI 46*n*, 57*n*, 91–2*n*;
other ref., I 242*n*, 257*n*, 340*n*; II
75*n*, 90, 104*n*, 149–52*n*, 155*n*,
176*n*, 182*n*, 184–6*n*, 189*n*, 190*n*,
194*n*, 200*n*, 202*n*, 204*n*, 219, 220,
325*n*, 379*n*; III.i 45*n*, 47–9*n*,
54*n*, 55*n*, 56*n*, 59*n*, 66*n*, 67*n*, 70*n*,
74*n*, 78*n*, 81*n*, 83*n*, 106*n*, 126*n*,
150*n*, 162*n*; III.ii xxxviii; VI
124*n*, 133*n*; VII 465; VIII 342
Speght, Thomas, his *Chaucer*, II 3,
9, 10, 326*n*; V 171*n*
Spence, Joseph, *Anecdotes* (in Vols.
VII–X Osborn ed. references
are given as well as Singer), I 8*n*,
28*n*, 50, 88*n*, 105, 127, 130, 134*n*,
154*n*, 198, 201, 202, 209*n*, 224,
254*n*, 263*n*, 280*n*, 330, 332, 347,
353, 364
II 7, 8*n*, 81*n*, 86, 90*n*, 91*n*, 92, 95,
121*n*, 209*n*, 220*n*, 231*n*, 237*n*,
268*n*, 357*n*
III.i xi, xii *n*, xiii *n*, xxiii *n*, xxx *n*,
79*n*, 153*n*
III.ii ix, x, xx–xxiii and *n*, xxviii,
xxxiv, xxxvii *n*, xl *n*, 16*n*, 26*n*,
28*n*, 33*n*, 34*n*, 47*n*, 66*n*, 97*n*, 101,
108*n*, 113*n*, 119*n*, 142*n*, 153*n*, 167,
169, 171
IV xiii, xvi, xxvi, xxix, 10*n*, 14*n*,
16*n*, 30*n*, 107*n*, 116*n*, 177*n*, 196*n*,
200*n*, 201*n*, 204*n*, 236*n*, 240–1*n*,
244*n*, 280*n*, 293*n*, 300*n*, 319*n*,
343, 347, 353, 356, 359, 360, 369,
373, 374, 378, 379, 381, 383, 390
V cited *passim*
VI 20*n*, 35*n*, 45*n*, 48*n*, 72*n*, 141*n*,
170*n*, 177*n*, 223*n*, 263*n*, 298*n*,
313*n*, 335–6*n*, 359*n*, 393*n*, 404*n*,
438*n*, 442*n*, 448*n*
VII xii, xxxv and *n*, xxxvi *n*,
xxxvii and *n*, xxxviii *n*, xli *n*,
xlii *n*, xlvi *n*, lxxvii *n*, lxxxii and *n*,

ccxxi and *n*, ccxxii and *n*, ccxxvi *n*
Essay on Mr Pope's Odyssey, I
466*n*, 473*n*; VII cxciv *n*; AP
annotations in *Essay*, X 594–605
Other ref., II xiv, 358; III.ii ix,
174*n*
Spencer. See Sunderland
Spencer, Sir John, II 371
Spencer, Theodore, III.i xlviii *n*
Spender, Stephen, II 295*n*
Spenser, Edmund, AP opinion of,
II 252; his conceptualizing of
romance, III.i lxiii–lxiv; a poet
of "Magnificence", III.i lxxiv;
in AP poems, IV 159, 203; AP
imitation of, VI 43–5; AP early
imitation of, VII xxv; AP bust
of, IX xiii; other ref., I 18, 19, 20,
50, 100, 132, 294*n*; II 163*n*, 221*n*,
320*n*, 365*n*; V 223 f., 227, 403*n*;
VI 20*n*; VII lxxviii, ccxxxix
WORKS:
Amoretti, II 212*n*; *Astrophel*, I 76*n*;
Colin Clouts come home againe, I
71*n*, 91*n*, 92*n*; *Daphnaida*, II
306*n*; Eclogues, I 48, 75*n*; *Epi-
thalamion*, I 73*n*; *Faerie Queene*,
I 181–4*n*, II 27*n*, 166*n*, 190*n*,
252, 283*n*, 307*n*; III.i 17*n*, 24*n*,
47*n*, 94*n*, 148*n*; IV 120*n*; V 9*n*,
129*n*, 376*n*; VII 176, 295; VIII
150–1, 172, 177, 187, 211, 255,
494; IX 358, 509, 510; *Hymn to
Heavenly Beauty*, III.i 49*n*, 160*n*;
Mourning Muse of Thestylis, I 76*n*;
Muiopotmos, I 63*n*; V 383*n*; *Pro-
thalamion*, I 60*n*; II 376; *Ruines of
Rome*, II 282*n*; *Ruines of Time*, II
365*n*; IV 320*n*; *Shepherd's Calen-
dar*, I 14, 31–3 and *n*, 43–5, 46, 51,
54, 60*n*, 63*n*, 71*n*, 73*n*, 76*n*, 78*n*,
90*n*, 91*n*, 93*n*, 95*n*; II 45*n*; IV
202*n*, 320*n*; V 224; VII liv and *n*

Sphynxe, in AP poem, I 414

Spingarn, J. E., I 17n, 209–211n, 215n, 216n, 219n, 227n, 239n, 240n, 244n, 248n, 250n, 255n, 258n, 264n, 272n, 275n, 285n, 286n, 288n, 293n, 297n, 313n; II 221n, 287n, 322n, 378n; VII lxxii n, lxxiii n

Spinoza, B., V 317n, 386n

Spinozism, alleged Spinozism in E. on Man, III.i xviii, xx; associated with principle of plenitude, III.i xxii; repudiated by AP, III.i xxii

Spitzer, Leo, III.i xxxiv n

Spon, J., Voyages, V 379n

Spondanus (Jean de Sponde), ed. Homer, VII xl, lxxxi, cvi, xxxviii, 55, 89, 93, 102, 133, 150, 200, 213, 217–18, 222, 230, 232, 265, 299, 301, 304, 310, 313, 386, 410, 440; VIII 39, 43, 106, 109, 113, 181, 356, 377, 386, 390, 497; IX 31, 39, 46, 209, 218, 222, 238, 245–6, 249, 256, 275, 310, 344, 351, 406, 416, 421; X 7, 93–4, 149, 232, 236, 252, 279, 291, 325, 345, 441, 476; ed. Hesiod, X 186

Sports of the nobility, V 400–3 and n

Sporus. See Hervey

Sprat, Thomas, Account of Cowley, I 215 and n, 217, 258n; History of the Royal Society, I 242n; IV 204n; his poems, III.i 55n, 109n, 130n; in AP poems, IV 204n, 205; other ref., VII xlix

Spurgeon, Caroline F. E., II 4 ff., 330n

Stack, Thomas, trans. Mead, III.i 19n

Stackhouse, Rev. Thomas, V 281n

Stafford, Mr, trans. Virgil, I 84–6n

Stafford, Mr (architect), III.ii 138n

Stagg, John (bookseller), V 462

Stagyrite. See Aristotle

Staines (Middlesex), in AP poem, IV 257; other ref., I 183n

Stair, John Dalrymple, 2nd Earl of, Biog., IV 357; in AP poems, IV 326 and n; other ref., IV xxxii, 39n

Stalker, J., II 175n f.

Stanford, W. B., VII ccviii n

Stanhope. See Chesterfield

Stanhope, George, trans. Epictetus His Morals With Simplicius His Comment, III.i xxviii n, xxv n, lxxi n: trans. Charron, III.ii 27n

Stanhope, H. (poet), V 41n, 430

Stanhope, James, 1st Earl, Biog., IV 386–7; in AP poems, IV 317 and n; AP acknowledgement to, VII 24; other ref., I 186n; IV 302n, 350; V 144–5n

Stanislaus I, King of Poland, III.ii, 93n, 103n

Stanley, Thomas, his History of philosophy, II 260n; III.i 17n, 112n

Stanton Harcourt (Oxon.), VI 198–200 and n, 234n, 242–4 and n

Stanyan, Abraham, in AP poem, VI 173, 175n

Stanyan, Temple, in AP poem, VI 173, 175n; author of Grecian History, VIII 250

Stapylton, Robert, VII cviii

Statius, Publius Papinius (1st c. AD), AP early imitation of, VII xxxv; in AP Preface, VII xlviii; AP use of style in Homer trans., VII lxvii; Parnell cites, VII

lxxxii; as interpreter of Homeric tradition, VII clxxxiii; other ref., VII ccxxxv; X 412, 418
WORKS:
Silvae, II 324*n*; III.i 165*n*; VII 52; IX 44; X 61; *Thebaid*, I 164*n*, 263*n*, 387*n*; II 144*n*, 153*n*, 173*n*, 196*n*, 202*n*, 204*n*, 208*n*, 260*n*; III.i 118*n*; V 205*n*, 340*n*, 468; VI 20*n*; VII 4, 6, 8, 174–83, 200, 238, 240, 243, 314; VIII 473, 494–5, 533; IX 381; X 19

Steele, Leighton, VII xv *n*

Steele, Sir Richard, AP corres., I 100, 117*n*; II 243 and *n*; VI 35*n*, 57*n*; publisher of *Poetical Miscellanies*, I 358, 464; VII xxxvi, cxi; *The Drummer* (1722), IV 339*n*; as AP collaborator, VI 102*n*; in AP poems, VI 123, 137, 139*n*, 140, 173; acknowledgement in AP Preface, VII 23; other ref., I 18, 59*n*, 99, 306*n*; II xii, 82, 200*n*, 219, 322*n*, 339*n*, 340*n*; III.ii 105*n*, 152*n*; IV 377; V 134*n*, 150*n*, 183*n*, 222*n*, 328*n*, 354*n*, 433; VI 102*n*, 177*n*. See also *Guardian*; *Spectator*

Steele, Robert, I 40*n*

Steeleids (political poem), II 219 and *n*

Steevens, George, II 188*n*, 333*n*, 348*n*; VII lxxxviii *n*

Steinman, G. S., *Memoir of the Duchess of Cleveland*, IV 75*n*

Stephanus of Byzantium (author of geographical lexicon, 4th c. AD), VII 182

Stephen, Leslie, II 310; III.i xxiv *n*, xliii–xliv, lxvii; V 388*n*; VII cxciv *n*

Stephens, Henry ("Stephanus"), VIII 195

Stephens, Thomas, I 331, 347, 349, 411*n*, 412*n*, 414*n*, 419*n*, 421*n*, 423*n*, 424*n*, 428*n*, 433*n*, 435*n*, 437*n*, 440*n*, 441*n*, 445*n*

Sternhold, Thomas (versifier of the Psalms), in AP poems, IV 215 and *n*; VI 290, 291*n*; other ref., IV 111*n*, 214–15*n*; V ix, 170*n*; VI 165–6*n*, 198*n*

Stevens, John, I 270*n*, 485

Stevens, Wallace, VII ccvi and *n*

Stewart, Dugald, III.i xliii

Stewart, Thomas, II 415

Stimson, D., trans. Copernicus, III.i 45*n*

Stobaeus (author of anthology, 5th c. AD), V 365; VII 335

Stoicism, pervasive in *E. on Man*, III.i xxviii, xxx, xxxv, xxxix, xlvi; anti-Stoicism, III.i xxxvi, lxix; as an "extreme" doctrine, III.i xl; mentioned in *E. on Man*, III.i 52, 67

Stoics, VII 396

Stourhead (Wilts.), VI 248–9*n*; VII ccxxvi *n*

Stow, John, in AP poems, *Chronicles*, IV 34, 35 and *n*, 198–9*n*, 199; other ref., *Survey of London*, I 310*n*; V 142*n*, 189*n*

Stowe House (Bucks.), III.ii 143

Strabo, *Geographia*, VII lxxvi, lxxxii, cvi, 43–4, 48–9, 55, 60, 75–7, 79, 91, 156, 171, 177–85, 224, 261, 368, 458; VIII 74, 104, 252, 349, 404, 409–10, 463, 565; IX 30–1, 33, 43–4, 86, 102, 109, 124, 134, 143, 155, 189–90, 302, 306, 337–9, 344, 348, 350, 372, 379, 396, 402, 415, 428, 430, 434–5, 437–8; X 53, 84–5, 117, 126–7, 180, 201–2, 204, 255, 259, 280, 338

Strada, Famianus, I 93*n*; V 97*n*

Stradling, J., trans. Lipsius, III.i 139*n*

Strafford, Thomas Wentworth, 2nd Earl of, III.ii 108*n*

Strafford, Thomas Wentworth, 3rd Earl of, in AP poems, VI 368, 392, 394*n*; AP corres., VI 249*n* 312*n*

Strand (London), in AP poem, V 99, 106, 297, 299

Stratford, William (correspondent of Lord Oxford), IV 121*n*, 365; V xxi

Stratocles (demagogue, 4th/3rd c. BC), VII 72

Straus, R., his *Unspeakable Curll* cited, V 110*n*, 121*n*, 165*n*, 199

Strephon, in AP poem, I 62 ff.

Stuart, in AP poem ("a S. reigns"), I 152

Stuart, Dorothy Margaret, VI 184*n*

Stuart, James, the Old Pretender, III.ii 93*n*

Stubbes, George (poet), in AP poem, VI 173, 176*n*

Stukeley, Rev. William (antiquary), V 438; VI 460*n*

Stygian, in AP poem, VI 66

Styles, Benjamin Heskin (financier), III.ii 137*n*, 144*n*

Styx, in AP poems, I 413, 427; V 140, 314; VI 33, 88, 370

Suckling, Sir John, I 239*n*; III.i 26*n*, 62*n*; IV 87

Sudbrook House (Surrey), III.ii 174

Suetonius, I 81*n*; III.i 142*n*, 145*n*; III.ii 144*n*; IV 117*n*, 191*n*; VIII 306, 381

Suffolk (the place name), in AP poem, IV 261

Suffolk Letters, IV 65*n*, 339, 358, 374,

391; VI 28*n*, 127*n*, 184*n*, 202*n*, 335*n*, 343*n*, 392*n*, 436*n*

Suffolk, Henrietta Howard, Countess of, in AP poems, VI 182, 184*n*, 250–1; her dog, Fop, VI 366–71*n*; other ref., VI 252*n*, 254*n*, 370*n*, 371*n*, 437*n*

Sühnel, Rudolf, VII li *n*, cxvi *n*, cliv *n*

Suidas (lexicographer), in AP poem, V 365 and *n*; other ref., 446; VII 29, 32–3, 40, 43, 45, 60–1; IX 213

Summers, M., I 299*n*

Sunderland, Anne Spencer, Countess of, VI 160*n*

Sunderland, Charles Spencer, 3rd Earl of, in AP poems, VI 181, 184*n*; other ref., VI 117*n*

Sundon Memoirs, III.i xvi *n*; IV 359, 393

Surrey, Henry Howard, Earl of, in AP poems, I 175 and *n*, 176*n*

Surtz, E. L., I 105*n*

Sutherland, C. H. V., V 472

Sutherland, James, VI xx, 359*n*; X 495, 501, 503, 504

Sutton, Richard, Biog., IV 387; in AP poem, IV 135 and *n*

Sutton, Sir Robert, Biog., IV 387; in AP poem, IV 298*n*; other ref., III.ii 99*n*, 100*n*; IV 135*n*, 349

Swan, John, *Speculum Mundi*, III.i 41*n*

Swift, Jonathan, Biog., IV 388; his visits to England (1726–7), VI 252*n*, 254*n*, 258*n*, 371*n*
AP corres., III.i xiii, 11*n*, 25*n*, 51*n*, 140*n*, 141*n*; III.ii xvi *n*, xix *n*, xxxiv, xxxvii, xxxix, xlvi *n*, 46*n*, 138*n*; IV xiii, xxii, xxiv, xxxix, xl, 10*n*, 19*n*, 97*n*, 119*n*, 170*n*,

212–13n, 215n, 217n, 258n, 281n, 318n, 323n, 324n, 353, 358, 368, 382; V ix, x–xi, xvii n, xxx, 62n, 68n, 160n, 188n, 311n; VI 164n, 250–1n, 266–7n, 309n, 322n, 345n, 351n, 440n, 442n, 454n; VII ccxx n

Other corres.: Bolingbroke's letters to, describing *E. on Man*, III.i xii ff., xxv n; other, I 198n; III.i 86n; IV 67n, 217n, 246n; V xiii, xx, xxii, xxiii, xxviii n, 9n, 20n, 129n, 160n, 189n, 413n, 443, 445, 454; VI 331n, 370n

His "imitations", IV xxviii n, xlii, of Horace *Sat. II vi*, 247–59; his opinion of AP *Epilogue*, IV xxxix; his view of Dryden, IV 217n; his connection with the *Dunciad*, V xiii ff., xx, xxv, xxxix–xl, 201n; attacked by the Dunces, V 113n, 165n, 208, 209 ff., 430, 455; as member of Scriblerus Club, V 387–8n; VI 115n, 116–19 and n, 241n, 414n; as AP collaborator, VI 115–18n, 119n, 258n, 370–1n, 414n; *Miscellanies* (Pope–Swift), VI 285n, 287n, 347n; AP imitation of his manner in Horace *Ep. I vii*, IV 265–73; VI 110–11 and n, 376; on trans., VII ccxx; AP acknowledgement to, VII 23

In AP poems, IV xxxviii, 31, 67–9 and n, 105, 115, 213–15 and n, 246 and n; 273; V 62 and n, 62–3n, 109, 112, 113n, 190, 190–1n, 270–1, 301, 336; VI 120, 251–2 and n, 253–5 and n, 266–81, 307, 309n

Other ref., I 18, 211, 291n; II xii, 7, 200n, 231, 255n, 286n, 310 and and n; III.ii 112n; IV 121n, 364;

V xlviii, 427–30 *passim*, 448, 473; VI 130n; VII xxv, xxvii, ciii, cxxiv; X 604

WORKS:

Battle of the Books, I 225, 226; IV 102n; V xlv n, 79n, 99n, 100n; *Dean and the Duke*, III.ii 173; *Description of the Morning*, III.ii 36n; *Directions for a Birth-day Song*, VI 338n; *Drapier's Letters*, III.i 77n; V 191n; VI 242n, 255n, 307n; *Enquiry into the Behaviour of the Queen's Last Ministry*, I 315n; epigrams, III.ii 145n; VI 331n; *Epistle to Gay*, IV 392; *Epistle upon an Epistle*, II 217n; *Essay on Modern Education*, III.ii 91n; *Examiner*, III.ii 26n; IV 284n; *Foolish Methods of Education among the Nobility*, III.ii 107n; *Gulliver's Travels*, II xiv, 105n; III.ii 24n, 50n; V 401n, 430; VI 116n, 266–81, 307, 371n; VII xxvii, cxxv; *Journal of a Modern Fine Lady*, III.ii 37n; *Journal to Stella*, I 131, 165n; III.ii 25n, 26n, 109n; V 98n, 137n, 457; VI 131n; *Legion Club*, III.ii 24n; *Letter of Advice to a Young Poet*, V 124n; *Letter to a Very Young Lady on her Marriage*, II 182n; *Libel on Dr Delaney*, III.ii 65n; *Logicians Refuted*, III.i 100n; *Mechanical Operation of the Spirit*, V 129n; *Mr Collins's Discourse of Free-Thinking*, V 144n; *Mrs Biddy Floyd*, III.ii 73n; *Ode to the Athenian Society*, II 408; *On Poetry*, IV 237n; *Poems*, V xv, 37n, 166n, 350n; VI 331n, 338n; poems ascribed to, VI 412n, 413n, 415n, 439n, 443n, 457n, 460n; *Proposal for the Universal Use of Irish Manufacture*, IV 213n;

sermons, III.i 87*n*, 123*n*, 131*n*,
133*n*, 136*n*, 145*n*, 154*n*; *Tale of a
Tub*, II 54*n*, 159*n*, 194*n*, 217;
III.i 21*n*, 57*n*, 61*n*, 122*n*, 147*n*,
148*n*; III.ii 17*n*, 24*n*; V xl, xlv *n*,
90*n*, 150*n*, 363*n*; VI 133*n*;
Thoughts on Various Subjects, III.i
66*n*; *To Mr Gay*, III.ii 102*n*;
Tritical Essay, III.i 112*n*
Swift, Thomas (grandfather of
Jonathan Swift), VI 252*n*
Swiney, Owen, I 200
Swiss, in AP poem, V 315 and *n*
Switzer, Stephen, *Ichnographia Rus-
tica*, III.ii 141*n*
Sydenham, Thomas (physician),
V 105*n*

Sykes, N., *Edmund Gibson*, IV 362,
382; *Church and State*, IV 308*n*;
V 404*n*
Sykes, W. (painter), II viii
Sykins [Sican], Mrs John, IV 97*n*
Sylph[–s, –id, –ids], in AP poem,
II 147, 150–4, 157, 163–4, 166,
171, 179, 183, 197, 211; other
ref., II 378–83
Sylvester, J., II 264*n*
Sylvia, in AP poems, I 65 ff.; II
128, 161; III.ii 54*n*; VI 286
Symaethis, in AP poem, I 365 and *n*
Sypherd, W. O., II 216*n*
Syrian, in AP poem, V 378, 379
Syrtes, in AP poem, I 443 and *n*
Sysiphus, in AP poem, VI 32

T

Tacitus, Cornelius (historian, 1st c. AD), II 264n; V 390n f.; VII 291, 337; X 151

Taenarus, in AP poem, I 415 and n

Taine, Hippolyte Adolphe, III.i 53n

Talbot. See Shrewsbury

Talbot, Charles, 1st Baron, Biog., IV 389; in AP poems, IV 174n, 175; V 357 and n; other ref., IV 382; V 401n, 455

Talbot, William, Biog., V 455; in AP poems, V 397–8n, 402; other ref., III.i 142n

Tallard, Camille D'Hostun, duc de, I 40

Tall-Boy, in AP poem, III.ii 56 and n

Tallemant, Paul, II 216n

Tanais, in AP poems, V 156, 324

Tantalus, in AP poems, I 424, 426

Tarquin, in AP poem, VI 108

Tartar[–ean], in AP poems, I 428; V 156, 324

Tasso, AP opinion of, II 252; as interpreter of Homeric tradition, VII clxxxiii; other ref., I 261n; II 221n

WORKS:

Aminta, I 30, 31n; *Gierusalemme Liberata*, I 30; II 252, 260n, 319n, 367n; VII 6, 176, 202, 332, 359, 380; VIII 114–15, 171, 186, 191, 208, 227, 242, 246–7, 310; X 61; *Godfrey of Bulloigne*, II 173–4n

Tassoni, Alessandro (author of *La Secchia Rapita*), II 108, 110, 147n, 159n, 174n; V 108n, 450

Tate, Nahum, Biog., IV 389; in AP poems, IV 109; V 72 and n, 277, 287 and n; VI 173, 176n, 284; his version of Psalms, I 253n; IV 215n; trans. Ovid, I 339; III.i 43n; trans. Simonides, III.i 67n; a poem, II 175n; other ref., IV 14n; V xlv, 149n

Tatler, I 240n, II 10n, 90, 149n, 161n, 167n, 171n, 176n, 180–2n, 186–90n, 194n, 200n, 204n, 209n, 218, 219n, 227, 232, 241, 259n, 264n, 265n; III.i 15n; III.ii 36n; V 381n, 384n, 398n; VIII 167

Taurus, in AP poem, II 72

Taylor, Jeremy (divine), in AP poems, VI 287, 288n; *Holy Living and Holy Dying*, III.i 94n; III.ii 55; other ref., II 209n; III.i 73n, 132n

Taylor, John (the "water-poet"), in AP poems, V xlv, 141 and n, 321

Taylor, Thomas, II 157n

Telamon, in AP poem, I 452

Telemus, in AP poem, I 366

Tempest, Alathea or Henrietta, in AP poems, I 47, 88 and n

Tempest, Sir Charles Robert, II 372

Tempest, Henry, I 88*n*

Tempest, Sir John, I 88*n*

Tempest, P., II 228*n*

Temple. See Cobham

Temple, Sir William, I 16 f., 18, 85*n*, 153*n*, 240*n*, 244*n*, 264*n*, 293*n*, 313*n*; II 148*n*, 231 ff., 260*n* ff., 378*n*, 408; III.i 53*n*, 84*n*, 88*n*, 99*n*, 113*n*, 114*n*, 123*n*, 124*n*, 129*n*, 134*n*, 151*n*, 170; VI 372*n*

Temple (London), in AP poem, IV 173

Temple-Bar (London), in AP poem, IV 49

Tenison, Thomas, Archbishop, III.i 94*n*, 96*n*

Tennyson, Alfred, 1st Baron, II 144*n*, 222; III.ii 142*n*

Terence, in AP poems, I 81 and *n*; V 364; his comedies, I 257*n*, 259*n*; III.i 26*n*, 113*n*, 145*n*; IV 60*n*, 77*n*, 324*n*; IX 44, 409; X 150, 270, 277, 362

Tereus, in AP poem, I 401 and *n*

Terrasson, Jean (critic of Homer), VII xl–xli and *n*, 121, 268, 328, 332, 338, 382, 429; VIII 316, 350, 365

Tertullian, in AP poem, II 74; *Apol.*, VII 63; *De Carne Christi*, IX 454

Teubner, B. G., the editions of classical works, VII 28, 32–4, 40, 46, 64, 69–70

Teucer, in AP poem, I 451, 452, 453, 454

Thales (the Cretan, 7th c. BC), VII 56

Thales (philosopher, 7th/6th c. BC), VIII 175

Thalestris, in AP poem, II 108, 132, 134, 135, 191 f., 199, 201, 203, 376

Thalia, in AP poem, V 345

Thame, in AP poem, I 71 and *n*

Thames, in AP poems, I 59, 67, 71 and *n*, 89, 165, 168, 169, 173, 181 and *n*, 183 and *n*, 185, 191 and *n*; II 127, 129, 159, 169; IV 114, 153, 159, 289; V 130, 133, 137, 140, 141, 191, 308, 309, 310, 314, 321, 336; VI 44, 225, 367, 382

Thamis, in AP poem, VI 43

Thebes [–an], in AP poems, I 409 and *n*, 411, 415, 417, 418, 420, 423, 425, 427, 428, 431, 432, 433, 434, 443; II 259; IV 225

Thebais, VII 54. See also AP Works, *First Book of Statius*

Themistius (rhetorician, 4th c. AD), V 296*n*

Theobald, Lewis, Biog., IV 389; V 455–6; in AP *Master Key to Popery*, III.ii 180 and *n*, 184; AP quotes La Bruyère on, V 206; in *Dunciad*, II xv; as character in text of *Dunciad* A, V 59–194 *passim*; by name in *Dunciad* A, V xvi, 49, 51, 54, 61*n*, 75 and *n*, 93*n*, 94, 97, 99*n*, 151*n*, 154*n*, 187*n*; displaced as hero in *Dunciad* B, V xxxii, 252, 269*n*; occurs in *Dunciad* B, V 279 and *n*, 290 and *n*, 415–17; AP epigrams on, V 138*n*; VI 302, 303*n*, 304–5*n*, 326, 327, 329*n*; in other AP poems, IV 108, 123, 175; VI 283, 450; his notes imitated or parodied, V 59*n*, 65*n* f., 80*n*, 81*n*, 90*n*, 122*n* f., 153*n*, 182*n*, 195*n*, 267; other ref., V 81*n*, 152*n*, 429, 435, 441, 443, 444, 447; VI 329*n*, 330*n* Translations, of Ovid, V 75*n*; his

Aeschylus, V 76*n*, 88 and *n*, 185, 186*n*, 335; his *Ajax*, V 81*n*; of Plato, *Dialogue of the Soul*, V 89–90*n*; as translator, V 84*n*, 85*n*, 90*n*, 113*n*, 365*n*
WORKS:
Cave of Poverty, V 64, 75*n*, 77*n*, 90, 431; *Censor*, V xxxix, 29, 73*n*, 75*n*, 77*n*, 186*n*, 431, 455; *Double Falshood*, V 99*n*, 180–2*n*; his pantomimes, V 68*n*, 76*n*, 88*n*, 176*n* f., 183*n*, 184*n*, 185*n*, 335*n*; *Shakespeare*, III.ii 150*n*; V xxiii, 83*n*, 268*n*, 280*n*, 297*n*, 427, 456; *Shakespeare Restored*, II xiv; V xi–xiii, xxxvi, xl, 40, 59*n*, 60*n*, 66*n*, 75*n*, 82*n*, 88*n*, 121*n*, 123*n*, 153*n*, 180*n*, 182*n*, 195*n*, 217*n*, 267*n*, 279*n*, 433*n*, 453, 456; VII xxvii; contributions to *Mist's Journal*, V 8*n*, 21, 29, 30, 38, 39, 45, 75*n*, 80*n*, 83*n*, 86*n*, 114*n*, 180*n*, 182*n*, 209, 211 and *n*, 213*n*, 231*n*, 233*n*, 279*n*, 435, 448, 456; to *The Daily Journal*, V 75, 76, 456; other works, V 87*n* f., 90*n*, 177*n*, 185*n*, 207–8, 210, 211, 365, 431, 455; VI 289*n*
Theocles, in AP poem, V 389
Theocritus, I 15*n*, 16, 18, 19, 20, 24*n*, 28*n*, 29 ff., 30*n*, 32*n*, 43 ff., 48, 49, 60*n*, 61*n*, 72–5*n*, 83*n*, 86*n*, 89*n*, 254*n*, 334; II 209*n*; V 81*n*, 223; VII 44, 49, 201; VIII 285; X 37, 73, 253, 367
Theodamas, in AP poem, II 29
Theodorus, Manlius, III.i 157*n*
Theon, V 393*n*
Theophrastus (philosopher, 4th/3rd c. BC), II 16*n*, 17*n*; III.i xxxvi, 119*n*; VI 123; IX 242; X 222
Theseus, in AP poem, II 258

Thetis, in AP poem, I 412 and *n*
Thisbe, in AP poem, II 40
Thomas, Elizabeth, Biog., V 456; in AP poems as Corinna, V 105–6 and *n*, 162*n*, 299*n*; sale of AP MSS, VI 28*n*, 90*n*; other ref., V 210
Thomists, in AP poem, I 289 and *n*
Thompson, Aaron, *British History*, VI 193*n*, 421*n*
Thompson, A. H., notes cited, III.i 22*n*, 83*n*, 94*n*, 152*n*, 155*n*
Thompson, Francis, VI xx
Thompson, H. K., III.i vi
Thompson, William, II 6
Thoms, W. J., III.ii 121*n*; VI 396*n*
Thomson, James, *The Seasons* and AP *E. on Man*, III.i xlvii, lxvi; *Liberty*, III.i 116*n*, 126*n*; *The Seasons*, II 6*n*; III.i xxviii *n*, 12*n*, 16*n*, 38*n*, 44*n*, 45*n*, 76*n*, 115*n*, 121*n*, 126*n*, 129*n*, 148*n*; IV 351–2, 368, 376; V 37, 157*n*; AP Prologue to his *Sophonisba*, VI 310–11; other ref., IV xxiv; V 440, 447; VII lxiii
Thoos, in AP poem, I 452
Thornhill, Sir James (painter), II viii; IV 113*n*
Thorold, Sir George, Lord Mayor, in AP poems, V 69 and *n*, 275*n*; other ref., V 135*n*, 167*n*, 205
Thorpe, C. D., III.i 72*n*
Thracian, in AP poem, VI 31
Thrale. See Piozzi
Thrasymed, in AP poem, I 459
Thucydides (historian, 5th c. BC), VII lxxxii, 44, 49, 52, 70, 72, 161, 175–6, 181, 384; IX 90, 141, 265, 309, 344, 433; X 127, 202
Thulè, in AP poem, V 89, 289
Thurmond, John, V 176*n*
Thyrsis, in AP poems, I 82 ff., 88 ff.

Tiberius, III.ii xx

Tiberius Rhetor (author of work on Demosthenes, 2nd c. AD), VII 144

Tibullus, Albius (poet, 1st c. BC), I 224; II 356, 357; III.i 26n; IV 175; VI 236, 420; IX 380; X 340

Tickell, Major-General Sir Eustace, VI 465n

Tickell, R. E., his *Thomas Tickell*, V xvii n, 30n, 33n, 439, 455; VI 206n

Tickell, Thomas, his *Guardian* essays, I 17–18, 42; V 222n; his poetry, I 128, 130, 154n, 188n, 190n, 192n; II 151n, 217n, 268n; III.i 30n; III.ii 97n; IV xxviii n; V 348n; VI 109n, 207n; trans. of *Iliad*, II xiii; IV 343; V 30n, 110n; VI 112n, 132n, 135n, 145n; VII xxvi, xxxviii, xlii, cvii; AP use of trans., X 495, 496; his ed. of Addison's *Works*, IV 339; V 30n, 236; VI 205n, 465; in AP poems, VI 140, 141n, 173, 176n; other ref., V xvii

Tidcombe, Lt-Gen. John, in AP poems, VI 26, 29n, 39, 40; other ref., I 100; VI 415n

Tillotson, Geoffrey, author of *On the Poetry of Pope*, I xiii, 55n, 132n, 137n, 337n, 344n; II 36n, 222n, 302n, 308n, 325n, 333n, 354n, 364n, 365n; III.ii 17n, 18n, 98n; IV 219n, 228n; V xlii n, 8n, 108n, 351n; VI xx, 240n, 242n; X 495, 500, 501, 502, 503, 504, 505, 506, 509, 510, 511

Tillotson, John, Archbishop of Canterbury, I 302n; III.i xxxiv n, 63n, 90n, 124n

Tillyard, E. M. W., III.i xlviii n, li n, 68n, 71n; VII cxciv

Tillyard, P. B., III.i 62n

Timanthes (Greek painter, 5th c. BC), VIII 360, 545

Timbs, J., *Club Life of London*, III.ii 91n; IV 143n, 326n

Timoleon, in AP poem, II 267 and n

Timomachus (painter, 1st c. BC), VIII 359

Timon, in AP poems, III.ii xxvi–xxx, xliii, 146 ff., 147n, 170–4, 175, 183–8; IV xiii, 8n, 9, 243, 358; VII ccxlviii, ccxlix

Timotheus (poet, 5th/4th c. BC), in AP poems, I 283 and n, 284 and n; other ref., VIII 35

Tindal, Matthew, Biog., IV 389–90; in AP poems, IV 241; V 144, 144–5n, 175, 316, 330, 390; other ref., III.i 112n, 119n; IV 124–5n; V 432, 473

Tinker, C. B., I 2; III.i vii

Tirrell, Walter, I 157n, 158n

Tisiphone, in AP poem, I 413 and n

Titan[–s], in AP poems, I 304 and n, 445; III.i lx, 135; VI 142

Titian, in AP poems, VI 157, 159n

Titus (Roman emperor), in AP poems, III.i lv, lxii, 79, 80n, 142 and n, 145n; VI 203

Tityus, in AP poem, I 445 and n

Tlepolemus, in AP poem, I 449

Toft, Mary (impostor), in AP poems, VI 259–64, 445, 446n

Tofts, Katherine (singer), VI 413n

Toland, John, Biog., V 456–7; in AP poems, V 144 and n, 175, 316, 330; other ref., I 304n; III.i 47n; V 198, 385n, 390n

Toledo, in AP poem, VI 136

Tollo, King, in AP poem, VI 290

Tolstoi, Leo, VII clxxxvi

Tom, in AP poem, III.ii 22

Tompion, Thomas (watchmaker), VI 22, 23*n*

Tonson, Jacob, the elder, informant for AP on Man of Ross, III.ii xliv *n*, xlviii, 113*n*

Tonson, Jacob, AP corres., I 14, 37*n*, 37–8; III.ii 113*n*; *Miscellany* (1684), I 67*n*, 84*n*, 85*n*; Tonson–Dryden *Miscellanies*, I 37*n*, 42, 352; II xii, 14; VI 76*n*, 139*n*; VII xxv and *n*, xxxv *n*, cxi; as AP publisher, I 41, 42, 358, 361; II 14, 56; IV 108*n*; V xxvi, 31; published Ovid trans., I 339–41, 384; VI 174–5*n*; secretary of Kit-Kat Club, VI 177*n*; in AP poems, V 66 and *n*, 105 and *n*, 274, 299 and *n*; VI 25, 129, 131*n*, 172, 174, 174–5*n*; other ref., V 30*n*, 126*n*, 273*n*; VI 465*n*

Tooke, Charles, trans. *Iliad*, VII xv *n*, cx, cxxxvi, cxlii–cxlv and *n*, cxlv–clvi and *n*; X 495; AP debt to, VII clix, ccxliv *n*; parallels to AP *Iliad*, X 498; text selection of his trans., X 556–60

Tooting (London), in AP poem, IV 173

Topham, Richard, III.ii 134; IV 288*n*

Topsell, Edward, his natural history, III.i 42*n*, 65*n*, 102*n*, 112*n*

Torricelli, Evangelista (natural philosopher), III.i 56*n*

Tot'nam, in AP poem, V 130, 308

Toulon, in AP poem, VI 27

Tournemine, R. J. de (Jesuit), III.i xviii

Tower of London, in AP poems, IV 293; VI 196

Townsend, Horatio, V 346*n*

Townshend, Charles, 2nd Viscount, Biog., IV 390; in AP poems, IV 185; VI 181, 184*n*; other ref., V 145*n*

Toynbee, A., *Industrial Revolution*, IV 390

Tracy, G. R., III.i 40*n*

Trapezuntius, Georgius (translator of Plato, Aristotle), VIII 204

Trapp, Joseph, Biog., V 457; trans. Ovid, I 344; *Lectures on Poetry*, II 353*n*; in AP poems, V 147*n*, 272*n*

Trapp, Joseph B., I xii, 322*n*; X xii, xxiii

Trask, W. R., VII lvi *n*

Travers, in AP poem, V 147*n*

Travers, Henry, II 6

Trays, in AP poem, VI 367

Trenchard, John (political journalist), V 134*n*, 441

Trent, in AP poem, IV 251

Trevelyan, G. M., I 300*n*; VI 28*n*

Tripos, in AP poem, I 435 and *n*

Tritons, in AP poem, III.ii 152

Trotter, Catharine (dramatist), V 162*n*

Troy [Trojan, –s], in AP poems, I 449, 452, 456, 457, 470, 472; II 131, 134, 182, 199, 271 and *n*, 272; V 85, 88, 283; VI 27, 230

True Briton (periodical), V 153*n*

True Character of Mr Pope, IV xxvi

Trumbull, Sir William, in AP poems, I 59 and *n*, 60*n*, 61*n*, 172; VI 169–70; AP corres., I 127, 171*n*, 331*n*, 353; III.i 160*n*, 162*n*; other ref., I 38, 41, 43, 126–7, 130, 141, 201, 202, 341, 342, 348, 355, 356, 358; II 287*n*; V 19*n*; VI 167*n*, 168*n*, 170*n*; VII xxxv and *n*

Tucca, Plotius (Virgil's literary executor), V 411; X 231

Tuke, Sir Samuel (dramatist), V 102*n*; VI 303*n*

Tullock, John, III.i 57*n*, 93*n*

Tully. See Cicero

Tunbridge Wells (Kent), in AP poem, V 327 and *n*

Turbervile, George, II 293*n*

Turberville, A. S., *House of Lords in the XVIIIth Century*, IV 332*n*; *Johnson's England*, IV 353

Turenne, Henri de La Tour d'Auvergne, Vicomte de, in AP poems, III.i 137 and *n*; IV 322 and *n*

Turk[–s], in AP poems, IV 79, 110; VI 143, 234, 284

Turnell, Martin, III.i lxxvii *n*

Turner, F., II 374*n*

Turner, Sir Gregory Page, IV 289*n*

Turner, Richard (merchant), III.ii 94*n*

Turnpike system, in AP poem, IV 36*n*, 37

Turnus, in AP poem, II 272

Tutchin, John, Biog., V 457; in AP poems, V 118 and *n*, 302

Tweed (river), in AP poem, III.i 82

Twickenham, in AP poems, IV 97; VI 44; AP life at, IV 17*n*, 65–7 and *n*, 96 and *n*; AP villa and embellishments, VI 213*n*, 225, 226*n*, 321, 383; VII xxvi, xlii–xliii; grotto, VI 226*n*, 248*n*, 394*n*;

VII ccxxiii *n*, ccxxiv, ccxxv; ornament planned for, VII ccxxvi *n*; AP idea of hospitality for, VII ccxxvii, ccxxix; engraving of villa, X xiii; garden illus., X xiii–xiv; other ref., VI 44, 249*n*, 317*n*

Twickenham Edition, VII xv–xvii, xx–xxii, cxi, cxii, cxliii *n*, ccxxiv *n*, ccxxvi *n*, ccxli *n*, ccxlviii *n*; X 494

Twining, Thomas, VII lv *n*

Tyber, in AP poems, I 185 and *n*; V 158, 325, 373

Tyburn (London), in AP poem, V 64, 273

Tydcomb. See Tidcombe

Tydeus, in AP poems, I 412 and *n*, 433 and *n*, 443

Tydides, in AP poem, II 271

Tyrawley, James O'Hara, 2nd Baron, Biog., IV 375; in AP poems, IV 85, 245 and *n*

Tyrconnel, John Brownlow, 1st Viscount, Biog., IV 350–1; in AP poems, IV 302, 302–3*n*, 322

Tyrian, in AP poems, I 163, 387; IV 239

Tyrrell, James (political philosopher), III.i 161*n*

Tyrtaeus (poet, 7th c. BC), VIII 219

Tyrwhitt, Thomas, II 251*n*

Tzetzes, Johannes (poet, 12th c. AD), VII lxxxi, 33; X 22

U

Uffenbach, Z. K. von (diarist), IV
28*n*

Ulrich (Ulric, the Turk), George
I's servant, III.ii 66*n*; VI 184*n*

Ulysses, in AP poems, I 380, 465,
466, 467, 468, 471, 472, 473; II
190; IV 33; V 142, 315; VI 51

Umbra, Lord, in AP poems, III.i
154 and *n*; III.ii 24 and *n*, IV 41;
VI 140

Umbriel, in AP poem, II 183, 196,
203

Universal Journal, VI 440*n*

Universal Spectator, III.i xvi *n*; V
xxxi, xxxiii *n*, xxxv *n*, 163*n*,
259*n*, 326*n*, 428, 448, 451, 452

University of California, the library, VII xxii

University of California at Santa
Barbara, VII xv and *n*

University of Texas, X 590

Upon a Ladies Visit at a Country Seat
(anon.), X 501

Uriah, in AP poem, VI 291

Urry, John, II 3, 4*n*, 326*n*

Ursinus, Fulvius, *Illustrium Imagines
ex Antiquis Marmoribus Expressae*,
IV 112*n*

Ustick, W. L., I 216*n*, 272*n*, 290*n*

Uxorio, in AP poem, III.ii 91 and *n*

V

Vadius, in AP poem, VI 204

Vaga, in AP poem, III.ii 114

Vaillant, Monsieur, mentioned in a letter, I 348n

Valeriano, Piero, I 321n

Valerius, in AP poem, II 74

Valerius Flaccus (poet, 1st c. AD), *Argonautica*, V 140n; VII 102; X 252

Valerius Maximus (historian, 1st c. AD), X 203

Valerius Probus, IX 211

Valla, Laurentius, X 441

Valliant, Jean-Foi, V 380n

Vanbrugh, Sir John, Biog., IV 390; in AP poems, IV 219 and n; other ref., II 154n; III.i 154n; III.ii 139n, 143n, 188n; IV 104n, 113n; VI 285n; VII ccxlvi

Vandalis [Wandle] (river), in AP poem, I 183 and n

Vandals, in AP poems, V 156, 324

Van der Vaart, Jan, III.ii lviii

Van Doren, Mark, VII 4

Vane, Anne (court lady), VI 342, 343n

Vanini, Giulio Cesare (free-thinker), V 376n

Van Keppel, Arnold Joost, I 301n

Vanneck, Joshua, Biog., IV 390-1; other ref., IV 181n

Varius Rufus, Lucius (poet, 1st c. BC), V 411; VI 152; X 231

Varro, Marcus Terentius, *De lingua Latina*, VIII 40; *Rerum rusticarum libri*, VIII 245; X 341

Vasari, Georgio, I 227

Vatia, Servilius, III.ii xxvii n, 171n

Vatican, in AP poem, V 78

Vaughan, Henry, III.i 1, lxxiv, 99n, 157n

Vauxhall Gardens, in AP poem, III.ii 176, 183

Veitch, John, trans. Descartes, III.ii 131n

Velleius Paterculus. See Paterculus

Veni's, in AP poem, VI 367

Venice, in AP poems, III.i 155; Venetian, III.ii 140; IV 263

Venus, in AP poems, I 67 and n, 76, 377, 395, 396 and n, 397, 398, 404; II 15, 30 and n, 72, 75, 211, 340; IV 151, 243; V 127, 159 and n, 306, 325, 374-5; VI 21, 106, 379

Verney, Richard, Baron Willoughby de Broke, V 93n

Vernon, Thomas, Biog., IV 391; in AP poem, IV 69; other ref., IV 64n

Veronese, Paolo, in AP poem, VI 157, 159n

Verres, in AP poems, IV 301, 321

Verrio, Antonio, in AP poems, I 177n, 178 and n; III.ii 151 and n

L

Versailles, in AP poem, III.ii 141*n*, 144 and *n*

Verses Upon the Late D—ss of M., III.ii 168

Vertue, George, I xiv; II 239*n*; III.ii lviii, 112*n*; VI 365*n*, 374*n*; X xii

Vertumnus, in AP poem, I 377 ff.

Vespasian, in AP poem, VI 203; other ref., I 411*n*

"Viator", signature in *Gentleman's Magazine*, III.ii 114*n*

Victor Amadeus II, King of Sardinia, III.ii 28*n*

Victor, Benjamin, III.ii 116*n*; V 67*n*, 416*n*

Vida, Marcus Hieronymus (author of *De arte poetica*), in AP poems, I 320 and *n*; other ref., I 169*n*, 244*n*, 246*n*, 253*n*, 261*n*, 262*n*, 266*n*, 281*n*, 282*n*, 315*n*, 318*n*, 322*n*; II 106, 204*n*; III.i 152*n*; V 9; X 119, 258

Vigilius, in AP poems, V 158 and *n*, 325

Villario, in AP poem, III.ii 145 and *n*, 146

Villiers. See Buckingham; Cleveland

Villoisin, J. B. d'Ansse de (ed. Homer), VII lxxiii–lxxiv

Virgil (Publius Vergilius Maro), neo-classic theory derived from, I 15–16, 18–20, 28*n*; AP pastoral theory related to, I 29–33, 48–50, 52, 59*n*, 352, 360; V 223–9; his mock-heroic poetry, II 106–7; in AP poems, I 254 and *n*; IV 104, 320 and *n*; V 82, 365; VI 27, 83, 157, 204, 207*n*, 376, 450; AP *Messiah* an imitation of, I 111–22 and *n*, 132, 137; AP *Virgil Restauratus*, V 217–21 and *n*; AP early imitation of, VII xxxv; compared to Homer in AP Preface, VII xlviii, 3–16 *passim*, 20, 22; X 410, 412; AP use of in Homer trans., VII lxvii, lxx; compared to Homer, VII lxxii; view of Homeric simile, xcvii; position in epic tradition, cxxv, clxxxiii, clxxxvi, ccvi; his nymphs, ccxxvi; interpretation of deities, clxxxix; 18th c. preoccupation with, clxxxiv, clxxxv; other ref., I 37, 228, 243*n*, 257*n*, 259*n*, 261*n*, 262*n*, 263*n*, 269*n*, 281*n*, 282–3*n*, 291*n*, 313*n*, 322*n*, 347; II 114; III.i 41*n*; V 204, 254, 256, 411*n*; VI 20*n*; VII lxii, 51–3, 191, 271, 317; X xiii, 414, 415, 417, 419–25 *passim*, 430, 439, 475, 598, 601

WORKS:

Aeneid, I 118*n*, 120*n*, 121*n*, 148*n*, 159*n*, 161*n*, 163–5*n*, 174*n*, 180*n*, 181*n*, 184*n*, 186*n*, 193*n*, 244*n*, 262*n*, 282*n*, 296*n*, 325*n*, 409*n*, 416*n*, 417*n*, 465*n*, 483

II 106, 145–212*n* *passim*, 227, 258*n*, 264*n*, 276*n*, 277*n*, 320*n*, 339*n*, 345*n*, 366*n*, 380, 398, 405

III.i 16*n*, 94*n*, 96*n*, 104*n*, 129*n*, 138*n*

III.ii 118*n*

V xxxviii, 51, 55, 60*n*, 61*n*, 63*n*, 64*n*, 71*n*, 85–9*n*, 98–100*n*, 103*n*, 106*n*, 107*n*, 109*n*, 115*n*, 117*n*, 118*n*, 120*n*, 121*n*, 127*n*, 130*n*, 137*n*, 139*n*, 140*n*, 150–2*n*, 154*n*, 155*n*, 160–2*n*, 164*n*, 167–70*n*, 176–8*n*, 183*n*, 185*n*, 186*n*, 194*n*, 205, 284*n*, 295, 329*n*, 341*n*, 351*n*, 356*n*, 363*n*, 373*n*, 376*n*, 391*n*, 406*n*

VI 242*n*, 371*n*, 385*n*

VII lviii *n*, lxxii, lxxvi, lxxvii, xcix, cxxiv, cxxvi, cxxxi–cxxxii, cxliii, clxxix, ccix and *n*, ccx–ccxi, ccxiii, ccxxv, ccxxxv, 53, 91, 102, 119, 125, 132, 139, 152–3, 167, 174–6, 188, 190–1, 195–6, 208, 220, 227, 229, 243–4, 246–8, 253, 265–6, 271–2, 274, 277, 282, 284, 290, 292, 295, 307, 309, 313, 316–17, 326, 330, 338, 342–5, 353, 357, 359, 371, 395–6, 400–1, 408, 411, 415

VIII 16–17, 20, 64–5, 86, 89, 107, 114–15, 122, 124, 129, 136, 150, 158, 173–4, 214, 242, 244, 254, 276, 307, 310, 324–5, 329, 334, 341, 358–61, 381, 395, 397, 404–5, 408–9, 414, 423, 434, 440–1, 462, 466, 486, 490, 531–3, 553, 578

IX 20–2, 24, 28, 34, 60, 63, 66, 93–4, 98–9, 104, 115, 121, 138, 154, 174–5, 181, 183, 187–8, 191, 199, 211–12, 214, 217, 223, 234, 236–7, 244–5, 251–2, 263, 279–80, 292, 301–2, 305, 320, 330, 333–4, 336–8, 348–9, 352–3, 356–7, 360, 362, 367, 373, 377–9, 382, 384, 386–7, 393–5, 397, 402, 410, 418–20, 426, 428, 444, 449, 455–6

X 5–6, 8–9, 14, 33–4, 61, 65, 69, 105, 115, 119, 188–9, 192, 201, 206, 231, 239, 298, 305, 312, 316, 347, 349, 368, 374, 378, 385, 387–8, 417, 418, 501, 502, 503, 504, 505, 509, 510, 511

Eclogues, I 42 ff., 60–9*n*, 71–80*n*, 82–7*n*, 89–91*n*, 93–5*n*, 99, 100–3, 105, 148*n*, 151*n*, 158*n*, 245*n*, 281*n*, 320–2*n*; II 193*n*, 260*n*, 332*n*; III.i 108*n*; V 81*n*, 86*n*, 106*n*, 129*n*, 130*n*, 136*n*, 140*n*, 143*n*, 154*n*, 159–62*n*, 186*n*, 191*n*, 222, 347*n*, 390*n*, 412*n*, 470, 472; VII lxxii, ccxvii, 200; VIII 355; IX 428; X 222, 250, 357

Georgics, I 67*n*, 73*n*, 77*n*, 85*n*, 113*n*, 121*n*, 132, 135–7, 138, 151*n*, 156–8*n*, 160–2*n*, 164*n*, 170*n*, 171*n*, 173*n*, 176*n*, 177*n*, 182*n*, 185*n*, 186*n*, 193*n*, 194*n*, 265*n*, 280*n*, 296*n*, 309*n*, 310*n*, 416*n*, 467*n*; II 106, 127*n*, 150*n*, 277*n*, 399; III.i 41*n*, 96*n*, 111*n*, 155*n*; III.ii 109*n*, 113*n*; V 53*n*, 71*n*, 77*n*, 122*n*, 130*n*, 133*n*, 361*n*; VII 153; VIII 167, 186, 245, 410, 433; IX 97, 153–4, 280, 313, 382, 403, 415, 452, 454; X 116, 148, 302, 387, 501, 502, 504, 506

Virro, in AP poem, III.ii 137

Virtuosi, in AP poems, V 338, 381 ff. and *n*, 398 f.

Visigoths, in AP poems, V 157, 324

Visto, Sir, in AP poem, III.ii 137 and *n*

Vitellius, III.ii 27*n*

Vitruvius, Pollio, I 292*n*; II 257*n*; III.ii 155; VII 44, 61; IX 356

Vitruvius Britannicus, VII xiii

Vleughels, Nicolas, VIII xxi

Voiture, Vincent, AP *Epistle . . . with the Works of Voiture*, I 311*n*; VI 62–5 and *n*; AP *Verses* imitating, VI 85–90 and 90*n*; AP *Rondeau* imitating, VI 61; other ref., II 154*n*

Volga (river), in AP poem, I 186 and *n*

Voltaire, praises AP poetry, II 105*n*; learns authorship of *E. on Man*, III.i xvi *n*; doubts existence of AP letter to Racine, III.i xxii *n*; cites Shaftesbury as source of

W

Wade, George (general), IV 381

Wagstaffe, William (physician), V 45, 46n, 102n, 466

Waingrow, Marshall, I xii

Wake, William, Archbishop of Canterbury, IV 306n; V 313n; VI 380n

Wakefield, Gilbert (editor of AP), his notes, I viii, 13n, 60–9n, 71–5n, 77–87n, 89–95n, 112–22n, 148n, 149n, 153n, 154n, 156n, 158–61n, 163–9n, 172–4n, 177n, 179–82n, 184–7n, 189n, 190n, 193n, 194n, 241n, 242n, 244–6n, 248–50n, 252n, 253n, 257n, 259n, 261–3n, 265–9n, 274n, 279n, 280n, 282n, 283n, 286n, 287n, 291n, 297n, 304n, 305n, 308–13n, 315n, 316n, 318–20n, 322n, 325n, 326n, 338n, 387n, 388n, 390n, 393n, 402n

II 144n, 153n, 154n, 156n, 157n, 160n, 166n, 172n, 173n, 177n, 182n, 190n, 192n, 210n, 212n, 215n, 241, 265n, 268n, 275n, 281n, 288n, 298n, 319–22n, 324n, 339n, 342n, 346–8n, 366n, 368n, 391n

III.i 11n, 14n, 18n, 23n, 24n, 27n, 28n, 30n, 32n, 35n, 39n, 40n, 41n, 43n, 57n, 58n, 60n, 67–70n, 72n, 82n, 88n, 95n, 96n, 98n, 108n, 110n, 111n, 113n, 114n, 129n, 131n, 135n, 138n, 140n, 146n, 147n, 155–7n, 164n, 165n

III.ii 15n, 25n, 37n, 70n, 83n, 91n, 93n, 96n, 104n, 116n, 120n

IV 12n, 60n, 62n, 111n, 174n, 208n, 244n, 325n; other ref., ix

V 61–3n, 71n, 77n, 80n, 87n, 98n, 103n, 107n, 109n, 111n, 130n, 133n, 148n, 153–5n, 157n, 160n, 186n, 287n, 288n, 310n, 367n, 387n, 405n, 470

VI 71n, 159n, 385n, 442n, 461n

VII xv n, lxxxiv–lxxxv n, lxxxvii–lxxxviii and n, cviii and n, cxiii n, cxxxiii n, cxciv n, cliv n, clvi n

X 494, 495, 500–6 passim, 508–12 passim, 575, 576–7, 578, 579

Wales, in AP poem, VI 256

Wales. See Frederick

Walker, Middleton (man-midwife), in AP poem, VI 259, 264n

Walker, Richard, Biog., V 457; in AP poems, V 363, 371 and n

Waller, Edmund, Go, lovely Rose, I 46, 82n; II 197n, 408; A Panegyrick to my Lord Protector, I 151n, 188n, 189n, 191n; IV 195n, 325n; Upon Roscommon's Translation of Horace, I 249n, 297n; his trans. of Virgil, II 333n; VII cviii; of Corneille, IV 216–17n; other poems, I 61n, 62n, 77n, 81n, 148n, 149n, 153n, 155n, 163n,

189n, 190n, 293n, 322n; II 158n, 383; III.i 23n, 45n, 89n, 113n, 164n; IV 87n, 308n, 325n; V 87n, 354n; VII 189; VIII 283; X 504 In AP poems, I 65 and n, 280, 280–1n; IV 159, 217, 325 and n; AP imitation of, VI 7–8 and n, 8–11 and n; AP *Waller*, VI 45–7 and n

Other ref., I 132, 133, 134–5n, 278n, 356; II 115, 160n; VII xlv, cxxvii, ccxxxv

Wallerstein, Ruth, III.i 72n

Walond, W. (composer), VI 36n

Walpole, Horace, 1st Baron W. of Wolterton (1678–1757) (brother of Sir Robert), IV 289n, 334 and n; V 311n

Walpole, Horace, later 4th Earl of Orford (1717–97) (son of Sir Robert), marginalia in copies of AP poems, I viii; III.ii 20n, 34n, 46n, 48n, 54n, 63n, 66n, 103n, 138n, 144n; IV ix; V 395n; on Martha Blount, III.ii 46n, 47n; comment in letters on Martha Blount, III.ii 73n; on Duchess of Buckinghamshire, III.ii 61n, 62n, 170n; other letters, III.ii 52n, 61n; V 401n; VI 342n, 343n, 379n; views on landscape gardening, III.ii 141n, 143n, 149n, 174; *Anecdotes of Painting*, III.ii 35n, 113n, 138n; VI 159n, 213n; relations with AP, IV xviii, xxvi–xxvii, 391–2; cited as authority, IV xx, 57n, 75n, 80n, 126n, 135n, 166n, 225n, 238n, 243n, 244n, 287n, 289n, 291n, 319n, 347, 366, 369, 370, 375, 376, 377, 382, 383, 384, 393, 394; V 350n, 351n, 373n, 375n, 376n, 379n, 392n, 401n, 474; VI 159n, 163n, 184n,

213n, 287n; marginalia in a Homer owned by AP, VII lxxvii n; other ref., II ix, 4; III.ii 168

Walpole, Sir Robert, 1st Earl of Orford, Biog., IV 391–2; his Excise Bill, III.ii 101n; IV 64n, 133, 334n; his tenure of power, III.ii 105n; in *Master Key to Popery*, III.ii 186; relations with AP, III.ii 137n, 186; IV xviii, xxvi–xxvii; character of his rule, IV xxxi; V 356n; the opposition to his government, IV xxxi–xxxvi, 38n, 194n, 228n, 309n; V 344–5n; compared with Verres, IV 302n, 321, with Jon. Wild, 315n; AP mentions in letter, V 19n; not "Sir Shylock" in AP poems, III.ii 137n; in AP poems, IV 21 and n, 36 and n, 38n, 39, 83, 101 and n, 299–300 and n, 320–1 and n, 322, 334 and n; V 285 and n, 393n, 402–3n, as Palinurus, 404n, 405 and n; other ref., I 130; V xxviii, 60n, 145n, 211n, 262 and n, 268n, 311–12n, 313n, 326n, 428, 441, 444, 448, 454, 456, 460, 473; VII ccxxxiii

Walsh, I., II 358n

Walsh, William, Biog., IV, 392; MS colloquy with AP on AP *Pastorals*, I xii, xvi, 477–82; corres. with Wycherley on *Pastorals*, I 13, 14, 37, 59n; other connection with *Pastorals*, I 37–41 and n *passim*, 46–7 and n; AP corres., I 7n, 13, 30n, 31n, 38n, 39, 47, 59n, 89n, 197, 198, 199, 223n, 259n, 271n, 273n, 278n; II 106n; VI 72n; his critical theory and practice, I 18, 48, 222; II 300; his reading of AP *Discourse*, I 20, 38, 51–2; dates of his friendship

with AP related to dating of poems, I 197–9, 201–2, 347; his poems, I 83n, 86n–88n, 90n, 91n, 95n, 174n; II 26n, 335n; IV xxviii; in AP poems, I 325 and n; IV 105; other ref., I 353; V 19n, 114n

Walter of Lille (Gautier de Châtillon, author of *Alexandreis*), IX 434

Walter (or Waters), Peter, Biog., III.ii 102n; IV 392; in AP poems, III.ii 85, 86–7n, 102; IV 5, 9, 13 and n, 68n, 69, 139, 141, 210–11n, 211, 297, 307, 315 and n, 333n; in *Master Key to Popery*, III.ii 185–6, 185n; other ref., III.ii 86n

Walthoe, John (publisher), V 287n, 328n

Walton, Brian, *Biblia Sacra Polyglotta*, VI 110, 111n

Walton, Izaak, I 163n

Wandle (river). See Vandalis

Wanley, Humphrey, AP corres., V 443

Wanstead House (Essex), III.ii 145n

Wapping, London, in AP poems, V 148; VI 44

Warburton, Eliot, *Memoirs of Horace Walpole*, V 148n

Warburton, William, Bishop of Gloucester, *Vindication of Mr Pope's Essay on Man*, III.i xxi–xxii, xxiii, xxiv, xxvi; his influence on AP, IV xli, 135n, 298n; gift of AP MS to Mason, IV 157; his *Enquiry into Miracles*, V 344n, 443; *Divine Legation of Moses*, V 448–9, 458, 459; erects monument to AP in Twickenham Church, VI 376n; AP corres., III.i xxvii, 50n, 129n;

III.ii ix, xl n, 11, 21n, 41, 48n, 77n, 83n, 100n, 106n, 162; V xxv n, xxx, xxxiii n, 251n, 315n, 353n; replies to Crousaz, VII xxviii; emendations to AP Homer notes, VII xix

His notes, I 3n, 63n, 81n, 88n, 89n, 93n, 95n, 114n, 116n, 148n, 151n, 158n, 161n, 162n, 164n, 166n, 167n, 193n, 197, 217n, 239n, 240n, 242n, 249n, 251–2n, 257n, 260n, 262n, 266n, 269n, 282n, 312n, 322n, 325n; II 87 and n, 95, 151n, 155n, 166n, 180n, 186n, 210n, 246n, 378n, 379n; III.i 34n, 57n, 72n, 110n, 116n, 124n, 145n; III.ii 16n, 19n, 22n, 27n, 43, 46–8n, 72n, 88n, 100n, 108n, 110n, 111n, 130, 144n, 154n, 166n; IV 6n, 55n, 96–8n, 101n, 102n, 125n, 203n, 212n, 221n, 242n, 272n, 278n, 285n, 287n, 299n, 304n, 306n, 319n; V *passim*; VI 98n, 150n, 155n, 207n, 356n, 379n, 380n

Editions of AP *Works* (1751), I v–viii, xv–xvii, 2, 125, 223n, 329; II xi, 8, 14, 121 and n, 140–1, 144n, 315n, 359, 395; III.i xv n; III.ii xiv; V 20n, 193n, 249; (1744 and earlier), III.ii ix–xvi and n; (1743), *Adv. to the Reader*, V xxxvii, 251 and n; *Ricardus Aristarchus Of the Hero of the Poem*, V xxxvii, 254–65 and n; his connection with *The New Dunciad*, V xxx f., and with *The Dunciad* (1743), V xxxvii, 249n, 251n, 361n, 368n

His editorial methods, III.ii ix, xiv ff., 6 ff., 76 ff., 88n, 100n, 106n; IV vii–ix, 93–4n, 106n, 162 and n, 190, 242n, 248, 266, 276,

304n; V 398n; VI xiii, xiv, xix,
98n, 163n, 206n, 225n, 251n,
299n, 331n, 356n, 363n, 364n,
379n, 385–6n, 387n, 388n, 398n,
399n, 401n, 416n, 457n; VII
ccxxxix
Other ref., II xv, 400; III.i xxv n,
xxx; III.ii xvii, xix n, 27n, 33n,
43n; III.ii 47n, 109n, 167; V 83n,
258n, 268n, 312–13n, 364n, 367n,
435, 453, 456; VI 149n, 223n,
460n; X 474
Ward, A. W. (editor AP, 1896),
I viii, 161n, 425n; III.i 46n, 61n,
115n, 144n, 150n, 151n, 154n; IV
ix, 126n, 258n, 269n, 337n
Ward, Edward (Ned), Biog., V
457; in AP poems, V 86, 86–7n,
152, 152–3n, 161, 165n, 198, 287,
291, 322, 326; other ref., V xlvi,
141n, 201n, 204n, 211 and n, 474;
his *History of Clubs*, VI 177n
Ward, John, Biog., IV 392; in AP
poems, III.ii 85 and n; IV 306–7;
V 152, 152–3n, 322; other ref.,
III.ii 60n, 104n
Ward, Joshua, Biog., IV 392–3; in
AP poems, IV 98n, 210n, 211,
240n, 241, 269n
Wardman, Alan, VII xxiii
Warmsley, Catherine, II 92, 375
Warner, T., Biog., V 457–8; in AP
poems, V 111 and n, 301
Warren, Austin, I 255n, 272n; II
301n; VII li n, lxxviii n, lxxx n,
lxxxi n, cxciv n
Warren, Robert (divine), V 174–5n
Warton, Joseph, edition of AP
(1797), I viii, 208n, 484; II 7n;
III.ii 12; IV ix; VI 412n, 413n,
419n, 448n, 458n; *Essay on Pope*,
viii, 102 and n, 208 and n, 293n;
II 240 and n; III.i xlii; III.ii

34n, 46n, 79; IV ix; his *Adventurer*
essay, I 290n; III.ii 101n; his
publication of AP *1740*, IV
330–1; other ref., II ix, 299n;
X 474
His editorial notes and com-
ments cited, I 60n, 63n, 71n, 88n,
149n, 161n, 172n, 192n, 255n,
257n, 265n, 278n, 308n, 310n,
315n, 316n, 322n, 326n, 389n,
402n, 438n; II 5 and n, 8 and n,
37n, 113n, 119n, 145n, 167n,
197n, 203n, 224 and n, 228n, 229–
30, 239, 255n, 271n, 274n, 293n,
306n, 333n, 336n, 341n, 345n,
346n, 355 and n, 357n, 376, 379,
405, 414; III.i xvii n, xxiv n, xxv,
xxvii, 16n, 41n, 45n, 50n, 54n,
85n, 87n, 93n, 95n, 115n, 120n,
122n, 124n, 126n, 128n, 140n,
148n, 149n, 152n; III.ii 35n, 46n,
50n, 54n, 55n, 63n, 64n, 68n, 98n,
120n, 128, 145n, 169, 173, 174;
IV xxxix, 12n, 98n, 164n, 168n,
242n, 278n, 321n; V xliii, 100n,
129n, 133n, 156n, 165n, 186n,
286n, 313n, 327n, 356n, 367n,
369–70n, 373n, 379n, 387n, 397n
f., 440, 467; VI 20n, 206n, 207n,
250n, 287n, 386n, 392n, 393n
Warton, Thomas (the younger), II
224 f.; 305n, 362n; X 474
Warwick, Edward Rich, 7th Earl
of, in AP poems, V 393 and n; VI
128, 131n, 173; other ref., VI
144n
Wasse, Joseph, Biog., V 458; in AP
poem, V 366
Wasserman, Earl, I 133n, 149n,
157n; VII ccxxviii and n
Watkins, Roy, VII xxiii
Watson, George, VII lii n, lxxiii n
Watson, James (bookseller), V 462

Watt, A. F., II 178n, 180n
Watts, Isaac, in AP poems, V 78–9n, 172; *Horae lyricae*, II 194n, 210n, 304–5, 333n, 342n; other ref., III.i 50n; VI 169n
Watts, J. (publisher), V 31
Waxwork shows, IV 42n, 43
Webb, Daniel, II 311n
Webb, S. and B., *English Local Government*, III.ii 156n
Webster, Edward, Biog., V 458; in AP poems, V 127n, 306n
Webster, John, III.i 40n, 112n
Webster, William, Biog., V 458–9; in AP poem, V 308 and n
Weekly Amusement, III.i xvi n
Weekly Journal, V xlvii n; VI 434n
Weekly Medley, V 430
Weekly Miscellany, III.i xvi n, xvii n
Weekly Register, VI 454n, 455n
Weever, John, II 69n
Weil, Simone, VII ccvi n
Welby, T. E., II 365n
Wellek, René, I 252n; III.i vi
Wells, J., II 232n
Welsted, Leonard, Biog., IV 393; V 166n; literary affiliations, I 18; his poems, I 325n; IV 100n, 112n; *One Epistle to Mr Pope*, IV xvii, 124n, 385; V 138n, 211, 212n, 440; VI 328n, 330n; praises *E. on Man*, III.i xv; abuses AP friends, IV 121n; in AP poems, IV 99n, 123, 123–4n; V xlii, xlv, 73n, 91n, 124, 125, 126 and n, 138 and n, 166 and n, 306, 328; VI 299n, 450, 461n; in *Peri Bathous*, V xvi, 166n; his *Triumvirate*, V 208; *Labeo*, V 211–12; other ref., V xlvii n, 26, 43, 112n; 134n, 151n, 153n, 174n, 322n
Welsted, Richard, in *Master Key to Popery*, III.ii 172n, 176n, 179;

other ref., III.ii xxix n, 128 f.
Welton, Richard (nonjuror), V 175n
Wentworth. See Strafford
Wesley, John, II 209n; III.i xxvii n
Wesley, Samuel (the elder), V 67n, 78–9n, 175n; VI 295n
Wesley, Samuel (the younger), in AP poems, VI 294, 295n; AP corres., VI 92n, 315n; other ref., IV 120n; V 73n, 79n, 118n, 350n; VI 325n
West. See Delaware
West, A. S., I 239n, 279n, 280n, 303n, 322n
Westminster, books by J. E. Smith on, IV 62–3n; in AP poems, V 191, 336; VI 388
Westminster Abbey, tombs and monuments in, VI 208, 209n, 238n, 281, 282n, 312, 313n, 317, 320, 349, 351n, 363n, 395–7n, 400, 401n; VII ccxxxii n
Westminster Bridge, III.ii 156n; IV 63n
Westminster Hall, V 130, 131n, 308, 357, 404
Westminster School, V 191, 285, 336, 355
Weston, Mrs Elizabeth, II 353n
Westphaly, in AP poem, IV 323
Wey (river), in AP poem, I 183 and n
Whaley, John, II 415n
Wharncliffe, J. A. Stuart-Wortley-Mackenzie, 1st Baron, V 393n
Wharton, J. J. S., *Law Lexicon*, IV 182n, 284n
Wharton, Philip Wharton, 2nd Duke of, in AP poem, VI 287, 288n; other ref., I 38; III.i 154n; III.ii 30 ff., 55n, 94, 174; IV 302n; V 73n, 392n f.

Wharton, Thomas, 1st Marquis of, III.ii 30*n*; VI 117*n*

Whatley, Stephen, Biog., V 459; in AP poems, V 73*n*, 137*n*

Wheeler, Sir George (author of *Journey into Greece*), VII 181

Wheeler, R., III.ii 113*n*

Whichcote, Benjamin (Platonist), III.i li, 124*n*, 125*n*

Whincoop, Thomas (divine), III.i 159*n*

Whip and Key (pamphlet), V 230*n*, 232*n*, 234

Whiston, William (divine), in AP poem, VI 25, 28*n*; other ref., V 73*n*, 175*n*; VI 415*n*

White, Holt, I 279*n*

White, John, I 155*n*

White's Chocolate House (afterwards White's Club), in AP poems, III.ii 91 and *n*; IV 42–3*n*, 43, 141, 143*n*; V 277–8*n*, 284, 286, 293, 296*n*; VI 172, 175*n*

Whitefield, George, Biog., V 459; in AP poem, V 308 and *n*

Whitehall Evening Post, IV 148; V 10*n*, 182*n*, 212, 459, 460; VI 200*n*, 227*n*, 243*n*, 247*n*, 262*n*, 339*n*; VII xliii *n*

Whitehall Journal, V 136*n*, 455, 459; VI 136*n*

Whitehall Palace, in AP poems, I 188 and *n*; III.ii 25; IV 63 and *n*

Whitehead, A. N., III.i xlvi, lxv

Whitehead, Paul, *Manners. A Satire*, IV xl; V 342*n*, 435; VI 379*n*; *State Dunces*, IV 317*n*; V 403*n*, 443, 454; other ref., IV 358, 378; V 399*n*

Whitehead, William, II 302*n*, 308*n*

Whiteknights Park (Oxon.), III.ii 47*n*

Whitman, Cedric, VII cxxxiv *n*, clxxxv

Wiffen, J. H., *Memorials of the House of Russell*, IV 143*n*

Wight, in AP poem, IV 140, 141

Wild, Jonathan, Biog., IV 393; in AP poem, IV 315 and *n*

Wilkes, John, I viii; IV ix, 307*n*; V 395*n*

Wilkins, A. N., V 467

Wilkins, John, in AP poem, V 384, 384–5*n*; other ref., II 341*n*; III.i 48*n*

Wilkins, William, Biog., V 459; in AP poems, V 111, 301; other ref., V 168*n*, 207

Wilkinson, C. H., VI xx

Wilks, Robert (actor), VI 98*n*, 230*n*

Will, in AP poem, III.ii 22

Willey, Basil, *Seventeenth Century Background*, III.i lxiv, 107*n*; V 387*n*

William I, I 138, 152*n*, 153*n*, 155–7*n*; X 601

William II (Rufus), in AP poems, I 158 and *n*; V 130, 308; other ref., I 140, 152*n*, 155*n*, 157*n*, 158*n*; X 430

William III, in AP poems, IV 169 and *n*, 227 and *n*; VI 253, 255*n*, 290, 291, 293*n*; other ref., I 61*n*, 152*n*, 157*n*, 159*n*, 177*n*, 179*n*, 189*n*, 206, 300–2*n*, 304*n*; II 396, 399, 400

Williams, Aubrey, I 231*n*; V 460, 464 ff., 469 ff.; VII xxxv *n*

Williams, Sir Charles Hanbury, *Poems*, III.ii 92*n*, 102*n*, 121*n*; IV 289*n*, 371, 382, 392

Williams, Sir Harold (editor of Swift), I 131; IV 248*n*, 252*n*; VI xx, 119*n*, 412*n*, 439*n*, 443*n*, 457*n*, 460*n*

Williamson, G. C., II viii, 371*n*

Willughby, Francis (ornithologist), III.i 102*n*

Wilmington, Spencer Compton, 1st Earl of, Biog., IV 354–5; in AP poems, IV 335 and *n*; V 147*n*; other ref., III.ii 181*n*; V 403*n*

Wilmot. See Rochester

Wilson, Arthur, V 359*n*

Wilson, Dr, Fellow of Trinity College, Dublin, IV 330

Wilton House (Wilts.), III.ii lviii, 48*n*, 135*n*

Wimpole House (Cambs.), III.ii 108*n*

Wimsatt, W. K., I xiii, xiv, 215*n*; II 387 ff.; III.i vi; VII xii and *n*, xxiii; VIII xii; X xii, xiii

Winchelsea, Anne Finch, Countess of, her poems, II 146*n*, 187*n*, 295, 323*n*; III.i 40*n*; in AP poem, VI 120–2 and *n*

Winchelsea, Daniel Finch, 7th Earl of, Biog., IV 360; in AP poem, IV 332 and *n*

Winchester School, V 355

Winckelmann, Johann Joachim, IX xiii

Windham, Ashe, VI 438*n*, 439*n*

Windham, William, IV 340, 367

Windsor, in AP poems, I 59, 67, 84, 148, 164, 165, 170, 174, 176, 184, 189; IV 257; VI 44, 392

Windsor Castle, II 399

Wing, Donald G., III.i vi; VII xxiii

Winnington, Thomas, Biog., IV 393; in AP poems, IV 334

Winslow, Ann, I 105*n*

Winstanley, D. A., I 307*n*

Winstanley, William, *Lives of the Poets* quoted, V *passim*; other ref., V x, xvii

Winton, in AP poem, V 355

Wissing, Willem (painter), III.ii lviii

Withers, George (poet), in AP poems, V 78, 79*n*, 92, 291; other ref., II 294; III.i 95*n*; V xlv

Withers, Henry, Lt-Gen., AP epitaphs on, VI 320–1

Withers, Robert, II 364*n*

Wits Paraphrased, II 293*n*

Wittkower, R., VI xx

Wolf, F. A., *Prolegomena ad Homerum*, VII lxxi, lxxiv, lxxv, lxxvi

Wollaston, William, III.i 11*n*, 66*n*, 89*n*, 106*n*, 136*n*, 139–41*n*, 149*n*

Wolseley, Robert (critic), III.i 15*n*

Wolsey, Thomas (cardinal and statesman), in AP poems, IV 301 and *n*, 321

Wood, Anthony (antiquary), V 321*n*

Wood, George Alistair, VII xxiii

Wood, J., II 411

Wood, Robert, VII lxxiv

Wood, Thomas (vicar of Chiswick), in *Master Key to Popery*, III.ii 182, and *n*; in AP poem, VI 340, 340–1*n*

Wood, William (ironmaster), in AP poem, VI 254

Woodward, John, Biog., IV 393; in AP poems, IV 28*n*, 29, 37 and *n*; other ref., III.ii 135*n*; V 371*n*, 449

Woodward, W. H., trans. Erasmus, III.i l 1*n*

Woolston, Thomas, Biog., V 459; in AP poems, V 164 and *n*, 175 and *n*, 330; other ref., V 83*n*, 176*n*

Woolwich, in AP poem, VI 44

Wooton, Thomas (bookseller), V 462

Worde, Wynkyn de (printer), in

AP poems, V 79, 79–80n, 281; other ref., V 82n, 83n, 88n

Wordsworth, William, his opinion of AP *Messiah*, I 102; on the epistle as a form, II 299n; *Tintern Abbey* and *E. on Man*, III.i lxvi–lxvii; his opinion of nature imagery between Milton and Thomson, III.i lxvi n; belief in an objective order beyond man, III.i lxvii; *The Prelude* a poem of magnitude, III.i lxxii; his poetic "world" compared with AP's, III.i lxxiv, lxxv–lxxvi; his style compared with AP's, III.i lxxvi–lxxvii, lxxviii; his romantic view of man, III.i lxxvii; other ref., III.i v

Worldly, in AP poem, III.ii 90, 97n

Wormius, Olaus, in AP poems, V 171 and n, 329

Worsley, Lady Frances, in AP poem, VI 158, 160n

Wotton, William, II 262n, 288n

Wren, Sir Christopher, in AP poems, V 188n, 189, 336; other ref., I 180n, 242n; II 396; V 428, 470; IV 62n

Wright, C. E., VI xx

Wright, H. G., VII cxxiv n, cxxv n

Wright, J. (printer for L. Gilliver), V xxvii, xxix n

Wright, John, trans. Buffon, III.i 42n

Wright, L. S., II 414 f.

Wright, T., *History of Essex*, III.ii 156n

Wright, Thomas, *Passions of the Minde*, III.i 68n

Wycherley, William, AP revision of his poems, I 201–2; V xxxix, 82n, 84n; VI 16n, 17n, 53–4n, 57n, 58–9n, 60n, 437n; *Lines to Mr Pope, on his Pastorals*, I 268n, 275n, 279n, 281n; *Plain Dealer*, II 170n; III.ii 24n; IV 98n, 110n; VI 145n; other works, II 205n, 400; III.i 77n, 145n; III.ii 108n; as AP collaborator, VI 38n, 53–60n; in AP poems, I 80, 308n; IV 201 and n; VI 26, 29n, 37, 37–8n; AP *Autumn. To Mr Wycherley*, I 41, 80 and n, 81n; AP corres., I 13, 14, 37n, 41, 42, 59n, 201n, 214n, 273n, 290n; II 289n; VI 76n, 102n, 139n; other corres., I 13, 14, 37, 59n; other ref., I 225, 298n; V xi, 19n, 32, 114n, 456

Wyld, H. C., I 75n, 317n; II 153n; III.ii 28n, 56n

Wyndham, Sir William, Biog., IV 394; in AP poems, IV 318 and n, 336 and n; V 357; VI 383, 384n, 385n; other ref., IV xxxi, xxxv, xli, 39n; V 352n

Wynne, Edward, *Eunomus*, V 401n

Wynne, Marjorie, I xii; VII xxiii

Wyvill, Christopher (poet), VI 421n

X

Y

Yahoo, in AP poem, VI 274

Yalden, Thomas, *To Mr Congreve*, II 9*n*, 217; *Temple of Fame*, II 185*n*, 217–18, 218*n*, 250*n*, 308*n*, 344*n*; trans. *Iliad*, VII cx, cxxxviii–cxxxix; X 495; parallels to AP trans., X 499; text selection from his *Iliad*, X 554–6

Yale University, printings of *Iliad* in the library, X 588, 590, 591–2; other ref., VII xv, xxiii; VIII xii

Yates, Edward, II 396, 399; IV 49*n*

Yeats, William Butler, VII ccxxiii

Yonge, Sir William, Biog., IV 394; in AP poems, III.i 154 and *n*; IV 115, 115–16*n*, 298, 303, 334; in *Master Key to Popery*, III.ii 184*n*, 186 and *n*; other ref., III.ii 178*n*; IV xix; V 281*n*, 428, 453; VI 439*n*

York (city), III.i 82

Yorke. See Hardwicke

Yorke, Charles (politician), III.ii xvii *n*, 89*n*; IV xx *n*, 327*n*

Yorke, Philip Chesney, *Life of Hardwicke*, IV xxxv *n*

Yorkshire, in AP poem, VI 256

Young, Edward, *E. on Man* attributed to, III.i xv; letters to Tickell, V xvii, 439, 455; in AP poems, V 109, 109–10*n*, 301; other ref., V xlv *n*, 100*n*, 101*n*, 392*n*; VI 442*n*; VII lxiii, cvii *n*
WORKS:
Busiris, IV 243*n*; *Epistle to Lansdowne*, V 179*n*; *Imper. Pelagi*, III.i 31*n*, 67*n*, 121*n*, 143*n*; *The Last Day*, III.i 27*n*, 32*n*; *Love of Fame*, II 158*n*; III.i 87*n*, 89*n*, 94*n*, 130*n*, 131*n*, 147*n*, 148*n*; *The Universal Passion* (seven satires), V 36 and *n*, 327*n*, 405*n*; *Two Epistles to Mr Pope*, IV 14*n*, 96*n*, 98*n*, 203*n*, 314*n*; V 15*n*, 183*n*; *Vindication of Providence*, III.i 26*n*, 67*n*, 69*n*, 72*n*, 89*n*, 159*n*

Young, Sir G., *Poor Fred*, IV 380

Young, John (of Glasgow), III.ii xv *n*

Younger, Mrs Elizabeth (actress), VI 129, 131*n*

Yvon, Jacques, V 472

Z

Zamolxis, in AP poem, II 264

Zembla, in AP poems, II 256; III.i 82; V 68, 275; other ref., II 410–11

Zeno, in AP poem, VI 151

Zenodotus (ed. Homer, 4th c. BC), VII 60, 127; VIII 144

Zephalinda, in AP poem, VI 124, 127n

Zephyretta, in AP poem, II 166

Zeuxis, in AP poem, VI 158

Zimmermann, Hans-Joachim, VII xvii n, xviii n, xxxviii n, lxxvii n, lxxxi n; X 575n

Zoilus (critic of Homer, 4th c. BC), in AP poem, I 292 and n; other ref., I 250n, 252n, 262n; VII 44, 61, 265–6; IX 305, 356, 455

Zoroaster, in AP poem, II 260 and n